60/-
D0410996
PEN

America in Modern Italian Literature

Modern

BY

America in Italian Literature

DONALD HEINEY

Rutgers University Press
NEW BRUNSWICK, NEW JERSEY

Library of Congress Catalogue Card Number: 64–24738
Printed in the United States of America
by H. Wolff, New York

a Federico e Vittoria,
amici e angeli custodi

Acknowledgments

The writing of this book would have been impossible without the help of the many people who lent their material assistance and advice. Particular thanks is due to the Italian writers themselves who were generous with their comments and opinions, and whose friendship was frequently more valuable than either: Giuseppe Berto, Italo Calvino, Livia De Stefani, Augusto Frassinetti, Giovanni Guareschi, Alberto Moravia, Fernanda Pivano, Vasco Pratolini, Nantas Salvalaggio, Giorgio Soavi, Mario Soldati, and Elio Vittorini. Other information was provided by scholars and specialists: the Hon. Davide Lajolo of the Italian Chamber of Deputies, Sergio Perosa of the University Institute of Venice, Giorgio Spini of the University of Florence, Biancamaria Tedeschini Lalli of the University of Rome, and Cipriana Scelba of the American Commission for Cultural Exchange With Italy. Finally, gratitude is due Professors Glauco Cambon, Sergio Pacifici, and Sergio Perosa for their intelligent reading of the manuscript and for their many helpful comments.

The research for the book was made possible through grants from the Penrose Fund of the American Philosophical Society and the American Council of Learned Societies. Assistance was also received from the Research Committee Fund and the John W. Park Scholarship Fund of the University of Utah.

A preliminary version of Chapters 3 and 4 appeared in *Twentieth Century Literature,* 3:3 (October, 1957), and the material is used by permission of *Twentieth Century Literature* and Alan Swallow. Parts of Chapter 8 have appeared as "Berto: Texas and Treviso" in *Cesare Barbieri Courier,* 7:2 (Spring, 1964), and Chapter 11 first appeared in *Western Humanities Review* 18:4 (Autumn, 1964) as "Moravia's America."

All translations are my own except where indicated by notes. In some cases I have utilized standard English translations as a check; descriptions of these editions will be found in the Bibliography.

Contents

ONE: ***The Legend***

TWO: ***Legend to Literature***

APPENDIX: *Three Documents*

ONE

The Legend

". . . an America pensive and barbaric, blissful yet quarrelsome, dissolute, fecund; burdened with all the past of the world, yet youthful, innocent."

—PAVESE

1 *Chateaubriand, the Movies, and Other Myths*

For over a hundred years Italy has occupied a special place in the American consciousness, just as the Italian consciousness has cherished a particular dream of America. To the middle-class American the names of artists like Michelangelo and Leonardo da Vinci are the essence of culture, and every summer their power brings to Europe long lines of tourists who tramp through the museums with their guidebooks, Americans who have never read Balzac or Goethe but who know that art is the Mona Lisa. And in the popular Italian mind, from the beginning of emigration in the nineteenth century, America has traditionally been a place where the streets are paved with gold and where the poor man can become a millionaire, like A. P. Giannini and Al Capone. Each country has built up a kind of mythology about the other which is only partly true. Hawthorne's *Marble Faun* is only the first of a long line of novels that express this American myth of Italy, and the picture is not very different a hundred years later in Tennessee Williams' *The Roman Spring of Mrs. Stone*. The myth of America is just as firmly rooted in the mind of the typical Italian peasant; the more ignorant and illiterate he is, the more he is likely to think of America as a kind of second Eden. The notion is there in the intellectual too, but it is deeper down. First his political opinions have to be systematically stripped away, and these are often anti-American. But underneath lies the same myth.

In common usage a myth is something made up, the opposite of truth. Often the word is used as a synonym of dishonest fabrication: "The allegations of my opponent are pure myth." But myths are not untrue; rather they may be described as profound distortions of the truth. The fact that Persephone descends every year for six months into the realm of Hades is a truth known to everyone who has ever bought an overcoat or watched leaves fall. The ideal subject for a myth is something which is near at hand and yet in some way veiled in mystery—the changing of the seasons, the miracle of reproduction, a mountain hidden in the clouds. The forces that the myth attempts to explain are real; it is simply that the means of their operation are not clear. The Italian myth of America is fabulous, exaggerated, sometimes nightmarish; but it is an attempt to explain a real place, a power whose magic is only half understood.

Unlike the classic myths, this legend is constantly being nourished and altered by new sources of information between the two cultures. The average Italian knows much more about America than the Greek knew about Mount Olympus. He can see pictures of it in his weekly magazines, and he can read the letters that his wife's cousin sends from Philadelphia; practically every Italian family has an emigrant relative or knows an emigrant in America. If he reads the newspapers, he is aware of America as a political power, a force that influences his daily life and in the end may even determine his destiny. Particularly if he is an Italian intellectual he is likely to see America as the center of an invisible empire of influence, an influence that is sometimes generous and idealistic and sometimes sinister. Whether he is an intellectual or a peasant he believes in the myth for reasons that go very deep into his culture and his own relation to it. His picture of America is often irrational because it is built on a basic inconsistency in his own nature. On the one hand he needs to believe there is a place where everybody is rich and all the work is done by machines; on the other hand he needs someone to blame for fallout, Coca-Cola, and the perverts in blue jeans who hang around in the Piazza di Spagna. In modern Europe the signs of America are everywhere, its influence is constantly felt, and yet there is something elusive and unattainable about this culture which seems superficially so ubiquitous. In the case of Italy the fascination is enhanced by the long tradition of emigration, and emigration of a special kind. Not only have millions of Italians emigrated to America in the last century but they have kept their ties with the homeland in a way that French or English emigrants, for example, have not. The typical Italian who went to make his fortune in America planned in the back of his mind to come back in ten or twenty years, as soon as he got rich. Sometimes he didn't get rich, and sometimes he didn't come back. But the first-generation emigrants in America failed to learn English or learned it only poorly; they kept their emotional ties with Italy, they sent back a continual stream of letters, packages, and money orders to their relatives, and sometimes they did come back themselves to buy a piece of land and retire. In every Italian village, particularly in the south, there is an "Americano" like this, a returned emigrant a little more prosperous than the rest. And yet it is not only this hope of emigration that keeps the legend alive. The peasant dreams of America not because he hopes to go there, but precisely because America represents something unattainable, fabulous, and for that reason consoling. If he had any real hope of going there he would stop dreaming and start planning. As it is he can always daydream about the Place of Abundance where he might go, and where everything would be different. The legend is durable and it has very little to do with the real America; it survived the virtual cutting off of emigration after the Depression and it has survived even the firsthand contact between Italians and American troops that took place during the Second World War. There is no other myth comparable to it in Italian culture. In spite of the efforts of leftist intellectuals to oppose a Russian mythology, a Russian folklore, a Russian literature to the American, there is no myth of the Soviet Union in the same sense. Even if the Italian peasant or worker is a Communist he has no particular desire to emigrate to the Soviet Union, and the juvenile delinquents in Rome wear baggy sweaters and jeans, not Russian peasant blouses. Myths come out of a national subconscious; they are not created by intellectuals and they are not disseminated by propaganda.

Literature is a valuable source for the study of this kind of myth, more so in a way than politics or journalism because it exposes the emotions in an intuitional state. Like religion, literature moves toward the heart of things where other forms of investigation tend to play on their surface. A great deal can be learned about what Italians think of America by studying history and sociology, by talking to emigrants, by investigating the accounts of travelers and journalists; but the information obtained in this way tends to be confined to stereotypes: Italians envy American automobiles but disapprove of divorce, they consider Americans puritanical but skillful in mechanical things, and so on. Literature offers insights that are less factual, more intuitive, and more deeply rooted. It tells us not only what people think about things but what they feel, and sometimes it shows us the intricate mechanism that lies under this feeling. The way the sociologist deals with a foreign culture is comparable to a medical examination; the literary critic performs something comparable to a psychoanalysis.

The modern Italian writer is not always pro-American, but he is usually interested in America, and more likely than not his style shows the influence of American literature. The American who reads his way through the Italian novels of the last twenty years will frequently hear the voices of Hemingway and Saroyan, and he will also hear his own country mentioned and discussed more than any other foreign culture. Or at least he will hear a strange place mentioned that is called America; often it seems to have little to do with the prosaic place where he marries his wife, raises his children, and eats his corn flakes. Eavesdropping on the private dialogue between Italian writer and Italian reader, he may have the strange sensation of overhearing a conversation about himself between two other people. Eavesdropping is rather dishonest but it is also fascinating, especially for those who—like all who hope to know themselves better—have a profound curiosity about the lives of others.

Naturally there is a certain danger in treating literature in this way. It is the danger always inherent in treating as a means what should be an end in itself. To Marxist critics literature is a "superstructure," a kind of spiderweb that society excretes and leaves behind it while it is working toward its economic and political ends. It is useful as a source of class attitudes and it can even be used as a weapon to carry out social reform, but it could be abolished completely without basically changing human institutions. To the Marxist, literature, philosophy, and the arts in general are only symptoms of processes that are at the bottom economic and political. If literature were only a superstructure of this kind it would have the importance attached to, say, stock market indexes and election returns. That it is not is shown by the fact that it often outlives the institutions that have produced it. No one takes Babylonian theology seriously any more or believes in Greek polytheism, but we still read *Gilgamesh* and the *Odyssey*. We do so primarily not because of the information they contain about Babylonian and Homeric society but because they are universal human stories, books of prophecy that seem to offer us some insight into our own problems and our own natures. This is the real reason why some men write works of fiction and other men read them. Cesare Pavese's novel *La luna e i falò* and Alberto Moravia's *La ciociara,* to take two examples, are works of literature in this sense. The fact that they also offer the American reader a glimpse of his own culture, like a glimpse of one's self from behind reflected in a mirror, is an accident the authors did not intend. Sometimes a book is valuable not only for what the author meant to say but for what he did not mean to say. In this case the critic is useful, perhaps, to explain to the writer what his book is about. In other cases a book written for one culture will have an entirely different value for another culture. The Hebrews and the Christians both read Isaiah, for example, but it was two different books to them. In this case the task of the critic is to reinterpret the book for the second culture and show the meanings it has acquired in the process of migration, as Thomas Aquinas did for Isaiah. *The Marble Faun* read by an Italian will not tell him very much about his own country he didn't already know, but it will show him Italy as seen by an American and in this way help him to grasp what his own culture is. The books of Elio Vittorini, Ignazio Silone, Alberto Moravia, and Mario Soldati are valuable in the same way. In Italian literature written under Fascism and since the Second World War there lies buried a complicated pattern of attitudes, prejudices, and emotions toward America. This mythology—for this is what it is, in the same sense that Greek mythology was the source material for classical literature—is useful not only because it shows how authors use their materials but also because it tells something about America that could not be learned in any other way. Like the Navajo rug-weavers, the Italian writers all work separately and they all weave the same patterns. The task of the critic is to point out the patterns.

Probably the intelligent Italian reading *The Marble Faun* will not be nearly as baffled as the intelligent American encountering a portrait of his own culture in an Italian novel—Soldati's *Le lettere da Capri,* for example, or Pavese's *La luna e i falò*. The American has an image of himself that is quite precise. He thinks of himself as pragmatic, humanitarian, democratic, and above all modern and civilized. Cesare Pavese's generation of young Italians in the Thirties dreamed of America in adjectives that ring strangely in American ears: "pensive and barbaric, blissful yet quarrelsome, dissolute, fecund; burdened with all the past of the world, yet youthful, innocent." [1] The American doesn't conceive of himself as particularly pensive, or particularly barbaric. But the portrait is unmistakably his. Instead of Babbitt, or the Man in the Gray Flannel Suit, it seems he is the Pensive Barbarian, brooding and fecundating in the primeval forest. And then he remembers that his own literature too reflects this archetype of the primeval: Longfellow, Fenimore Cooper, and even *Huckleberry Finn.*

The myth of the primeval forest goes deep, in Europe as in America. From the time of its first discovery America was fixed in the European subconscious as a new Eden, a recovery of innocence. It is no accident that in legend the first explorers searched not so much for gold or wealth as for the Fountain of Youth. This attitude persisted, through the eighteenth century and beyond, not because of anything that America was in itself but because it was something that Europe needed to believe in for reasons of its own. Overcivilized cultures, from the Hellenistic Greeks to modern Europe, have traditionally ended in a nostalgia for the simple and primitive, a longing for the Fortunate Isles. In the history of literature this is called pastoralism, and it tends to recur in cycles. In modern times the notion was crystallized by Rousseau and the romantics, but behind it lay the whole tradition of the pastoral which went back to Theocritus and before. When America became involved in this pastoral tradition, it was more or less through an accident of history; it happened that the New World was discovered at a time when Europeans needed to believe in the primeval and the Noble Savage, in a return to innocence, and this need simply fixed on America as a convenient object. America to the European mind was a myth from the beginning, a myth the Europeans believed in because they needed to believe that somewhere there was a land free from the plagues and famines, the dynasties and social classes, the hypocrisies and cynicisms, of the Old World. If there were no America it would have been necessary to invent one, as the Greeks invented the myth of Atlantis.

When the nineteenth-century European imagined America, it was partly that of Tocqueville and partly that of Fenimore Cooper, the most widely read American author on the Continent before 1900. But more influential than either *Democracy in America* or the Leatherstocking Tales was François-René de Chateaubriand's *Atala,* a curious short novel that would not otherwise be very important. In no other work of literature is the concept of the Noble Savage expressed so perfectly, and this was made possible partly because Chateaubriand chose the New World as his setting. Like many other commentators on

America, before and after, he began with an imperfect knowledge of the country he was describing. When he came to the United States in 1791 he was already steeped in Rousseau's *Rêveries du promeneur solitaire,* in Ossian, and in Bernardin de Saint-Pierre's *Paul et Virginie,* that French best seller of the eighteenth century with its exotic island setting and its idealized, almost perversely chaste eroticism. He brought his own romanticism with him and he saw everything through Ossianic spectacles, a little larger than life and a good deal more noble. The ostensible purpose of his trip was to look for the Northwest Passage, but he soon discovered the impracticality of this and instead he spent seven months traveling chiefly in the settled regions of the eastern seaboard. According to his memoirs, which are not always to be trusted, he pushed westward as far as the "Tenase" and visited the land of the Cherokees. Among his other adventures he described a meal of buffalo cutlets roasted over an open fire, and one of the more expensive cuts of steak, charcoal-broiled in the "American" manner, is still called a Chateaubriand in France. This dish invented by savages, charred on the outside and pink on the inside, was the first contribution of America to European gastronomy.

Soon after his return to Europe Chateaubriand wrote the two short novels *Atala* (1801) and *René* (1802), both originally intended as episodes in his vast *Génie du christianisme.* The American setting of *Atala,* a vast primeval forest, shadowy and vaguely ominous, is drawn more from romantic imagination than from the United States Chateaubriand actually visited. The tale is recounted by the blind old Sachem Chactas to the young Frenchman René, who has fled from a dark past in his native Brittany. In his youth in the virgin Louisiana territory, Chactas is captured by his enemies the Muscogulges, who prepare to put him to death. Rescued by the maiden Atala, he flees with her through the forest. Although the two soon fall deeply in love, Atala is reluctant to give herself to him, and finally she reveals why. She had been secretly baptized a Christian, and her Christian mother bound her by a vow to the Virgin never to marry. In her despair over her doomed love she takes a fatal potion and dies, consoled by the wise old missionary Père Aubry and mourned by her Indian lover. The tale closes with her funeral, an elaborate set piece of romantic description. *René,* the second novel, concerns itself with the mysterious past of its hero in Brittany. Chateaubriand obviously intended for René and Atala to stand as contrasting figures, representing Europe and America, respectively. Where he is complicated she is simple; his unhappiness is that of decadence, hers is a pensive and melancholy innocence. If they are both unhappy it is simply because it was the literary fashion of the time and because Chateaubriand was a specialist in melancholy.

These two tales were widely read all over Europe; in their time their vogue was almost equal to that of *Werther.* Four translations of *Atala* appeared in Italy alone between 1801 and 1805, and for the rest of the century it dominated the Italian notion of America among cultivated readers. To the Italian scholar Enrico Nencioni, writing in 1897, the "noble and melancholy René" was the spiritual godfather of American poetry, "the first to see and hear the poesy of the immense prairies, the seas of grass, the ocean-like rivers, the virgin forests." [2] Because Chateaubriand had traveled in the United States, the tale was accepted as an authentic picture of America, almost as an American book. The American writers who were read in Italy before 1930 tended to be those whose image was similar to Chateaubriand's, or at least not contradictory to it: the primeval Cooper, the decadent and romantic Poe. Fenimore Cooper's novels were translated as early as 1828, and Poe was widely read, usually in the French translation of Baudelaire. The writers who did not fit the pattern of Chateaubriand were often oddly distorted; the first translation of Hawthorne's tales appeared in 1900 under the title *Racconti del Farwest,* although Hawthorne never wrote anything of importance with a setting west of the Appalachians. Even after Whitman was championed by critics of the stature of Papini and Nencioni at the end of the century he was considered an ingenuous primitive, and the industrial and democratic side of *Leaves of Grass* was ignored. Of Thoreau, Emerson, and Holmes nothing was known in Italy until the twentieth century; there was no place for scholarly Boston gentlemen in the forest of Atala.

This notion of America as primeval forest persisted in Italy into the Thirties, long after it had ceased to be a fact—although by the end of the century Cooper's Natty Bumppo and Chateaubriand's Atala had evolved into the cowboy with his pony and the cowgirl with her durable virtue. In 1910 the biggest event of the international opera season was the New York premiere of Puccini's *La fanciulla del West,* based on David Belasco's *Girl of the Golden West* which Puccini had seen on Broadway in early 1907. The opera was soon produced in Italy and made the round of the world's opera houses, although it failed to establish itself in the standard repertory. Today the plot of this opera seems almost like a parody of a Western. It begins with the burly miners who shout "Hello!" in English almost all the way through the first act, and it rises to a climax in the nostalgic farewell of Minnie and Johnson to California, a duet imitated from the famous "Addio monti" apostrophe in Manzoni's *I promessi sposi:*

> Goodby, beloved country;
> Goodby, my California!
> Mountains of the Sierra, snows, goodby!

After Puccini came the cowboy films and the paperback Westerns. The cult of a Wild West which had already begun to disappear became almost as popular in Italy as it was in America, and even more fabulous, since it bore no relation to any reality the Italians had ever known. The words cowboy, saloon, whiskey, sheriff, and Far-West are commonly used in English even by Italians who know no other word of the language. In 1955 a Milan newspaper published a set of themes written by schoolgirls from thirteen to fifteen years old in a small Lombardy town on the subject, "If I could choose, in which country of the world I would like to live." The choices ranged from Kenya to the North Pole, but by far the most popular country was America. Like their Italian elders, the little girls tended to confuse the real United States with the Argentine pampas, the

Gran Chaco, and the Wild West of Puccini in their image of "America." "I would like to inhabit the American pampas where the Indians and cowboys are, and fight against the former and exterminate them like a fabulous warrior and gallop in the immense prairie, flanked by twenty or more Negroes. After that, to be the mistress of an immense plantation of cacao, coffee, and cotton and have many Negroes for my servants who would tell me their stories and the stories of their land and the many legends that make it even more fabulous and beautiful. To go to America to see the wild horse tamers and try my hand at it too and then afterwards go to a saloon to drink whiskey and sing the beautiful songs of the Far West which bring back the melancholy of your own land." And another little girl: "I would like to ride over the endless prairies, have a pony just for me and catch an Indian with a lasso. At night, after riding all day long, I would gather around the fire with my friends and sing songs of the Far West. My pony would be named Belik. I would like to go in a saloon and, like the cowboys, arrogantly order a glass of whiskey." [3]

Perhaps it is not surprising that Italian children should share the same make-believe of the Wild West as their American counterparts, since they saw the same movies. But American children, of course, do not play at being gondoliers or Renaissance condottieri, and this is an interesting difference between the two myths. The American myth of Italy is basically touristical; it is fed by American Express tours, the memories of GI's, and the glossy pages of *The National Geographic.* Italy seen through the haze of old kodachrome slides is a postcard land, colorful but slightly backward, where the gondoliers all sing "O sole mio" and the favors of passionate black-eyed girls can be bought for nylon stockings. Also the land of pickpockets, spaghetti, and importunate ciceroni. The Italian notion of America is at the same time more naïve and more complicated. Although there are always some who emigrate, for most Italians America has been until recently a land it is possible to visit only in books. Where the typical American is quite likely to have a firsthand experience of Italy, either as a soldier or as a tourist, his Italian counterpart knows only American literature, American films, American jazz, and the pictures of America in the Sunday supplements. The two Italian writers who were the most influenced by American literature and who were the leaders in diffusing American culture during the Thirties, Elio Vittorini and Cesare Pavese, never visited the United States. If they had actually come to America perhaps the private myth they carried in themselves might have been destroyed; it was at least partly destroyed in the few like Mario Soldati who came. The Italian intellectuals who lived under Fascism needed this myth because it offered them their only hope of escaping from the cultural sterility around them, the sense of being imprisoned in the ruins of their own history. To a generation submerged in the fakery of official Fascist rhetoric, America offered the possibility of a return to the primitive and elemental, a return to innocence. When Pavese, in 1930 an unknown university student translating Melville, discovered an America that was "pensive" and "barbaric," "blissful yet quarrelsome, dissolute, fecund," he had focused his emotions on a myth that had relatively little to do with the real United States. Perhaps he was at least subconsciously aware of this, but in any case it did not really matter. The land he had discovered was the mythical America of Chateaubriand, which he had encountered again in the pages of Whitman and Melville. The shaggy Walt who was "not tamed" and sounded his barbaric yawp over the roofs of the world was the answer to Mussolini making a speech in Piazza Venezia. The Pensive Barbarians persisted in the European consciousness because they expressed a need and not a fact, the need of Europe to believe in the possibility of its own rebirth.

The part played by emigration in forming the Italian image of America was of great importance, perhaps more important than any other factor, especially among the poor and uneducated. It influenced not only those who went but also, in a way more strongly, those who stayed behind. With the possible exception of Ireland, Italy has sent a larger proportion of her population to the United States than any other country in the world. Especially in southern Italy there are towns where practically every family has a son, an uncle, or a cousin in America. The great mass of this emigration took place in a period of about fifty years beginning in the late nineteenth century. The peak occurred in the twenty years from 1890 to 1910; in a single year of this period three hundred thousand Italians emigrated to America, more than the population of Venice. The flow was cut off after the quota laws were strictly enforced in the Twenties, but in 1938 there were more residents of Italian descent in New York City than there were people in Rome. New York had become the largest Italian city in the world.[4]

The effect of this Italian influx on American society was important and widespread. But Italy was also changed by the phenomenon of emigration, in the way any organism is changed when it gives a part of itself to another organism, when it establishes a link with something outside itself—a formula which might serve as a definition of love, or of dependence and servitude. America became a part of the Italian consciousness in a manner comparable to the other facts of Italy's environmental experiences: Catholicism, poverty, sunlight, the Roman heritage. "Among the hundreds of myths cherished by the peasants," says Carlo Levi, "one stands out among the rest by providing the perfect avenue of escape from grim realities. It embodies fable and fact, concrete existence and romance, necessity and imagination. It is their version, magical and real at the same time, of an earthly paradise, lost and then found again: the myth of America." [5] The Myth, in fact, had formed even before the main wave of emigration had begun; in a sense the Myth was the cause of the emigration and not the other way around. As early as 1853 the inhabitants of the Italian village of Vasto expressed it in a petition they sent to the Bourbon minister of the interior protesting the deforestation of their lands.

> Your Excellency: His Majesty's faithful subjects beg to inform Your Excellency that the woods belonging to both charitable institutions and private individuals are being cut

> down and the land cleared for cultivation, to the detriment of our pastures. For lack of firewood the undersigned and all other inhabitants of the Abruzzi region will be compelled to emigrate to California.[6]

It did not occur to them to mention emigration to the Kingdom of Naples or to another European country; and this was before every village in Italy had at least one native son in America. By the time of Levi's exile in southern Italy, in the mid-Thirties, the Myth was reinforced by an elaborate network of contacts with American relatives. Letters, photographs, money, packages of food and American gadgets, arrived in a steady stream from those who had been fortunate enough to emigrate in reality to the earthly Eden. Those who remained in Italy dreamed and mythologized. The objects that arrived from America were viewed as powerful symbols, virtually as fetishes. In the Thirties in southern Italy the dollar bill—that paper facsimile of the American Myth—was used as a token of religious sacrifice, particularly to honor the Madonna. The peasants pinned it to the clothing of religious statues and burned it during the fireworks displays on the feast days of local saints.[7] Their popular songs, their superstitions and folklore, expressed this mythology of an America where the streets were paved with gold and the common man drove around in automobiles. But the Myth was real; there were those who had gone off to live it in actuality, and letters and money orders arrived to prove it.

For the most part these emigrants, especially those from the south, were poor and uneducated. Few of them left any systematic written accounts of their experience, and what happened to them and what they felt about it can only be pieced together from letters and folklore. One who did write a book was Angelo Pellegrini, who emigrated from a small Tuscan town to America as a child with his family in 1913 and eventually became a scholar and a professor at the University of Washington. In spite of its occasional bitterness his *Immigrant's Return* (1951) reads like a fable of the Dream of Emigration. In the Pacific Northwest town where the family settled, life was crude and hard but abundant. Pellegrini never forgot his first American breakfast in New York: ham, eggs, potatoes, toast, coffee, cream, sugar. Anyone who smiles at his materialism has perhaps never been hungry in the way Italian peasants in 1913 were hungry. Pellegrini is realistic, and he has the objectivity of a scholar. As the son of a peasant he knows that materialism is better than want, and he saves his special irony for the European intellectuals who criticize American vulgarity: "The critics who have accused us of kneeling before the Dynamo, and who have unabashedly told us of their own spiritual superiority, have done so in the ease and comfort of their studies, with servants at their beck and call. . . . I am not aware that there has ever been a St. Francis among them." [8]

Pellegrini fulfilled another well-known part of the fable: After he had become an American he went back for a visit to his native village with his pocket full of dollars. It was this experience that brought home to him the true significance of what had happened to him. On the ship he met a Florentine merchant who was an inexhaustible source of anti-American clichés. The food on the ship was indifferent, and Giancarlo, who was coming back from a business trip to America, had the answer. " 'Ah, vedrete a Firenze! Che vino! Che cucina!' . . . He explained that the ship had taken on her supplies in New York. Which meant, of course, that the meat, the fowl, the fruit were storage products—frozen for Heaven knew how long! The wine, too, was American wine deceptively bottled. He expostulated learnedly on America. All commerce! All dollars! No soul! No heart! All hurry and frustration. 'L'Americano ha tutto che il cuore desidera; ma non sa godere niente.' " [9]

As a matter of fact, when Pellegrini reached his Tuscan village he found the wine was sour because the peasants harvested the grapes before they were ripe, afraid their neighbors would steal them. But even before this he discovered that Giancarlo, like the Italian intellectuals, was not St. Francis. His trunks were full of American contraband which he hoped to get through customs: two dozen portable radios, a hundred and eighty cartons of cigarettes, a hundred and fifty pairs of nylons, five dozen cigarette lighters, lighter fluid, three dozen sheets, fifty shirts, an assortment of drugs and cosmetics. "Wherever he is, I salute Giancarlo. May the good Lord protect him from the degradation of commerce, dollars, and frustration." [10] Without a certain level of material substance there is no spirit and men live like animals. As a child Pellegrini was sent out on the roads with a cart to gather manure with his bare hands. But the real significance of America is not that it enabled him like Giancarlo to have fifty shirts and two dozen radios, but that it had given him the possibility of fulfilling himself that he would never have had as an Italian peasant. It was hunger that had brought his family to America. But once he was there anything was possible; he studied, wrote books, and became a professor. "I had realized long before that emigration to America had meant for me the difference between growth and stagnation; that it had changed the whole course of my life; that it had given me freedom to pursue the profession of my choice; and that it had made me quite happy. But I had never felt the weight of this truth with such convulsive immediacy as I did during the days we spent with the people who had been my childhood friends. In the barrenness of their existence I saw what might have been my own destiny." [11]

Pellegrini's case was exceptional; very few rose as high in American society as he did in the second generation. The trouble is that only those who were exceptional wrote books. Jerre Mangione's *Monte Allegro* (1942) probably comes as close as any other book to portraying the experience of typical immigrants. Set in the Italian colony in Rochester, New York, it shows the well-known three-generation pattern of Americanization: the unassimilated grandparents, the half-assimilated parents, and the Americanized children. A great book might be written on this theme along the line of *My Ántonia,* but unfortunately Mangione does not go this deep. The treatment is light and the style anecdotal, and the result is a kind of Italian *Life with Father.* A book written in a different style, more scholarly and more bitter, is Panuzio's *The Soul of an Immigrant* (1921). Constantine Panuzio was born in the province of

Bari in 1884 and first came to America as a merchant seaman. Like Pellegrini, he went on to become a university professor, a sociologist at UCLA. But he climbed a steeper path than Pellegrini and was treated to more kicks and blows on the way. His autobiography is almost totally critical of America, documenting in bitter detail all the brutality, cruelty, and injustice he had experienced. This too is part of the myth, another and darker side of it. Among the small number of loan-words that have passed into the Italian language from English are *linciare,* to lynch, and *linciaggio*, a lynching. The Sacco-Vanzetti case has passed into the Italian national consciousness, not only among intellectuals as in America but among illiterate peasants and people who have never read a book. When these two Italian immigrants, a humble shoemaker and a fish-peddler, were executed in 1927 in Massachusetts for a crime they almost certainly did not commit, a legend was created which became in the Italian mind a parable of "justice" as it is dealt out to the immigrant in America. Another case almost forgotten in America is still remembered in Italy. In New Orleans in 1890 a group of nineteen Sicilian immigrants who were accused of the murder of a police chief were taken from jail by a mob, and eleven of them were killed. This lynching was virtually advertised beforehand in the papers; the day before the *New Orleans Times-Democrat* had announced a mass meeting and advised its readers to "come prepared for action." After the lynching the same paper congratulated the mob, commenting, "Desperate diseases require desperate measures." This incident was widely publicized in Italy and resulted in a wave of anti-American feeling. The consul in New Orleans protested to the federal government, and the Italian minister in Washington was recalled to Rome; in Italy there was even a brief war scare.[12] These incidents and others like them helped to establish the notion which still persists in Italy today that lynchings of Negroes and "foreigners" are a daily occurrence in America. The Italian emotionalism over the Chessman execution in 1960 and the Soblen case in 1962 can only be understood as part of this pattern. The innocence of both Chessman and Soblen was never questioned by most Italians, journalists and intellectuals included. Both cases were accepted as typical of the persecution of Jews, immigrants, and artists in America. It was no use for American papers to point out that both Chessman and Soblen had been convicted by legally constituted courts. So had Sacco and Vanzetti. The typical Italian, intellectual or peasant, does not have a high regard for American justice.

Pietro Di Donato's *Christ in Concrete,* a best seller in America when it appeared in 1939, was even more widely read in Italy, where it was translated in 1941 as *Cristo fra i muratori.* Its literary quality is not remarkable; probably its popularity in America was more a symptom of a bad social conscience than anything else. In Italy it was read for other reasons. At the time it appeared—at the beginning of the Second World War—it coincided exactly with what Fascist propagandists wanted Italians to believe about America and about the fate of immigrants in the country that had murdered Sacco and Vanzetti. Its characters are Mulberry Street immigrants from the Abruzzi —the young hero Paul, his mother Annunziata, his father Geremio who is buried in liquid concrete in the fall of a scaffolding, his brother Luigi who loses his leg in another construction accident, his godfather Nazone who is pushed from a building to his death by a brutal foreman. In spite of this chain of horrors the novel is in its general lines autobiographical. Di Donato's own father died like the father in the novel, and many of the other stories are based on actual incidents. If the novel is unconvincing it is because he does not succeed in making these atrocities credible as, for instance, Rölvaag's *Giants in the Earth* does, and because he is too obviously angry. No one is ever punished for the negligence or outright criminality implied in Nazone's death, and the Italians who are crippled on construction jobs are left to starve. The style is marred by an amateurish Greenwich Village experimentalism, and even the Italian spoken by the characters is jarringly inaccurate. But the novel caught on in Italy not only because it was encouraged by the propagandists but because it expressed something the Italian mentality wanted to believe. It crystallized the whole disenchantment toward the Dream of Emigration that had begun to grow in the minds of Italians in the years after Sacco and Vanzetti and the Depression. "Discovered by an Italian—named from Italian—but oh, that I may leave this land of disillusion!" [13] cries Nazone shortly before his death. The message was not that Italians fall off buildings or even that race prejudice exists in America. It was that dreams are flimsy, reality is bitter, and America—the America of golden streets and easy abundance—does not exist. For those who stayed behind, the ones who had envied their prosperous American cousins, it was something they had wanted to believe all along.

Not all Italians had relatives in America and not all read *Cristo fra i muratori,* but they all went to the movies. Here they saw another America, the most fantastic of all. Some of the films were bad, but this did not really matter. The important thing was that the America they showed was believed in, and that these flimsy shadows on a screen dissolved away even the bitter stories of returned emigrants. In the movies they saw an America where the material problems had been solved and people were free to make love or get rich, to be gangsters, reporters, or aviators as the impulse struck them. Whether or not there was such a place, it was lovely to think about. Anybody who had a coin in his pocket could live in this place for an hour, in the movie theatre, and shut out Fascism for a while. This was an America where the dream never turned sour. Unlike Nazone in *Christ in Concrete,* Harold Lloyd never fell off the building; he hung on by his fingernails and in the end he married the banker's daughter. The films were fantastic and yet in a way they were real, more real than American literature which was only words on a page. The films showed real buildings, real skyscrapers, real streets, and the actors were flesh-and-blood people who lived somewhere in the world in a place you could go to. While the American intellectuals were attacking the vulgarity of the films and the Hays Office was trying to censor them, Hollywood was showing the young Italians exactly the kind of lives they wanted to live. The very "vulgarity" of the

all; but they never got around to doing anything. The heroes of the Westerns talked very little. They brooded, they chewed blades of grass, and when they acted they acted swiftly and impulsively. Instead of making speeches on balconies they saddled up and rode away to cut off the bandits at the pass. The cowboy stood for unreflective action. He was the real Nietzschean, and not Italo Balbo with his goatee and his rhetoric borrowed from D'Annunzio. In this way a lot of young Italians became anti-Fascists without knowing it, simply by going to the movies. The last film to arrive from America before the war was Frank Capra's *You Can't Take It with You,* released in Italy as *L'eterna illusione.* It was exactly America the Italians of 1939 wanted to believe in: a promised land where all the races of Europe flowed together in a kind of parody of the melting pot, love was madcap and effortless, and the problems dissolved at the end of a shower of dollars. "Many of us understand only today," the critic Pietro Bonfiglioli wrote in 1954, "that to applaud a film of Ford or Capra, to surrender to the amiable fiction of a democratic-paternalistic idyll like *You Can't Take It with You,* meant in the darkness of our collective unconscious to reject the mobilization of emotions, the psychological breast-beating of a declamatory Romanità to preserve in the back of our minds one uncorrupted corner where we could still permit ourselves the foolish and harmless whim of an inviolable intimacy. It meant rejecting complicity for a moment, rescuing the possibility of an innocence." [16]

It was not really a political message that the Italians found in the films; what attracted them was a desire for an American kind of happiness that was basically bourgeois. The "inviolable intimacy" that Bonfiglioli wanted to preserve was something Americans took for granted: the right to forget about politics and enjoy their private lives in security and comfort. This was what the businessmen meant when they said that the best propaganda America could drop on Europe would be the Sears Roebuck catalog. Unfortunately they were probably right. If the average Italian had to choose between the grandiose and crumbling Baths of Diocletian and the bathroom in an American film he would have no trouble deciding which he wanted. By 1960, probably, he had it. The material progress that seemed "American" in the Thirties came to Europe too after the war as an inevitable result of the new peacetime prosperity. The electric shavers, chromium plumbing, refrigerators, neon signs, modern kitchens, and supermarkets were things the Italians had seen in the movies before they saw them in their own country. Because of this optical illusion they seemed to come from America, and America was blamed for them by the spiritually minded and praised by the materialists when it did not really deserve either. A great deal of what is called "Americanism" in Europe and the rest of the world today is only the natural development of an industrial technology. It is impossible to insulate a culture against this kind of progress; it would have come to Italy eventually even if there had been no war and Fascism had continued. Even the less admirable elements of modernism, from jukeboxes to comic books, are inevitable in the same way. To stop them would be like trying to stop the invention of printing, which in its time was blamed for causing the end of courtly literature and producing a technological unemployment of troubadours. Progress always seems vulgar to the refined, but the man in the street wants it anyhow. This is what America represented for Italians in the years of the Economic Miracle.

Among those who deplored this "Americanization" of Italy were the American tourists. Those who had known Italy under Fascism and came back ten years after the war hardly recognized it. In the suburbs of Milan and Rome new apartment houses had sprung up, modern, functional, and steam-heated. The shops were full of refrigerators, vacuum cleaners, televisions, Kleenex, nylons, electric razors, transistor radios. There were the same supermarkets as in America, the mozzarella and salami wrapped in neat pliofilm. There were even the same Rice Krispies, except that in Italy they said "Pif Paf Pof" instead of "Snap, Crackle, and Pop." Here and there the traces of Fascist slogans were still visible on the walls ("Believe! Obey! Fight!"), but they were almost hidden under the Coca-Cola signs. In the elegant new apartment quarters of Rome, Due Pini or Monte Mario, the American could easily imagine himself in Evanston or Beverly Hills.

This was the last of the many ways the Italians had "discovered America." After the movies and the letters from emigrants, after the American literature of the Thirties, came the flood of mass-produced goods that transformed the face of Europe as it had transformed America. Naturally the high-minded could only deplore this. In the nineteenth century Henry James was annoyed to find a cab-stand in front of the Duomo in Florence, and the American in 1960 was not any happier when he found a Coca-Cola dispenser in the Colosseum. Unfortunately when the so-called underdeveloped countries discover progress they often seem to seize on the most material and vulgar aspects of it. It was not really pleasant to turn on a radio in Italy and hear rock-and-roll instead of Verdi. But if there had been no America for the Italians it would have been necessary to invent one, and instead of Coca-Cola and rock-and-roll there would have been something else. The critics who attacked this "vulgarization" of Italy were strange bedfellows: American tourists, old-fashioned Crocean aesthetes, certain elements of the clergy, Italian leftist intellectuals. The typical Italian Marxist of 1960 found himself in the odd position of defending abstract values against materialism. In general most Italian intellectuals, and not only the leftists, deplored this avalanche of mass culture that spread over Italy after the war, and in general America was blamed for it. But under the surface there was an ambiguity in their attitude. The leftists admired not only the classlessness but also the material efficiency of the United States, and the socialist Italy they imagined was not very different from the prosperous America of the Sixties.

At the opposite pole from the leftists was the slick Dolce Vita world of the night clubs. Before the First World War the paraphernalia of expensive pleasure in Italy had been French; after 1945 the pleasures of the leisure class seemed more and more to be imitated from old Fred Astaire films. While the housewife was coveting American kitchens the café society of Via Veneto was turning from vermouth and Alfa Romeos to whiskey, Cadillacs, and Negro jazz. American slang was chic in the Roman film world: "Okay," "Hello, Baby." A lot of this superficial Americanism of fads was due to the continual flow of people between the two film capitals; half the actors in Rome were American or had been in Hollywood, and those who hadn't tried to look as though they had, by wearing American clothes and ordering dry martinis in the clubs with names like Bricktop's and Florida. Federico Fellini's *La dolce vita* in 1959 made the final comment on what had happened to the Roman leisure class in the Italy of the Economic Miracle. There were many themes in this film, or rather a single theme with many aspects, but under them lay the conflict between an older and traditional, often decadent Roman society and the wave of modernism that collided with it after the war. In one scene, in a night club called Caracalla's, the sentimental melody of "Arrivederci Roma" is shattered by a trumpet blast which leads into a wild samba, led by a bearded American in jeans and a leather jacket. There are many other Americans in the film, and they are invariably portrayed as uninhibited and energetic, if sometimes vulgar. In contrast to them the hero Marcello is passive and "verbal"; he talks instead of acting. The orgy at the end of the film, the scene that symbolizes Marcello's final fall, is accompanied by a particularly idiotic jazz record and the prattling of an American dancer. In an earlier scene Marcello fails for all his Italian charm to seduce the blonde and superb Anita Ekberg; instead he is knocked flat by her "fiancé" Robert, an American who has been gloomy and silent until this moment when he moves to a violent action. It happened that the part of Robert was played by Lex Barker, called Sexy Lexy in the film world, a first-rate actor who had begun his movie career by playing Tarzan. According to his friends Fellini is an admirer of Tarzan films, and it was partly for this reason that he cast Barker in the part. Although Fellini is adept at creating emotion in his films he is in many ways an anti-romantic; his view of the world is hard and incisive and it would be hard to find a creative artist who is more different from Chateaubriand. But after a century and a half his America is not very different from the one in *Atala*. America is the return to the primitive, and its national hero is Tarzan, strong, silent, and virtuous, still the Pensive Barbarian in Chateaubriand's forest.

2 *The Travelers*

Two books by Italian visitors to America were widely read in Italy in the Thirties: Mario Soldati's *America primo amore* (1935) and Emilio Cecchi's *America amara* (1939). They were important enough in influencing what the average Italian in those years thought about the United States that they are worth examining in detail. Neither Soldati nor Cecchi was a Fascist party member or even particularly sympathetic to Fascism, but the small number of Italian visitors who came to America in the Thirties came under peculiar conditions. It was not easy to get a passport to travel abroad, and in any case they were not granted to suspected anti-Fascists or to writers connected with dubious publishers. To leave Italy in the Thirties it was at least necessary to have a clean political dossier, also to behave with a certain prudence while you were abroad and not make excitable statements about what was going on in Italy. If the traveler wrote a book he did so knowing it would be published by a censored press. Under these conditions the books Italians read about America all had the same flavor about them. Even when their authors were sympathetic to Anglo-Saxon culture they were not likely to say anything about America that basically contradicted Fascist propaganda. When the books were published the Fascist critics tended to gloat over certain details and thereby throw a false emphasis on them: the racial prejudice, the materialism, the vulgarity, the lack of culture. Often this was not what the authors intended, but the net effect of these books was to reinforce the stereotypes the Italians already had about the United States and its people.

Mario Soldati first came to America in 1929 as a student of art history with a scholarship to Columbia. Although he did not mention it when he applied for his passport he came with the notion of staying if he could; he has described this first trip to America as "an attempt at emigration." He found himself in New York with not very much money in the worst years of the Depression, and his experience was not a pleasant one. When his scholarship ran out after a year he found a job in a squalid cafeteria near the university, where he was put to work washing dishes with an antiquated machine that shook and fumed "like a Buster Keaton Ford" and finally broke down and flooded the kitchen. With this and other odd jobs he managed to stay on for another year. When he went back to Italy he became involved in the motion picture world and worked off and on as a scenarist and director from 1933 to 1958. Meanwhile he had made two more trips to America, in 1932 and 1933. *America primo amore* appeared in 1935, but it was based chiefly on the impressions and experiences of that first visit, when he had been a hungry student without friends and with only an imperfect knowledge of English. It was the only detailed account of daily life in America until Cecchi's book appeared four years later, and it was widely read and on the whole favorably reviewed.

After the false starts in the Thirties as art historian and scenarist Soldati finally found his métier as a novelist, and a first-rate one. *America primo amore* is a novelist's kind of travel book: impressionistic, vivid, and highly personal. His title, literally "America First Love," made it clear from the beginning that he offered the book not as a sociological or political study but simply as the story of a personal encounter. First loves are an ecstatic experience, but they are also emotional and unrealistic and they frequently end in disenchantment. Throughout the book Soldati's emotional relation to America is obvious; he writes about the United States the way any fairly sensitive novelist would write about the girl he was in love with when he was twenty. The mood is disillusioned, often ironic, but rigidly honest and never totally hostile. Introducing a new edition of the book in 1956 he wrote, "It is hard to tell the story of a love without bitterness." [1] If the Fascists found in his America many elements of the "decadent plutocracy" of their propaganda—a sterile puritan culture, inhumanly mechanized, cut off from the twenty centuries of tradition that lay behind Italian civilization—this was an accident he had not intended. Unfortunately it was also what made the book popular in Italy.

When Soldati landed in New York he already knew more about America than most Italians; he was an admirer of Henry James and Poe and he was thoroughly steeped in American movies. In spite of this preparation the country he found himself in seemed more strange than Persia or China. Here and there he saw a piece of Europe, a reflection of Barcelona or Naples, and sometimes he recognized Henry James' New York or the gangsterland of the movies. But the secret of the Americans continued to elude him; the Anglo-Saxon glance was "azure, intransigent, and mysterious." [2] In one chapter, one of the most revealing, he describes his initiation into American love. To an American there was nothing remarkable about the experience: a blonde and rather immature girl who had come to New York from Texas, a banal Brooklyn flat. But to the Italian the setting was surrealistic: "the invisible but sensible metallicity of the ambience; iron girders, heating tubes, electric wires: a tightly-woven cage thinly covered by the plaster of the walls. And the acrid odor of burned rubber, the dry electric-powerhouse air that is the atmosphere of every American house." [3] When he lowered his glance, he saw not a human but a blurred mass of blonde hair, faceless and anonymous: It was not a woman he was embracing but *an American,* America itself.

Meanwhile all was not going as he had planned. In Europe

he would have arrived at his goal by this time, but for some mysterious reason the blonde partner continued to repulse him. "Oh, this is not a childish kiss," the face under the blonde hair protested. This remark baffled the Italian; he could not see why it should be a childish kiss, since neither of them was a child. Like the Italians in James, he could only fall back on the rationalization of all Europeans confronted by the mysterious innocence of Daisy Millers. "The Anglo-Saxon women and especially Southerners see in the Negro an incarnation of guilt, and approach even the Mediterranean races, the Spanish, French, and Italian, with an obscure sense of sin. In the kisses of their own tall blond men they savor the perverse innocence of childish and familiar love; in the kisses of dark emigrants they fear—and covet—the male force of the adult and foreigner." [4] What was happening was probably much less profound. The Italian had confused two American folkways, necking and seduction; the American girl was ready to play at one but drew the line at the other. His error, the same error that Giovanelli made in *Daisy Miller*, was to mistake freedom of manners for lightness of morals. He concluded that love in America was infantile, the game of perverse children. But it would have required only a little reflection to see that "This is not a childish kiss" is not a remark made by a child.

He was not very much more successful in his courtship of the American university. He was used to the European university system, and the professors at Columbia and Berkeley seemed to resemble postal employees more than intellectuals. In a land without cultural traditions the aesthetic approach to literature was unknown. Chrétien de Troyes and the medieval romance were treated by American professors with the same mechanical precision as the history of railroad unionism. Leaving the campus, these file-card technicians went home to houses where they were put in aprons by their wives and set to peeling potatoes. "Come on Billy dear . . . there's your apron there. You better get to it at once." And Billy obeys. "Blessed life. Billy has attained his ideal. It took a little work, or rather a little patience, those two years between his student days and his first important position. But after all, a little bootlicking here and a little there, and never express an opinion, never never judge, and at twenty-five Billy already had his chair." [5]

Amid a slight air of confusion (he twice refers to the American national drink as the "high bowl") Soldati plunges on through the wilderness of American social life. Italo-Americans were even more depressing than professors. Under a glass bell of nostalgia they conserved what they imagined was Italian culture, the culture of a Sicilian barber of the Nineties. While the phonograph endlessly repeated "Funicolì Funicolà" and "O Sole mio," the dinner went on amid a stream of bad jokes in worse Italian. The wine was terrible; how could Italians have lost their taste so quickly? When Soldati made a mistake in English he was called a greenhorn, and when he asked what this meant he was taunted: "Mario . . . in Italia vui siete nu signore, ma accà vui siete nu cafone! . . . in Italy you may be a gentleman, but here you're only a yokel." [6] The joke was good-natured, but all the rest of the evening "Nu cafone!" rang in the ears of the art student from Turin. Even the happiness of Americans was the gaiety of savages taunting their enemies.

When the art student had nothing else to do, he could always walk about in New York, the city "where sandwiches are the only nourishment and subways the only means of locomotion." [7] An unexpected invitation to lecture on Italian art in Denver gave him a chance to travel west, and he saw Chicago, "a metropolis defeated, dirty, triste, where millions of men live in misery and degradation. And for this reason there is perhaps no city which better represents America." [8] His Chicago hotel was air-conditioned; that is, he explains to his Italian readers of 1935, the air was *confezionata,* synthetically manufactured. Here he finally found the America of the gangster movies; on a Chicago street he was robbed by two Negroes who took his twenty-five dollars and his shoes and disappeared into the night, leaving him barefoot with his hands pressed to a dirty wall. At this point he seems justified in remarking, "Our life is not so adventurous, but neither is it so squalid. It is quieter, more civil, more human." [9]

In spite of all the bitter anecdotes Soldati's book is not basically anti-American. Somehow he manages to convey an awe for the dimension and vitality of the New World, an attraction that is almost erotic, as the metaphor of his title suggested. On the surface what he has to say is mostly critical. The America he saw was a land of quarrels and neuroticism, a culture in which under a thin layer of frivolity nobody was really happy. The centuries of puritanism seemed to have repressed everything that made life worth living. And yet five years later he remembered his first impression of Times Square as a kind of adolescent fever, comparable to his first pleasure in the arms of a woman. "It was a joy so sudden and unexpected that it had already passed before I was aware of it. And if, beginning with that night long ago, I have remained faithful to Venus even in my torment and frustration, it is because I long again for that moment; only that moment will satisfy me and without hope of finding it I cannot live on." [10] He came back to America twice before he wrote his book, and after the war there were more contacts with Americans. By the time he published *Le lettere da Capri* in 1954 he was a well-known and prominent novelist, but he had not forgotten his first love. This novel, on the Jamesian theme of international misunderstandings between Europeans and Americans, was basically only a retelling of the encounter in the Brooklyn flat he had described twenty years before in *America primo amore*. Meanwhile the America he had discovered in 1929 had inevitably come to Italy too. Most of what he criticized in *America primo amore*, from the petty crime to the air conditioning and sandwiches, was easy to find in the Milan where he lived in the Sixties, where he chose, in fact, to live in preference to Rome. Milan is sometimes described as the Chicago of Italy; it is not popular with most American tourists because it is too "Americanized."

Where Soldati had been an unknown student, Emilio Cecchi came to America already a distinguished writer and critic. Not only was he an authority on art history but along with Mario Praz he was a leading Italian specialist on Anglo-Saxon culture. His *Scrittori inglesi e americani*, an essay collection published in

1935, was virtually a textbook of English and American literature for the Italian students of the Thirties. He knew English thoroughly and had translated, among others, Shelley, Chesterton, and Bernard Berenson. In short it would be hard to imagine an Italian better qualified to write a book about the United States. *America amara,* the book he wrote, was so anti-American that it seems unbalanced if not downright dishonest to the reader who examines it in the post-Fascist era. Cecchi was not a Fascist in any ordinary sense, and the reasons for his attitude are complicated and a little obscure. Essentially he was an academician who stood for the conservative and traditional values that antedated Fascism. His principles were a respect for the purity of language and for the dignity and stability of the Italian literary tradition; in politics his ideal was the "Carabiniere on horseback," a stable social order maintained by police force. This did not tend to make him sympathetic with experimental or revolutionary literature, for example the American naturalism of the Twenties. Vittorini, who was sympathetic to this American literature and was influenced by it in his own writing, says of Cecchi, "Actually he was and still is an old-fashioned man, a nostalgist for past times. His incomprehension of America is the incomprehension of an old-fashioned man toward a more modern state of things. . . . If he was not a Fascist it was because he was essentially more old-fashioned than Fascism." [11] But the fact is that his respect for the Carabinieri on horseback continued even after the Carabinieri were serving the Fascist government. In 1942 he was a member of the Italian delegation to a Nazi-sponsored writers' conference in Weimar, a meeting which was addressed by Goebbels and during which the writers were told by another Nazi speaker that their common enemies were "Bolshevism, democracy, Judaism, and Americanism." [12] Cecchi seems to have conducted himself with a certain dignity at this meeting; he did not wear a black shirt and he did not salute "romanamente," in the Fascist manner. But at least in this period he did not distinguish himself as a prominent anti-Fascist. By the time of the Weimar meeting *America amara,* which he had published in

1939, was at the height of its success; it was reviewed favorably by Fascist critics, and it had replaced Soldati's book as the semi-official Italian picture of America.

The contrast between the two books begins with the titles: Cecchi's is literally "Bitter America." He is like Soldati in that he is writing from firsthand experience of the things he describes, but he came to America on somewhat different terms. His book is based on two long visits to the United States and Mexico in the Thirties; he traveled widely, met American scholars and writers, and lectured on art history at Berkeley. Throughout the book he maintains a consistent image of himself: the cultured, urbane, slightly ironic traveler in a land of ingenuous barbarism. He mentions his distaste for sensational journalism, but he adds, "It is necessary to describe things as they are." [13] Everything he describes is documented, and the bias is simply in his manner of selection. Of the twelve photos he chooses to illustrate American culture one is an execution, two show corpses of gangster victims, and one is a particularly lurid lynching scene. His favorite American author was Poe, but he was also interested in Faulkner; in his criticism he extols Faulkner's savage power and views it as an expression of the conflict of paganism and puritanism in American society. But in admiring Faulkner it is not necessary to admire the culture that provides his material; Faulkner's function, in fact, was simply "to manipulate this ferocious material and add to it the cruelty of his own temperament." [14] To Cecchi it was not American literature that was decadent but American culture itself, and literature simply reflected the fact.

Occasionally his comments are sound if a little cranky. American food he found hygienic, attractively served, and sometimes even pleasing to the palate, and many Americans will share his low opinion of restaurant bread. He mentions Berenson who compared the skyscrapers of New York to the towers of San Gimignano, but prefers the opinion of James who thought they looked like a comb with many teeth missing. He quotes with approval Clemenceau who summed up the Americans in two short barks: "They can't generalize. And they make terrible coffee." [15] After Poe and Faulkner he found Melville the most typical American author; at the bottom it was the primordial America of *Moby Dick* that attracted him as it attracted many other European intellectuals. But he was caught in a basic dilemma; the deeper part of him wanted to believe in the America of Melville, but on the surface he spent his time looking for the America of the gangster films and Faulkner horrors. He found both Americas, since both were there, but neither was in exactly the form he expected. When he finally reached the unspoiled wilderness in California the "immobile and inarticulate gravity" [16] of Muir Woods made him nervous, and he was grateful for the history and tradition that separated the Europeans from nature. America was too big, too new, and too raw. On the peak of Tamalpais he felt like "a gay but decrepit flea on the back of an unweaned elephant." [17] It was because Americans were born into this stupendous nature and immersed in it all their lives that they failed to see its significance; they rejected its one great poetic expression in *Moby Dick*, which they insisted on treating as children's literature. In this way he was able to take the position of admiring primitive literature without admiring primitives. But it must have been a humiliation all the same for the eminent critic to feel like a flea, even a gay one.

It is when he comes to economy and politics that Cecchi seems the most Fascist or crypto-Fascist. He visited America in the middle of the New Deal period, and he saves his most pointed sarcasms for the Brain Trust and the "mysterious Jewish gray eminences" [18] of the White House. Unlike many European intellectuals he admired American mass production—at least the Ford plant produced automobiles, copiously and cheaply—and even came to its defense against the leftist attacks of Upton Sinclair and the CIO. His chapter on the New Deal is called "The Destruction of Property." The whole politico-economic part of the book is unbalanced, and the latent anti-Semitism is Cecchi's most unattractive side. It is probably only a coincidence that the book was published the year after the racial laws of 1938, which Mussolini had finally agreed to under pressure from the Nazis.

He is sounder, although equally cranky, when he sticks to

literary criticism. His criteria are those of the nineteenth-century aesthete, not very different from Santayana's. He had never shared the admiration of other Italians like Vittorini and Pavese for the American writing of the Twenties, and he consistently treated American literature as a kind of spontaneous barbarism, to be admired for the same reasons Ossian was admired in the nineteenth century. In *Scrittori inglesi e americani* he characterized the age of Melville and Poe as "a crisis of barbaric infantilism." [19] The experimentalism of the Twenties and the new narrative language of Hemingway he found puerile, a "literature in short pants." The few kind words in the literary sections he reserves for Thornton Wilder, for Willa Cather, and especially for Robinson Jeffers' *Roan Stallion,* with its dark pagan sensuality that reminded him of the Leda myth. In spite of his admiration for the Ford factory he was still searching for the America of the Pensive Barbarians.

At Berkeley he spent several months living in the faculty club and lecturing on Giotto and Masaccio to bright-eyed coeds, the kind of art majors that are found on most American campuses. Scholarship in the area of the humanities, as far as he could tell, was almost entirely mechanical; here he makes the same criticism as Soldati. A colleague in the art department dispensed easy formulas for judging a painting: design 30 percent, color 25 percent, composition 18 percent, chiaroscuro 15 percent, "sentiment" 12 percent. Cecchi commented that this was to be expected from a culture essentially physical and practical, where the whole realm of moral speculation and aesthetic values had hardly been discovered. He admired American progress in the physical sciences. While he was at Berkeley, Ernest O. Lawrence was engaged in his famous work in the structure of the atom, and Cecchi made a disturbingly prophetic remark: "The thought occurred to me that if Lawrence succeeded in his experiments in atomic energy, if he found the right formula, the air about us might at any moment become as unstable as dynamite." [20]

The student life on the campus merely reflected the rest of American culture. The purpose of fraternities seemed to be to inculcate a puerile mass instinct, a kind of innocuous conspiratorial romanticism. The more democratic side of campus life—the camaraderie of students and faculty, the lack of classroom discipline, the nonsense of student politics—rubbed his European class consciousness the wrong way. Although he never made the point, most of the students he encountered would never have found their way to the university in the Italy of 1930. He explained the students who waited on tables at the faculty club as "needy youths who earn the few odd dollars that at Columbia and other universities are given to Negroes." [21] In the culture he was accustomed to people who were obliged to wait on tables did not go to the university. A few pages later he reported that to maintain at Berkeley a son who "wants to enjoy himself a little" a father might spend from three to four hundred dollars a month.[22] American students were either too rich or too poor for him. Here his dilemma was simply the inconsistency of Fascist propaganda; America was simultaneously the "decadent plutocracy" and the land of mongrel leveling.

In the classes in art history his students were mainly women. Apparently he did not quite grasp the reason for this: that in a nation with a pioneer past women are the traditional bearers of "culture." He did, however, arrive at some conclusions about the coeds. There was no denying their "clamorous beauty"; they were the long-legged and energetic heroines of a thousand American films from Mary Pickford to Jean Harlow. They looked as though they would respond to amorous advances like electric bells, but when they spoke—for example when they raised their hands in class to ask which was the Virgin in the Annunciation scene and which the angel—they had the voices of kittens. All the coquetry, the swishing of skirts, the collecting of boy friends, was mere kittenish play. On Saturday nights after football games the campus police beat the bushes with flashlights looking for couples, but there was nobody there. "Puritanism sees in the sexual urge above all the peril of the flesh and an invitation to vice . . . any expression of sentiment or sensuality is hedged and circled about with such suspicion and rigor as to cause a genuine social and psychological paralysis. Reared in such an atmosphere of bleak virtue, youth moves toward its first sexual encounter disarmed and disoriented." [23] His view of American marriage is the same as Soldati's: the matriarchy where professors are put into aprons by their wives to peel potatoes. Cecchi even had a theory to explain why this did not happen in Europe. Catholicism, with its tradition of Mariolatry, had sublimated the male tendency to exalt the feminine, and the result was twenty centuries of art and literature. Protestantism, in suppressing this tradition of the Cult of Mary, had encouraged or permitted a deification of physical woman. In default of a Madonna, men had turned to worshiping their wives, who became like all angels unsexed. In its extreme form this situation produced the religious sibyls and "female popes" like Aimee Semple McPherson, a phenomenon Cecchi dwells upon at some length.

Like Soldati, Cecchi expected the impossible from America, and his private view of it would not stand up to reality. Setting out to find the America of Poe and Melville, he found the America of Sister Aimee. One experience might sum up his whole encounter with America: On a pilgrimage to Poe's tomb in Baltimore he blundered by mistake into a Presbyterian service and was cordially invited to "join our meeting." He barely escaped the outstretched hands. When he finally found Poe's grave it was not very well kept and the streetcars rattled past the cemetery; America had not known how to honor its greatest poet. Just once by the Pacific, at the end of his visit, he caught a glimpse of the America of Melville. The last memory he records in the book is that of a whale emerging mysteriously and unexpectedly from the sea off Monterey. It was a sight not seen very often from an Italian beach. As he stood doubting whether he had really seen it the shape appeared once more in the waves, this time farther off, and then "it swam vigorously toward the setting sun, toward the invisible doors of a world without history." [24] He records the incident without comment, and these were the last words he had to say about America.

After the war and the end of Fascism there was a period of

rather confused enthusiasm in Italian publishing. In the new freedom all the forbidden books were brought out and printed: Resistance novels, books by Jews, Marx's *Capital*, translations from Soviet literature. After twenty years of reading the complete works of Mussolini and the memoirs of General Badoglio the public appetite was insatiable. A number of books about the United States appeared, some of them leftovers from the Fascist period. Both Soldati's and Cecchi's books were reprinted after the war, and a new collection of Cecchi's American and Mexican pieces appeared in 1959 under the title *Nuovo continente.* Another well-known commentator on the American scene was Giuseppe Prezzolini, for many years holder of the chair of Italian literature and director of the Casa Italiana at Columbia University. Prezzolini had a curious and in some ways contradictory past as an intellectual before he came to America. He had begun as an old-fashioned liberal socialist; with Papini in 1903 he founded the review *Leonardo,* and he went on to direct the even more important socialist-humanitarian *La Voce* (1908–1914). With the advent of Fascism he retained his intellectual independence, at least in his own mind, but by 1924 he was writing a book on the theory of Fascism, and the following year he published a biography of Mussolini, which some of his critics felt was not really necessary even if the Duce had once been a socialist. In New York in the Thirties his nominal function was to serve as an ambassador of Italian culture, but in practice he often seemed, at least to anti-Fascists, to serve as a kind of intellectual spokesman or semiofficial apologist for the regime. This did not tend to make him popular with Italian refugees from Fascism in America, for example Gaetano Salvemini, who engaged in a chronic polemic with him from another university chair at Harvard. Prezzolini stayed on in America after the war, although his comments on the American scene after 1945 became increasingly petulant. His essays, many of them written for Italian newspapers in the Thirties, were collected in several volumes after the war: *America in pantofole* ("America in Slippers") in 1950, *America con gli stivali* ("America with Boots On") in 1954, and *Tutta l'America* ("All about

America") in 1958. Because of his long tenure at Columbia, Prezzolini had more firsthand contact with America than any other Italian commentator. But his conciliatory, or compromising, attitude toward Fascism caused him to be read with a certain skepticism by Italians, especially by intellectuals of the left, the ones who tended to be most interested in America. One of his positive contributions was to blast away at several well-known Italian misconceptions: that in America the streets are paved with gold and immigrants become rich overnight, that Americans are cultural ignoramuses, that Italians are born lovers and American women easy conquests. As time went on he became particularly annoyed with Italian-Americans. He had been obliged to deal with them for years as director of the Casa Italiana, and his patience was beginning to wear a little thin with Calabrian peasants who could not recite three lines of Dante but considered themselves the hallowed defenders of Italian culture. Professor Prezzolini was an old-fashioned scholar with conservative tastes. In a 1959 essay in *The Italian Quarterly*, a summary which was almost totally pessimistic about future relations between the two cultures, he referred to Italian-Americans as "a wall of incomprehension between the Italian and American people." [25] And in a 1963 book, *I trapiantati* ("The Transplanted") he finally disposed of the subject once and for all. After thirty years of observation he concluded that emigration was "a great tragedy." The emigrant lost his own culture, however crude and flimsy it may have been, and he never succeeded in adapting to the slick and traditionless culture of the skyscrapers. Even if it partly succeeded, the adaptation, or attempt at adaptation, was paid for with humiliation, suffering, and blood. One of the most trenchant sections is that on the Mafia and organized crime in America. *I trapiantati* was beautifully written and essentially sound in its judgments, but the reader could not help feeling the impression that Prezzolini had never really liked America, the country where he had spent almost half his life and on which he had become, more than any other Italian, a kind of semiofficial expert.

Most of the new books on America to appear after 1945 were

by younger writers with younger attitudes, more inclined to sympathize with American culture. The first book on America published after the Liberation was Antonio Sorelli's *Questa è l'America,* printed on bad paper by a small Milan publishing house in 1945. Sorelli had not visited America since the war, and his book was based on impressions several years old plus the few scraps of information he could pick up in Italy in the first months after the Liberation. Much of what he had to say was out of date, but if he was weak on facts he was strong on enthusiasm. The prewar America he described was a kind of Garden of Eden with modern plumbing; the shopgirls were all pretty, the machines were infallible, and even the food in the Automat was good. What he remembered most of all was the hot water. In America, he reported to the Italians who had known fuel shortages for five years, your bath was always ready because "even in April" instant hot water came out of the tap. As for the bathrooms themselves, they were sybaritic. "It is an article of faith for every good citizen of the Union that, modest or not, he must have a bathroom to himself as the prime necessity in his life. In the case of those who can afford it the bathroom is like a salon, with furnishings of the utmost refinement. Sponge-rubber cushions, gleaming mirrors, cosmetic devices to bring envy to the most refined woman of the Orient." [26]

Sorelli had obviously read *America amara,* the standard text on the subject, and one of his aims was to refute Cecchi point by point. He borrowed several details from Cecchi without indicating the source: the comparison of the skyscrapers to San Gimignano, the statistic that more traffic is carried vertically in elevators in New York than horizontally on the streets. He often goes out of his way to admire things Cecchi criticized, for example Aimee Semple McPherson, in his opinion a remarkable woman, even though "certain malicious chroniclers" found her private life less than exemplary. As for the so-called robber barons and other industrial giants criticized by these same birds of ill omen, "it must be recognized that they were the ones to appreciate the boundless resources of the continent." If only for this, he concluded absolutely without irony, we should be ready to wink at the millions or billions they have put away for themselves.[27] In this America of genial capitalism there are no classes on the trains and millionaires and workers ride together. Indians and Negroes enjoy complete freedom, although it is true that some whites preserve a "proud detachment" toward the colored races. In sex relations he seems to have encountered the usual enigmas. Like other Italians he often seems to be writing about a personal experience he does not tell us quite all about. For example, if an American woman who has agreed to go to the theatre with you fails to show up, you do not ask why. If you did, she would reply with "an amiable but evasive smile." [28] The reason, he hazards, is that Americans are not hampered by old-fashioned European notions of politeness. In this Land of Oz even the rudeness is delightful.

One of Sorelli's most curious chapters describes how the rich educate their young. The millionaire's son starts in the lowest ranks among the factory workers, picking up scraps that fall from the machines. In this way he builds his character and learns respect for the common man. Naturally when he comes home in the evening, matters are on a different basis. "When he has finished the day's work, he takes off the overalls. Underneath is the millionaire's clothing and the silk shirt. Outside is his car, and his friends waiting for him with their girls; he goes out with them to enjoy himself for a few hours and spend a little money, certainly not the money he has earned." [29] This system, he adds, seems to have good results—a fact that can be confirmed by anyone who remembers the films in the Thirties in which the hero marries the poor girl who had thought all along that he was only a factory worker like the others. Sorelli's chapter on the factory system is called "Manual Labor Is Not Degrading."

The spirit of 1945 was one of great and simple enthusiasms. As a symptom of this spirit Sorelli's book was an interesting cultural curiosity, but it was not very useful as an encyclopedia of fact. The book that eventually replaced Cecchi's as an authoritative source of information about America was not published until 1953. This was Guido Piovene's *De America,* based on a series of articles written for a Milan newspaper during a long visit to America in 1951 and 1952. Like Soldati and Cecchi, Piovene was a traveler with a literary background, a novelist and critic and former director of the UNESCO division of arts and letters. His political past was complicated and drew a certain criticism on him after the war. As a young journalist in the Thirties he had written for the Fascist press, defended Mussolini's military ambitions, and even indulged in anti-Semitism: all the more gratuitous, as his later critics pointed out, because he was financially independent and had no need to descend to this to earn his living. In the preface to his 1962 volume *La coda di paglia* ("The Straw Tail") he defended himself against these charges, or at least explained his view of the whole matter. In a Fascist atmosphere, when the whole intellectual ambience and climate of ideas was conditioned by the regime, it was difficult or impossible to see matters objectively as they could be seen after 1945. In Piovene's opinion his whole generation of intellectuals had tails of straw—their compromising and ambiguous past—and they simply had to accept the fact and go on from there. He described his own political evolution from a lukewarm Fascism to a sympathy with the Soviet Union and the PCI (Italian Communist Party), and concluded in effect, like Rousseau, "Let him who reads this examine his own heart and say if he can that he was the better man." This argument was understandably not very convincing with those Italian intellectuals who had been leftists in the Thirties and had gone underground for their beliefs. A pitched battle broke out over *La coda di paglia*, which meanwhile continued to sell briskly. A second storm broke in 1963 over the rumor that the coveted Viareggio Prize for fiction would probably go to Piovene for his novel *Le furie* ("The Furies"). Since the funds for the prize came from the Olivetti family, founders of Italy's most progressive industrial firm and Jews who themselves had suffered under Fascism, another—well-substantiated—rumor sprang up that if Piovene was awarded the prize, there would be no funds for a Viareggio Prize in 1964. The judges ended by awarding the prize to another novelist, Antonio Delfini, and then resigning. Piovene was left with his tail of straw and the royalties from two best sellers. This typical Italian literary polemic went on for several months.

Piovene was thus accused by his leftist critics of having assumed a "leftism of expediency" to cover up his own political past. If this was so Piovene was not the only one; there were other figures with a Fascist past in the PCI and the various socialist parties. Some of these were even more violently anti-American than their colleagues who had been leftists in the Thirties, and the reason was obvious: At the bottom they were nationalists, and they remained so whether they were Fascists or Communists. This did not seem to be the case with Piovene, who was individualistic in temperament and not always inclined to accept the Party view of the matter, whatever the party. For a leftist he viewed America with a remarkable objectivity, the same objectivity with which he described his own country in a later book, *Viaggio in Italia*, in 1957. He spent over a year on the research for *De America*, traveling by automobile and devoting more time to the west and south than any other Italian visitor had. His book was over five hundred pages long in fine print, with excellent photographs. In spite of his copious journalistic research, he observed everything with the eye of a novelist; he manages to give the impression that he is more interested in the American character and human interest than in piling up statistics. He also had the advantage of an indestructible good humor, a good will that carried him even over the inevitable rough spots—once he was accused by a youth in an Ohio café of being a "displaced person" who ought to go back where he came from. But he had enough objectivity to see that the traveler in a country richer than his own is always ready to convert the slightest accidental rudeness into a personal humiliation. On the whole he found Americans friendly. The stranger who lost his way or even paused indecisively for a moment would invariably be approached by someone who asked, "May I help you?" The demand was insistent, polite, and sometimes bothersome. This, he pointed out cogently, was probably the true origin of what was called American imperialism.

Although Piovene was an intellectual traveling in the company of intellectual and often affluent friends, he had enough intuition to grasp that America is essentially a heterogeneity and that there is no one "typical" American or "typical" American region. His experiences ranged from a Negro Baptist church meeting to a visit to Ezra Pound in an insane asylum. He noted the turnpikes with their identical Howard Johnson restaurants serving identical food every twenty miles, the heavy-handed kidding that cops reserve for pretty women, the girls who have their little toes amputated so they can wear smaller shoes. The west was the Wild West of the movies, but Virginia reminded him of his native Veneto, even to its cooking. At a New York party, in an apartment overflowing with books, he found still another America. A young pianist played his latest composition, and whenever the piano stopped, the sound of a flute could be heard from the next room. The hostess explained that her daughter was practicing for a Christmas recital at her college. When she went to investigate she came back to report that the flautist was nude except for a brassiere: a vignette from Salinger or Flannery O'Connor.

Piovene visited several American universities, including Harvard and Smith. He divided them generally into two types: the continental, which concentrated on the intellectual development of the student, and the English, which was concerned also with forming the student's character. Harvard was almost entirely on the continental model, but Smith was more typical of America: The Italian intellectual gazed somewhat bemused into a swimming pool where girls were learning how to rescue the drowned. But in the campus theatre other students were rehearsing Aeschylus. He reported correctly that students who worked their way by waiting on tables were "on the whole admired." He met one eminent professor who had earned his education this way without encountering the least humiliation, and an Italian student at Harvard who worked in a hotel and was invited out socially by the guests he met. His conclusions on American education were rather more amiable than those the average American would be likely to make.

He was equally open-minded about America's faults. Racial

segregation still existed, Taos was full of "nuts," Americans tended to be intellectually lazy and politically undeveloped. As for anti-Communism in its more naïve forms ("You been able to get rid of them Communists over there in Italy yet?") he noted it as a characteristic American phenomenon but he was remarkably mild about it for a writer who considered himself a fellow traveler. About American sexual life he said the same things as other Italians, but he said them more objectively and with greater insight. "That relations between men and women in America proceed with a slight limp is a well-known fact, a subject for jokes even among Americans." [30] He met the usual number of neurotic women, and was made nervous by a luncheon of several hundred females where he was the only male, but this did not lead him to make any generalizations about matriarchal society. Like most other Europeans he found a deep-rooted puritanism under the surface in American attitudes toward sex and morals. Alcohol was the invariable preliminary to love; the encounter took place in a half-conscious state and then was immediately forgotten. But Piovene guessed that for this reason the American young were not emotionally marked by their sexual experience, which on the whole was greater than that of Europeans. Virgins were rare—he concluded nonexistent—and yet somehow all Americans were virgins. Sin was dissolved in a fog of alcohol and left no traces but a slight hangover.

Piovene missed nothing; he observed the drunken Navajos lying along the highway outside Gallup, and in Salt Lake City he noted the renegade Mormons who hung around the state liquor store and asked strangers to buy whiskey for them. Los Angeles seemed to him "an antique desert rejuvenated and forced to smile." [31] His rare sarcasms he saved for Hollywood; he compared the fame of a movie star to that of a race horse, whose name is known to everyone but who has to obey the stable boy. But in this same city he met a mechanic who had a degree in philosophy and commented learnedly on Racine and St. Thomas. S't't'm's? The Italian was baffled. Ah, San Tommaso. One of the mechanic's sons was a pilot; the other was studying to be a professor. Over his workbench was a nude pinup from a magazine. "I keep it there where I can see it," he explained to Piovene, "to remind myself of my wife during the day." [32] There was no typical worker in this complicated country. Who was the typical woman, the nude flute-player or the busy club-woman? Piovene is the anti-generalizer. He warns against seizing on descriptions in the work of certain pessimistic American writers as the true image of America. The United States was a complicated organism, on the whole healthy, but like all healthy organisms full of germs. It remained to be explained why the organism lived and prospered. "This American literature of desperation, in speaking the truth, performs a critical function. But beware of taking it for the final word." [33]

Gianfranco Corsini, the author of *America allo specchio* ("America in the Looking-Glass," 1960), was a correspondent for the Rome daily *Paese Sera* who made two long visits to America in 1958 and 1959. After Piovene had written the standard encyclopedia most later books on America were specialized; Corsini's was political and economic. In spite of the fact that he wrote for a paper that was often anti-American, or at least hostile to American foreign policy, his tone was moderate and his observations usually sound. Like many other Italian leftists, he confessed, he had gone through a youthful crush on America that had left its traces even after the Bomb and NATO. "For the Europeans who grew up under the shadow of the American myth, for all those who have hidden a sheriff's badge under their desk or shouted *Americans go home* in the street, who have read Hemingway along with Leopardi and felt themselves in the same generation rescued and menaced by America, it is hard to free one's self from the preconceptions: America dolce, America amara." [34]

Corsini was more successful at freeing himself from the preconceptions than Cecchi. He commented favorably on the end of isolationism and the new interest of the American public in foreign policy, but he found in 1959 "a general sense of insecurity" that seemed inconsistent with the high American standard of living. He blamed the chronic anxiety more on the installment plan than on an unsatisfactory sex life. He recorded the figures on paperback books: fifty-five million in 1958. Many of them were murder mysteries, but some of them were Aristotle and Einstein. He devoted considerable attention to C. Wright Mills, David Riesman, and other domestic critics of the American scene; like Piovene he knew that the United States was made up of diversities and that there was no "typical" American. Although it would be an exaggeration to call his book sympathetic, it amounted to a systematic dismantling of the traditional stereotypes about America, particularly the economic and political.

A similar book, perhaps a little more pro-American, was Giorgio Spini's *America 1962*, subtitled "New Tendencies of the American Left." Spini was a professor of history at the University of Florence and a socialist who had been active in the Resistance, a typical Italian intellectual of the democratic left. He came to America twice as a university lecturer: a semester at Harvard in 1958 and another at Wisconsin in 1961–62. In *America 1962* he set out to attack two images simultaneously: the anti-American stereotypes of the Italian leftist press, and on the other hand "certain pretty pictures, full of shining healthy faces and toothpaste smiles, which advertise Coca-Cola and baby food in popular magazines in the United States." [35] This book had only a small printing, but its readers were the key Italian intellectuals, including the leaders of Spini's own Italian Socialist Party. By "American left" Spini meant simply everything that was in opposition to the bourgeois norm: intellectualism on the campus, pacifism and social gospel in the churches, the Freedom Riders, even slum clearance and the intelligent moderation of James Reston. He found plenty to attack in American culture, from the Birch Society to "that Egyptian pyramid of idiocy which is the *Reader's Digest*." [36] But he also saw everywhere evidence of an intelligent and effective opposition to these things, even though some of the Americans he described might be a little perturbed to hear themselves referred to as "left." Probably because his main experience of America was that of university life he tended to overestimate the liberal reaction, as campus Americans themselves sometimes do. There was a chapter on "Revolt on the Campus," mainly devoted to the 1960 student demonstrations in San Francisco, and another on the liberal press from *The Nation* to Vance Packard. America as he saw it was often superior to its own view of itself; the solid Republicans piously repeated their faith in reactionary ideas while they went on building a modern and progressive collectivist society. The American conservative who read this book might get a slight jolt. But the shock was even greater for the Italian leftist who liked to think of America as a nightmare of lynchings and capitalistic exploitation. Spini admitted that a country so large and complex, one destined to play so important a rôle in the future of humanity, was not easy to be objective about. If he had a bias it was pro-American, and he confessed this quite frankly. "After all this is not the book of a disinterested spectator. It is my weakness not to be able to forget that my country, if it is tolerably free at all today instead of ruled by a Nazi Gauleiter, owes more than a small part of this freedom to America; and that if my people have not starved to death it is because there was a time when they ate American bread. I understand perfectly well that this attitude of mine is not fashionable at the moment, but I have not been able to change it." [37]

By the time Spini wrote his book in 1962 America was no longer an exotic and unattainable land as it had been when Soldati came in 1929. In the new prosperity of the Economic Miracle more and more Italians were crossing the Atlantic to see it for themselves. In the summer of 1962 over seven thousand Italians visited the United States by air alone, and transatlantic liners on the southern route often seemed to carry as many Italians as Americans. Some of these were businessmen, some were students who were beginning to come to America in increasing numbers, but many were simply tourists on their vacations. Under these conditions it was no longer possible to write a book about America with the air of Marco Polo returning from the end of the world. The skyscrapers had been described a hundred times and all the obvious generalizations made about American sexual mores. The new travel books were less pretentious and more informal, confining themselves to anecdotes and personal impressions. One of the more entertaining was Nantas Salvalaggio's *America a passo d'uomo,* literally "America at a Walking Pace" (1962). Salvalaggio was a novelist and journalist who spoke English perfectly and had spent long periods of time in America as a correspondent. In 1962 he was editor of *Panorama,* a monthly published jointly by Mondadori and Time-Life, and visited New York frequently. When he wrote about America it was almost with the air of an American interpreting it for Italians. Where Cecchi had criticized the frantic pace of life in New York, Salvalaggio merely commented: "The European siesta may be the greatest refinement of the old continent, but it is also the reason why America is twenty years ahead of other countries." [38] This had a familiar ring; it was the growl of the typical American Babbitt trying to buy a razor blade in Rome at two o'clock in the afternoon. In New York everything was always open, everything hummed, and everything was air-conditioned. In fact the air conditioning worked too well; in the restaurants in Manhattan you froze in the summer and roasted in the winter. But Salvalaggio warned that foreigners should beware of irony. What was seen in New York in 1962 was the future of Milan, and of half of Europe; it would not be long until the Italians too would have the privilege of being too cold in the summer and too hot in the winter, and of having things done by machines they wanted to do themselves.

One of Salvalaggio's chapters was called "Pizza on Broadway." He heretically declared it was better than in Naples. And why? Organization, modern methods, and sanitary kitchens. Sometimes the efficiency made him a little nervous, but it made some Americans nervous too. He visited a factory and found the workers on the production line were not allowed time to sneeze, let alone clean their glasses. Who understood any longer the *otium* of the Latins, the classic leisure of Cicero and Horace? But unlike Cecchi, Salvalaggio was not sure he was in favor of *otium.* Europe was leisurely and poor; America was busy and rich. The plumber who came to fix the stopped sink on Saturday wore an elegant blue overcoat, shiny black shoes, and a homburg; he was on his way to a party. When he finished with the sink he washed his hands in the bathroom without asking permission, and his bill was fifteen dollars. "But the doctor only charges ten dollars a visit," objected the Italian. "So do I," said the plumber cheerfully, "but it's Saturday and this is overtime. Because I came here to you I'll be late to dinner." [39] It would be hard for an American to claim that Salvalaggio did not know what he was talking about.

Giorgio Soavi's *Fantabulous,* also published in 1962, was an equally easygoing and insouciant portrait of America. Soavi, a novelist and poet more or less in the vein of E. E. Cummings, was the author of an exuberant novel called *Gli amici malati di nervi* as well as several volumes of verse. His visit to America in 1954 lasted only three months, but two books came out of it: *L'America tutta d'un fiato* ("America All at One Breath"), a volume of poems and photographs, in 1959 and *Fantabulous,* a collection of prose sketches and impressions, three years later. Some of the poems in *L'America tutta d'un fiato* were in English, which he handled with a certain vernacular flair in the manner of Cummings or Kenneth Fearing:

> And then she said
> "we had such fun,
> did you have fun
> Giorgio? oh you are
> such a nice guy
> as a friend."
> Yes I was
> a stimulating person
> in the American grain [40]

Fantabulous (title borrowed according to the author's statement from American advertising) was a new version of the same impressions in a kind of crew-cut prose. Some of the sketches were semifictionalized; one of them, "The Long Island Guest," was later published as a short story by *Cosmopolitan,* and it would be interesting to know what the typical American woman thought of her portrait as seen by an Italian. The narrator of the story, making an effort like Soavi himself to be "a stimulating person in the American grain," finds himself at a Long Island house party with a hostess who is a kind of twentieth-century Daisy Miller slightly influenced by Zelda Fitzgerald. He gets no farther with this brittle but decorative lady than Giovanelli did with Daisy, and in addition (un-Jamesian detail) he has to fend off her homosexual cousin Theodore. But even the cousin is boyishly likeable—"Don't you even want to *try*?" he inquires wistfully—and the whole weekend is wrapped in a wonderful alcoholic innocence. Soavi was the first Italian to be really enthusiastic about American women. They are all pretty and all charming, even while they lock the bedroom door and leave him standing on the other side in his bare feet. They manage somehow to be both childish and depraved at the same time, like America itself. To Cecchi the writer who best caught the spirit of American life was Poe; to Soavi it is Nabokov. In the cemetery in New Orleans in 1954 he encountered a pair of little girls who fascinated him for some obscure reason and later when he read Nabokov's novel, he realized what he had seen: "two Lolitas at the seaside." [41] Even eight years earlier he sensed that the little girls were symbolic of something or other about America, perhaps its innocence or perhaps its perversity, or perhaps both, and he took their photograph and included it in *L'America tutta d'un fiato*. The picture shows two quite ordinary little girls perhaps ten years old wearing shorts and carrying Japanese parasols; there is nothing extraordinary about them except that they are wearing lipstick.

3 *The Americanisti*

The official aim of Fascism in the creative arts was "cultural autarchy," an art and literature totally free from foreign influences. While the chemists were working on synthetic rubber and ersatz gasoline to achieve economic autarchy, the artists were supposed to be creating a culture free from the contamination of Paris and New York, which were referred to in terms like "Judeo-Masonic democracy" and "decadent plutocracy." The ideal was a kind of plaster copy of the glories of ancient Rome with a glossy modern surface borrowed from the Futurism of E. F. T. Marinetti, who had come to the support of the Fascists in 1922 with his *Futurismo e Fascismo*. Western art was not only unpatriotic but immoral; there was always a puritanical strain in Fascism and one of Marinetti's ambitions was to end the tyranny of sex over the arts. The chief Horrible Examples were Proust, Picasso, Joyce, Stravinsky, and the American naturalists. "Artists must prepare themselves for the new imperialist function which must be carried out by our art," the Italian Minister of Fine Arts declared in 1926. "Above everything, we must categorically impose a principle of *Italianità*. Whoever copies a foreigner is guilty of *lèse-nation* like a spy who admits an enemy by a secret doorway." [1]

The other side of the artistic program was that domestic artists with any true originality were censored, which produced a rather confused situation. Publishers who printed translations were always in danger of censorship, and at the same time they were forbidden to publish Italian writers who were suspected of anti-Fascist ideas, and this included most of the good ones. (It ought to be made clear that the suspicion was directed mainly at novelists and essayists; poets like Eugenio Montale and Giuseppe Ungaretti were left relatively free.) Jewish, English, and American writers were the ones that suffered the most from censorship. Some American authors were forbidden categorically, and others might or might not be suppressed after they were published. For a publisher this was a greater disaster than prepublication censorship, since by this time he had invested a large amount of money in the manufacture of the book. Sometimes the censors couldn't seem to make up their minds. Fernanda Pivano's translation of *Spoon River Anthology* was first granted a publishing license, then the book when it appeared was seized by the police, then finally it was allowed to circulate with a different cover. Other books—translations and original novels—went off to Rome to be approved by the censors and simply never came back. Fortunately neither censorship nor "cultural autarchy" was very efficient. Not everything was submitted to the censor before publication; for example magazines and reviews were not, although sometimes an issue was seized by the police before it could be distributed. Furthermore not everything that was potentially subversive was censored. The censors were bureaucrats and not literary critics, and often they were a little dense. In the confusion some extraordinary things managed to be published; the two most remarkable examples were Moravia's *Gli indifferenti* and Vittorini's *Conversazione in Sicilia,* the two most important novels to be published in Italy in the second quarter of the century. The real damage of censorship was not that it suppressed all creativity but that the writer operated in an atmosphere of uncertainty where he never knew what would be allowed. For this reason everything written under Fascism, even novels that had nothing to do with politics, had a curious tentative or diffident quality, a vagueness or a tendency to abstraction. The effect was apparent not only in *Gli indifferenti* and *Conversazione in Sicilia* but in clandestine anti-Fascist writing like Pintor's essay "Americana," which was not published until after the war. Even when they were writing illegally the Italian writers had the air of treading on eggs; it was the spirit of the times.

Meanwhile, by discouraging domestic creativity the censorship only served to turn the attention of a culture-starved public to foreign writers, foreign books, and foreign films. These were censored only when they were patently bolshevik or when they were considered anti-Italian, like *A Farewell to Arms* which was thought to throw discredit on Italian military valor. This policy, the invention of politicians who had no notion of how one culture influenced another, resulted in one of the most remarkable enthusiasms for foreign books in the history of literature. In the Thirties the anti-Fascist journalist and author Antonio Gramsci wrote from the cell of a political prison, "The public seeks its own literature abroad because it feels it more *its own* than the so-called national literature. . . . Every people has its literature, but this may come from another people, that is, the people in question may be subjected to the intellectual and moral hegemony of another people. This is the most striking paradox of certain monopolistic tendencies of a nationalistic and repressive character: while they construct grand plans for hegemony, they do not notice that they have become the objects of foreign hegemonies." [2]

As it happened, American literature at this time was in a period of vigorous activity, and it was above all the American naturalists who were read and discussed in Italy in the Thirties. Caldwell, Steinbeck, Saroyan, and Sinclair Lewis were the most popular, and even writers like Hemingway who were not available in translation were read in English; it was relatively easy to order books from abroad through the mail. For the young Italian writers who grew up in the Thirties, those who rejected the cultural pretensions of Fascism, these books were a profound experience. It was the first contact they had with the artistic revolution that was taking place in the rest of the world, a movement from which Italy was isolated. The fact that they overvalued this American literature and often made mistakes—for example preferring James M. Cain to Faulkner—did not really matter. They read the Americans half-clandestinely, in an atmosphere of conspiracy that made the books seem even more fascinating than they were, and when they could not get translations they learned English in order to read them in the original. Even more important, when they began to write they imitated the Americans. The process that resulted was similar to what had happened in the early Renaissance when the classics were "discovered" in Italy: first reading and translation, then imitation, then a genuine phase of creativity influenced by foreign models. The most typical writers of the Thirties, Vittorini and Pavese, came to be called "Americanisti" even before the end of Fascism made it possible for them to publish their most important work. When the main wave of the new Italian fiction arrived, after 1945, the mark of American writing was obvious. But even earlier, in the mid-Thirties, it was clear what was happening. For two centuries America had been a cultural colony of Europe, and now for the first time the tide had turned and was flowing the other way. This annoyed the Fascists and many Italian critics who were not Fascists, those who were merely academic-minded and jealous of the centuries of tradition that lay behind Italian literature. Who were these upstarts anyhow, these colonial merchants who were setting out to teach the sons of Dante how to write books? In 1932 Carlo Linati's *Scrittori anglo-americani d'oggi* reflected this petulant view of American culture popular among many academicians and scholars, even those who were nominally anti-Fascist. "European civilization has behind it thousands of years of history, a body of political and moral development, revolutions, natural struggles, downfalls and rebirths of empires, immense labors of religion, custom, ideology, a whole past of marvelous aesthetic creativity. . . . It is inconceivable to surrender all this treasure into the hands of Babbitt. The European soul aspires to something more profound than the ability to construct machines, or to amuse itself in leisure. It aspires to the grace of culture, to refinement of emotion. It lives in a world of thought, analysis, passion; not only does it glory in its artistic, musical, and poetic genius but it is nurtured by it. Tradition is its second nature . . . the American, on the other hand, is by nature deprived of roots." [3] This was written two years after Sinclair Lewis had won the first American Nobel Prize for Literature. The passage is all the more remarkable because Linati was by no means pro-Fascist or anti-Anglo-Saxon; in fact he was one of the earliest Italian interpreters of Virginia Woolf and a personal friend of Joyce. It simply happened that, at a certain point in history, he shared the mistrust of the Fascist regime for the "American vogue"—in his case not on political grounds but out of respect for the Italian cultural and academic tradition. It happened also that the Fascists found his opinions useful. Whether this meant that Linati, and the academicians like him, aided the Fascist cause is a complicated question, and one still being argued among Italian intellectuals.

In spite of such hostile criticism, official or unofficial, the new American books were read as fast as they could be obtained. The literary reviews of the Thirties, particularly those with leftist tendencies, were full of articles on Melville, Lewis, and Sherwood Anderson. Pavese's first article on Lewis was in 1930, his translation of *Moby Dick* in 1932. The fact that these books were read half-clandestinely and that the reviews that discussed them were often suppressed only contributed to the legend. Reading American literature became for a generation of Italians a form of resistance, a secret revolt against their elders. To a certain extent the phenomenon happened in other European countries as well; Auden's poetry and the postwar novels of Sartre showed the influence American writing had exerted all over Europe in the Thirties. If Italian literature was affected more than any other, more than the French for example, it was partly because the French were jealous of their position as the literary leaders of Europe and more defensive about foreign influences; but also because the French did not have this twenty years of clandestine reading at a time when their own writers were censored and repressed. To the young Italians of 1930 American literature was not only a literature but a crucial personal experience; they read it almost the way the Christians had read Paul's letters in the catacombs.

To these young students and intellectuals the American books were the antithesis of official Fascist culture. In spite of its pretensions to modernism Fascism was essentially a senile ideology; it looked backward, to the Roman Empire, and not forward. The America the young Italians discovered in their books was youthful and vigorous, "primitive" in the sense that it offered the possibility of an escape from a corrupt civilization and a return to innocence. Basically this longing for the primeval had nothing to do with Fascism and antedated it; it was simply the dream of the Pensive Barbarians that had fascinated European intellectuals since the time of the first discovery of America. In 1908 Giovanni Papini had called Whitman "a good plebeian who sings without shame all the things of the world," and went on to prophesy the revolution in Italian writing that was to take place in the Forties. "We—and I mean especially we Italians—are too literary and well-mannered. We are gentlemen even toward the earth, which has no need of politeness, and in our poetry, which suffers from overeducation. . . . It is not enough to open the windows; we must go out of the house, out of the city and feel and love things intimately, the most delicate things and even those that are soiled, and express our love without regard for anyone, without pretty words, without restricting meters, without too much respect for venerable traditions, proper conventions and the stupid rules of polite society. We must regain a little of our barbarity, even our savagery if we want to rediscover Poetry. If Walt Whitman cannot teach us at least this, there is no point in translating him and talking so much about him." [4]

The vogue of American literature in the Thirties was assisted by a quite incidental fact: that the younger generation of Italian writers, their own creativity discouraged by the regime, turned to reviewing and translation for economic support. This resulted in a good many more foreign books being read and translated, in spite of the censorship, than would otherwise have been the case. The typical would-be writer in Italy in 1930 made his living by translating, usually from the English or French, or by criticism and reviewing. An important outlet—and source of income—for these younger Italian writers was the Terza Pagina or third page of the Italian newspaper, traditionally devoted to literary and cultural matters. Translation too was important economically, but it was also important in another way, in the part it played in forming the style of this new literary generation. A high proportion of these young translators went on to become important novelists and critics. One was Cesare Pavese, who wrote a thesis on Whitman at the University of Turin in 1930 and in the five years that followed translated Melville, Lewis, Sherwood Anderson, Dos Passos, and Faulkner. The most important of Pavese's early works was undoubtedly his translation of *Moby Dick,* which was published by Frassinelli in 1932 when he was barely out of the university. For the young Italians of Pavese's generation this one novel more than any book stood for America and the Myth of America. In the same period Pavese, as a reviewer for *La Cultura,* was writing articles on most of the Americans he had translated and others including Gertrude Stein and Edgar Lee Masters. In 1935, as a member of the Turin anti-Fascist circle that had gathered around the publishing house of Giulio Einaudi, he was arrested and exiled under police supervision to the small town of Brancaleone in Calabria. His first volume of poetry, *Lavorare stanca* ("Work Is Tiring"), appeared while he was still in exile; the publisher was Alberto Carocci, editor of the Florentine review *Solaria,* which was in chronic trouble with the censors until it was finally suppressed in 1937. By the time he came back from Calabria Pavese had begun to write fiction. Most of his early stories and novels remained unpublished, some of them until after his death. His first published novel was *Paesi tuoi* (roughly "Native Ground," translated into English as *The Harvesters*). This short narrative, a tale of rural violence in the manner of Steinbeck or Anderson, was written in 1939 and published in 1941 when it passed almost unnoticed in the confusion of the war. The third and creative phase of the American influence had begun.

It is hard to establish how much importance Pavese's early translations and criticism had in forming his style. In later years he was annoyed by the suggestion that he had learned to write from the Americans. "It is too simple to believe that translation has the effect of training your hand to the style you translate from. Translation—and I speak from experience—teaches us how we ought *not* to write; it makes us aware at every step of the way a different sensibility and culture express themselves in a given style, and the effort of rendering this style cures us of any temptation we might have to experiment with it ourselves." [5] When he wrote this in 1950 he was in an irrational and pessimistic anti-American mood, and like all creative artists he was defending himself from the implicit charge of having followed his models too closely, of having "imitated" them. But probably it was true that he was influenced more in his selection of theme than in style. What struck Pavese above all about the Americans was that they seemed to have regained their contact with the earth and with region, everything that was summed up in the Italian word *paese*. Pavese was born in the small Piedmontese village of Santo Stefano Belbo but reared and educated in Turin. His temperament was not urban and all his life he felt restless and uprooted in the city, although it was not until around 1931 that he began to relate this to his reading and to his own nature as an artist. When he read *Winesburg, Ohio,* it seemed to him that he had found an allegory of his own relation to the soil and an explanation of his rootlessness. His first essay on Anderson was called "Middle West and Piedmont." Later, in *Paesi tuoi,* he wrote a thinly disguised account of his own rediscovery of Santo Stefano Belbo. The country setting is far from idyllic or pastoral; a dark atmosphere of violence hangs over it from beginning to end. But the violence of the country is natural, almost innocent, after the mechanical cruelty of the city. In one passage the narrator remembers seeing blood on the wheel of a tram after an accident; it was shocking, but in the country the sight of even human blood was natural, simple, "like slaughtering an animal." Writing this book was for Pavese a kind of birth, violent and painful like all births. But it was necessary for him to write it before he could fulfill his own nature as a writer, and for this the example of the Americans was necessary. His attitude toward American literature was thoroughly subjective; he found in these writers what he wanted, or what he needed for himself, and he seems to have missed the point that Masters and Anderson were really part of a "revolt against the village" rather than a return from the city to the country. As for Hemingway he seemed to have no roots and was more at home in Europe than in America; Pavese was interested in his style but not in his personal philosophy or themes.

Elio Vittorini, the second of the two important Americanisti of the Thirties, came from a markedly different background. The main difference was that he lacked Pavese's university training; in fact he was not an intellectual at all in the usual sense but a self-educated worker. Born in Sicily in 1908 the son of a railroad employee, he spent his childhood in a succession of "little railroad stations with wire grills on the windows and the desert all around." [6] He had the minimum of schooling: five years of elementary school and three of trade school. As soon as he was old enough to support himself he left Sicily and went north, where he worked on a road gang and helped build a bridge near Udine. By 1927 he had begun to write. His first stories were published in Carocci's *Solaria,* which had already become the center of an anti-Fascist literary group in Florence. As a writer for this literary review he found himself in the middle of a pitched political battle. The Solarians were attacked by the same Giovanni Papini who had called for writers to "open the windows" twenty years before, and referred to in the Fascist press as jackals, hyenas, grave-diggers, and Jew-lovers (for publishing an article on Kafka). In this way, at the very beginning of his literary career, Vittorini was involved in politics whether he wanted to be or not.

In 1930 he found a better job, as a proofreader on the Florentine daily *La Nazione.* He worked from nine-thirty at night to five-thirty in the morning—"very bad for my health"—and in his spare time, in the little proofreader's cage, he taught himself English by translating *Robinson Crusoe* with a dictionary, one word at a time. With this beginning he went on to become one of the most eminent Italian translators and critics of American literature of his generation. His first published translation in 1934 was a novel of Lawrence. He went on to translate *Light in August, Tortilla Flat, God's Little Acre,* and several nineteenth-century Americans including Poe. Many of these early translations appeared serially in the weeklies *Oggi* and *Omnibus.* When he could afford it he went to the movies, mostly American, although he was also an admirer of René Clair. Meanwhile he was still writing criticism for *Solaria* and other "subversive" literary reviews—that is, those that published or criticized foreign writers, Jews, and Italian authors who were suspected of lacking enthusiasm for the regime: *Pégaso, Il Bargello, Letteratura.* Many of these pieces from the Thirties have never been collected; others were reprinted, some in shortened form, in his *Diario in pubblico* in 1957. The articles on American literature show a wide range of interest from the colonial period to the twentieth century and an erudition a university scholar might envy. Among his other accomplishments he managed to stay out of jail all through the Thirties and the difficult period of the war.

He did not, however, avoid the usual troubles with the censor. His most important work as a critic of American literature was a book that was suppressed before it was published. In 1940 he was asked by the Milanese publisher Bompiani to edit an anthology of American literature, and for this book he wrote a set of prefaces with a painstaking and detailed historical background. He spent most of 1940 and 1941 on this task. When *Americana* was already printed and bound it was seized by the police, and it was finally distributed to the bookstores in another version with Vittorini's prefaces deleted. A small number of uncensored copies were rescued and ended up in the hands of Vittorini's friends, among them Pavese and the young literary critic Giaime Pintor, who was later to write an important review of the book which was printed only after the war. Except for these clandestine copies Vittorini's prefaces have never been published in their entirety. A selection appeared in *Perspectives* in 1954, and another version, almost complete except for the section on the Thirties, was reprinted in *Diario in pubblico* in 1957. Considering the fact that they were suppressed before they were published, these prefaces exerted one of the most remarkable influences in the history of modern literature. In a letter to Vittorini in 1942 Pavese wrote, "The whole American century and a half is reduced to the essential evidence of a myth which we have lived, and which you here tell." [7] Fragments of the prefaces were passed around clandestinely in anti-Fascist literary circles, and the censored version of the anthology was widely read. By 1945 *Americana* had replaced Cecchi's *Scrittori inglesi e americani* as the best-known Italian book on American literature.

By this time Vittorini had already acquired a second and more important reputation as a novelist. In February 1933 *Solaria* had begun serializing his first novel *Il garofano rosso* (*The Red Carnation*). The theme was the psychological fascination that Fascism exerted on youth, especially the sexual-sadistic element. It was not surprising that when the third installment appeared the censors seized and destroyed the issue. Later, when he finished the novel and arranged to have it published by Mondadori, the manuscript went off to Rome for approval and nothing was heard of it for several years. Finally in 1938 it came back definitely rejected by the censor. But five years after the writing Vittorini had lost interest in *Il garofano rosso*, which now seemed to him tentative and insincere and on the wrong track in style. In Florence the review *Letteratura*, the successor to the suppressed *Solaria*, had already begun publishing the installments of his second novel *Conversazione in Sicilia*.

In this remarkable novel Vittorini had finally found his voice. Later, in a preface to *Il garofano rosso* when it finally appeared in 1947, he explained his dissatisfaction with the first novel and his search for a new narrative language that had preceded the writing of *Conversazione in Sicilia*. What he was seeking was a "musical" element which would free the novel from its realistic limitations, something that would do for the novel what the music did for the operas of Verdi. In the opera there is no inconsistency in hearing a chorus sing, "Let us depart, let us depart!" and never getting around to departing. It is the *emotion* of departing that the opera succeeds in conveying. "The musical drama has the power, denied to the novel, of expressing through its complexity some splendid general emotion, indefinable by nature and independent of the action, the characters, and the emotions portrayed by the characters." [8]

What was needed was a technique for surmounting and transcending realism, a step into the "fifth dimension" that Hemingway spoke of in *Green Hills of Africa.* Unlike Vittorini's first novel, *Conversazione in Sicilia* is not a realistic book. The style is pared, imagistic, antiphonal; in its use of refrain and the careful selection of rhythms it resembles poetry more than it does conventional fiction. One critic has described the technique as "the style of repetition and rebound." [9] Whatever precise influence Vittorini's years of translating and criticism had on him, it is clear that without Hemingway and Steinbeck this style could not have come into existence. In such passages as the narrator's dialogue with the knife-grinder ("Haven't you got a cannon to sharpen? Haven't you got a sword to sharpen?") he borrows the rhythmic musicality of Hemingway's conversation between the two waiters in "A Clean Well-Lighted Place," a technique which is also found frequently in Steinbeck's early Monterey stories:

> Pepe smiled sheepishly and stabbed at the ground with his inheritance, that knife, his father's knife. The long heavy blade folded back into the black handle. When Pepe pressed the button, the blade leaped out ready for use. The knife was with Pepe always, for it had been his father's knife.[10]

In this example from Steinbeck's "Flight" the word *knife,* the dominant motif, is reinforced with the verbal counterpoint of *blade, handle,* and *button,* as the similar words *blade* and *grind* are repeated in Vittorini's knife-grinder dialogue. Such parallels could be multiplied endlessly, although there is no demonstrable reason why they could not be coincidence. Such coincidences do happen—O'Neill's resemblance to the German expressionists is a good example—and students of comparative literature are always ready to rush in and prove "influences" where they did not really exist. In the case of Pavese and Vittorini there is more evidence than mere parallels in style, not only the period of translation when both writers were steeped in American literature but the statements of Vittorini and Pavese themselves. There were other influences on both writers, and one critic has even traced Pavese's themes to Proust.[11] But, right or wrong, Vittorini and Pavese are destined to be remembered in literary history as the Americanisti of the Thirties. In general Pavese was more influenced in theme and Vittorini more in style. But this is too simple; Pavese's style as well often resembles Anderson and Hemingway, and Vittorini in his criticism often discusses the themes of American writers, particularly Faulkner. The thematic influence is not as apparent in Vittorini's fiction, probably because it is better assimilated than in Pavese, but also because Vittorini found no one "theme" in American writing, or did not find it as simple as Pavese did. Having made the transition himself from a Sicilian primitivism to a highly civilized Milan, he was not so ready to see matters in terms of a neat contrast between American "barbarism" and European civilization. In 1938 he wrote, probably with Pavese's cult of the primitive in mind, "Today there are men of culture in almost every land and language of the world. In almost every country, therefore, there is a conflict between civilized men and barbaric men." [12]

Pavese and Vittorini shared one basic idea: they both conceived of literature not primarily as the telling of a story but as the poetic recovery of a state of nature, the effort of a mind pursued by "abstract demons" to regain contact with the things of the earth. If Vittorini was an urban writer and Pavese a rural one, this was a superficial difference that did not affect the basic similarity. Both of them understood that it was not *in the word* but *behind and through the words* that literature must convey its true meaning. They recognized the Americans as "symbolists" in this sense long before the notion that Hemingway was a realist had been demolished by Carlos Baker and Malcolm Cowley. "Symbols are born in Hemingway without labor pains, by elision, suggestion, and recurring image: as Minerva was born from the brow of Jove," Vittorini noted in 1941.[13] And in 1938 Pavese wrote, "The message of the Americans is a sense of mysterious reality under the words." [14] This preoccupation with verbal values was no mere linguistic preciosity; its purpose was to get at reality, and reality was man's relation to his physical environment. These three anti-sentimentalists—Hemingway, Pavese, and Vittorini—are at the bottom nature poets, and their relation to nature is essentially an emotional one. It was to express this emotion that the rhythmic-lyrical style was necessary.

> And then instead of going on to Arusha they turned left, he evidently figured they had the gas, and looking down he saw a pink sifting cloud, moving over the ground, and in the air, like the first snow in a blizzard, that comes from nowhere, and he knew the locusts were coming up from the South. Then they began to climb and they were going to the East it seemed, and then it darkened and they were in a storm, the rain so thick it seemed like flying through a waterfall, and then they were out and Compie turned his head and grinned and pointed and there, all he could see, as wide as the world, great, high, and unbelievably white in the sun, was the square top of Kilimanjaro. And then he knew that there was where he was going.[15]

In the famous climax to "The Snows of Kilimanjaro" the sensory reactions of the protagonist are portrayed photographically, without comment, and yet an emotion toward the sensory impressions builds imperceptibly, from underneath, until it breaks out in the unexpected sight of the snow-covered mountain. Not only the imagery but the syntax and rhythm contribute to the climax. The long descriptive passage (the locusts, the rainstorm) consists of only two sentences, in a flowing and liquid rhythm achieved through the comma splice and the frequent use of the connectives *and* and *then.* Then, at the end, the emotion produced is neutralized by the stark bluntness of the conclusion: "And then he knew that there was where he was going." A parallel is not hard to find in Pavese.

> I was tranquil then, as though I had been bled. But Gisella didn't come, and I lit up and smoked and the stubble was a little white and a little black, as the moon came and went, and the wind rose and the crickets screeched in the canes, and all the dogs were asleep. Then I was sleepy too.[16]

This passage from *Paesi tuoi* follows the airplane flight in "Kilimanjaro" even to the structure. The factual "And then instead of going on to Arusha they turned left" is paralleled by "I was tranquil then," the neutral state of emotion that serves as a starting point. This is followed by a set of sensory impressions in which the emotion rises to a climax, two sentences in Hemingway and one long sentence in Pavese. The sudden appearance of the mountain, "great, high, and unbelievably white," corresponds to "the wind rose and the crickets screeched in the canes." Finally the short calm conclusion, an acceptance: death in Hemingway, sleep in Pavese. Conventional punctuation is sacrificed to the rhythm of the paragraph; the missing comma after Pavese's "smoked" is a small but significant example of what he learned from the Americans. This passage would be a parody of Hemingway if it were not so well written, and if Hemingway had not so often parodied himself. *Paesi tuoi* is Pavese's most "American" novel in style, the most obviously imitative. In *La luna e i falò* ten years later the influence is better assimilated, and unless the reader is aware of Pavese's earlier development as a writer it would almost pass unnoticed.

Vittorini is a city writer and he seldom uses nature in this way. Even in the rural chapters of *Conversazione in Sicilia* his settings tend to be interiors, or street scenes like the dialogue with the knife-grinder. But he treats city imagery in the same rhythm that Pavese uses for the country, and often the resemblance to Hemingway is striking. His description of Milan under the air raids of 1943 ("Autobiografia in tempo di guerra") resembles the Gorizia of *A Farewell to Arms*: the dusty streets, the closed shops, the nostalgic memory of how the city had been in peacetime.

> The city gave us heat from itself, for it was burning, and it gave us its dust, its ashes; but it gave us nothing of its former animation, no noises from the crowd, the trams, the automobiles, the sound of shutters pulled up and down, nothing of its morning and its afternoon, nothing of its evening; and I have to say that all this was the way we wanted it, there inside, to be able to think of Porta Venezia with its plane-trees on fire, and all the cafés, all the stores, all the hotels and movie theatres closed, the lines of trams stopped and their trolleys down, nobody selling books any more under an umbrella, no custodian for the bicycles, nobody coming up the stairs from the underground lavoratory, no flower girl offering gardenias, no stands with sliced melons, no more newspaper stands with the names of Spain and China, not even the memory of dance-hall orchestras, but only the expanse of red asphalt in the flames, in the summertime, and the little prostitutes who come and go saying, no longer in anger, only lamenting, "O Christ, aren't there any men left? Isn't there even one more man? Isn't anybody a man any more?" [17]

This may be as much like Saroyan and Dos Passos as it is like Hemingway, but in any case there is nothing like it in Italian literature before. It also resembles an aria of Verdi, from the parallel development of the opening to the climax in which the refrain is repeated three times with slight variations. In this American style Vittorini had found "something that would do for the novel what music does for the opera."

Pavese and Vittorini were interested in American literature primarily for what it said to them personally, as individuals and as writers. Neither had any desire to be a literary prophet or *chef de cénacle.* In spite of this it soon became apparent that they were the centers of a recognizable literary movement, that this movement was anti-Fascist in politics and vernacular and "Hemingwayesque" in style, and that it looked to the example of America both for its ideals and for its literary techniques. A kind of scripture for the movement was provided by the *Americana* anthology, especially the small number of uncensored copies that were circulated clandestinely. The first important effect of this book was the impression it made on Giaime Pintor.

Pintor was born in Rome in 1919 of a well-to-do and prominent Sardinian family. He spent part of his adolescence in Sardinia, then returned to Rome in 1936 as a university student. Although he was formally enrolled in the faculty of law he quickly showed an interest in literature; by 1938 he was translating Rilke and other German poets, and a year later he was contributing to *Letteratura.* Even earlier he had begun to form his political ideas under the influence of liberal professors at the University of Rome. It was at this university, which had been rebuilt and modernized by Mussolini as a center of Fascist learning, that the first anti-Fascist riot in Italy took place: in 1938 the students whistled and shouted down Virginio Gayda, editor of *Il Giornale d'Italia* and an official spokesman for the regime, who had been sent to make a speech justifying the Nazi invasion of Austria. This happened at other universities as well; frequently the students formed liberal ideas while they outwardly supported the regime and even belonged to Fascist youth organizations like the GUF. Later these students served as the nucleus of the intellectual underground of 1943–1945, and one of them was Giaime Pintor. Shortly after he finished his university degree, in early 1940, he entered the army as a junior officer.

Pintor's father was a high state official and an uncle, Pietro Pintor, was a general who in 1940 was named president of the Franco-Italian armistice commission. When this uncle was killed in an air accident in December, Pintor, through the influence of friends, was assigned to the armistice commission in Turin to serve as a translator and general cultural aide. This assignment was to play an important part in his life; in Turin he met Pavese, and soon he was a member of the anti-Fascist literary circle of Giulio Einaudi and his friends. The Einaudians were suspicious at first, rightly so considering Pintor's position on the military commission and the fact that up to this time he had been known mainly as a critic and translator of German literature. But even before coming to Turin he had made his anti-Fascist sympathies clear to anyone who read between the lines. Early in 1940 the Fascist minister Giuseppe Bottai had founded a literary review, *Primato,* with the idea of attracting the young intellectuals who up to that time had been more or less hostile to the regime. Pintor and others were asked to contribute, and were soon sending to *Primato* articles marked by an elaborately ironic and thinly concealed anti-Fascism, although it seems to have taken Bottai some time to notice this. Of an anthology of Nazi poetry Pintor wrote, "In the light of our notions of poetry these five hundred pages are as blank and pristine as the leaves of a calendar." [18] In a later article he compared the sentimental decadence of Ernst Jünger's *Auf den Marmorklippen* to Vittorini's *Conversazione in Sicilia* which was published the same year, concluding that Jünger had "nothing to say to our generation" and that the German soldiers who carried him in their knapsacks along with Goethe were making a serious mistake and ought to throw away one or the other.[19] Another slightly too sarcastic piece about the Nazi writers' conference in Weimar in 1942 was refused by the editors. But when the Einaudi house was attacked by the Fascist press for publishing Dickens, Tolstoy, and other Judeo-Masonic writers Pintor came to its aid with an essay on "Protectionism in Culture" that somehow got past the *Primato* editors. He ended by implicitly comparing the Fascists to the Caliph Omar, who burned the Alexandrian Library because the only book worth reading was the Koran. About this time Bottai seems to have come to his senses and realized what was happening. He himself was considered a "liberal" Fascist and as such was suspect in party circles. Later, in 1943, he was one of those who voted to depose Mussolini and barely got out of Italy alive.

Pintor's duties on the armistice commission called for frequent travel, and he used these trips to make contact with other anti-Fascist groups in Europe. He became a close friend of Pavese and a consultant for the Einaudi house, and whenever he was in Milan he had long conversations with Vittorini. Under these influences he began to clarify his ideas and to understand his personal relation to the Europe that was collapsing all around him. First of all he realized that he was not an "intellectual" in the usual European sense of the word. In observing the relation between French cultural life and the fall of France he began to understand what decadence was: the elegant nihilism of a Drieu La Rochelle who collaborated with the Nazis, the dilettantism of a Montherlant who saw war as "a kind of corrida for unemployed intellectuals." The German equivalent was a romanticism that had turned sickly and ended in aestheticism, political reaction, and degeneration. "The posthorn of Eichendorff sounds once more in the verses of the bad poets of the Third Reich." [20]

So far in his writing Pintor had had little or nothing to say about American literature. But under the surface his whole intellectual development was carrying him toward the idea of America as the concrete antithesis of everything he had rejected in European culture. It was inevitable that sooner or later he would "discover" America in the way that Pavese and Vittorini had, and that it would have a similar profound effect on him as an individual and as a writer. The crystal that precipitated the reaction was the *Americana* anthology. Vittorini had given him an uncensored copy of the book, evidently in 1941, and he seems to have kept it for almost two years before he turned to reading it seriously. On a trip to Germany in 1943 he took the book along to read on the train with the idea of writing a review of it. As he read it, with the gray Bavarian plain passing by the train window, the book crystallized his ideas not only about America but about the whole cultural predicament of Europe and his own relation to it: his dislike of European intellectualism, his contempt for the academicians who had accommodated themselves so deftly with the enemy, his own search for a new and fresh literary language. He understood now what Vittorini had found in American literature and what this had to do with the writing of *Conversazione in Sicilia.* Under the immediate emotional effect of the anthology he wrote, instead of the review he had planned, an essay which is one of the most remarkable tributes ever paid to America by a European. It was never published in his lifetime; after the Liberation it appeared in the literary review *Aretusa,* titled simply "Americana," and it was reprinted in 1950 in the collection of Pintor's essays published by Einaudi as *Il sangue d'Europa.*[21] Before 1945 it was read only by the small number of anti-Fascists, most of them members of the Einaudi group, who happened to see it in manuscript. But a clandestine legend began to form around this essay as it had around the *Americana* anthology itself; in this way it probably had a greater effect than if it had been published openly. The "Pintor legend" became part of the folklore of the Resistance.[22]

Meanwhile the events of the war were carrying Pintor rapidly along with them. When the Mussolini regime collapsed in the summer of 1943 he went to Rome, visited the Badoglio command at Brindisi where he found "nothing changed among the military," and finally decided to offer his services to the Anglo-American command in Naples. It was not only an intellectual and professional decision but a deeply personal one. Before 1943, as a student and later as a critic and translator, he had been basically anti-Fascist but skeptical of politics, and had asked nothing more from life than literature as an honest vocation. But the war had distracted men from their personal habits and forced them to come to grips with the basic realities, made them realize that "there is no possibility of salvation in neutrality and isolation." [23] With his political ideas and his military training he was ideally suited to be a Resistance leader. He was briefed by Allied Intelligence, and on the first of December, 1943, he led a group in an attempt to pass through the German lines and make contact with the partisans around Rome. In the mountains south of Cassino, near the town of Castelnuovo, he was killed by a German mine. The last words he wrote were in a letter to his brother which was circulated in typewritten copies after his death among the partisans. "If I should not come back don't be inconsolable. One of the few certainties I have acquired in my experience is that no individual is indispensable and no loss irreparable. A living man can always find sufficient reasons for joy in other living men, and you who are young and alive should let the dead bury the dead." [24]

Pintor wrote "Americana" believing that it would never be published. He used to say of it "with his customary detached smile" that the Fascists would consider it an act of intelligence with the enemy and that after the war it would seem like an opportunistic adulation. Because of this it is one of his few writings not distorted by the atmosphere of censorship; he wrote for himself and freely expressed his ideas and emotions, leaving confused what still seemed to him confused at the time. The style suffered from this confusion and from his own obvious personal involvement in what he was writing about. The essay was saved by his sincerity, and by the prophetic judgment he showed about the historical movements he described. Much of it was devoted to a systematic indictment of Germany and German culture for the predicament that Europe then found itself in. "Every German girl discovers over again the same autumn sunsets her great-grandmother discovered, goes into ecstasy over the same landscapes, finds *fabelhaft* and *wunderbar* the same archeological relics. A fascination with wilderness, exoticism, the blue sky of Italy are still today the limits of an aesthetics which has served these incorrigible philistines for more than a century. Not one of them has grasped that a factory on the outskirts of Berlin is just as much 'nature' as the cliffs of Capri and that a window glimpsed from an unterbahn train has even more right to be admired, even on the same standards by which we admire a baroque garden." [25]

It was these people, with this "fundamental vice" deeply imbedded in their character, who were now on the point of dominating European culture. In reading *Americana* he had come to understand that the natural antithesis of this Germany was America, and America as it was reflected in Europe. "No people is closer to the American in the youthfulness of its blood and the candor of its desires, and no people celebrates its own legend in words more different. As always, the ways of corruption and purity are dangerously close, and a chronic madness seems to distract the Germans from their path and involve them in difficult and inhuman adventures. Thus these two peoples, who only a few years ago met amicably on athletic fields and competed in industrial production, face each other today as the protagonists of a cruel struggle. Each has taken on itself responsibility for the future of the world, and each is ready to batter down the last obstacle to the fulfillment of its destiny. For this is the real significance of the war which is now being fought." [26]

In this struggle Italy, at least official Italy, played a rôle that was more ignominious than tragic. Pintor took Cecchi as a model of the intellectuals who had managed somehow to accommodate themselves with Fascism while imagining they were preserving their intellectual independence. But it was not necessary to wear a black shirt in order to serve the enemy. In retreating within the alleged superiority of the European academic tradition they were essentially defending a decadence, the Europe of false baroque façades whose balconies were so convenient for the speeches of dictators. Cecchi's highest principle was the notion of defending the purity of language. There was no denying that *America amara* was perfectly written, but it was the book of an intellectual nationalist and therefore, in a certain sense, of a provincial. "This indefatigable traveler is one of the least equipped men in the world to adapt himself to the surprises of travel, one of the most obstinately shut up in the prejudices of his own country." [27] For this reason, even though Cecchi had lived in America and taught in an American university—even though he knew America superficially better than Pintor and his friends who had never been there—he could never grasp the real importance of American culture in the destiny of Europe. Where Cecchi had painstakingly assembled a chamber of horrors and pointed out corruption and decadence, Pintor and his generation had heard "a voice profoundly similar to our own, the voice of true friends and immediate contemporaries." [28] In the childhood of an Armenian-American Saroyan they recognized their own childhoods, with the simple objects, bicycles and newspapers, that had a power of enchantment denied to fairy tales and fables. The path of American literature was the path Europe was to follow, and the failure of the older generation of critics was that they had stubbornly refused to see this. Even Cecchi with his keen ear for style had never grasped the importance of the stylistic revolution of Hemingway, Faulkner, and Sherwood Anderson. To these "academicians" America was still the nightmare landscape of Poe, inhabited by vulgar materialists. For this was the gravest and most terrible of the accusations that had been brought against America, that it was a "materialistic civilization." In this phrase the cultural aristocrats of Europe, the scholars who wrote in comfortable studies where they never had to soil their hands, summed up the whole humanism of comfort and physical security that America offered to the rest of the world. Since Italy had culture but no bathtubs, it was obvious that if America had bathtubs it could not have culture. Furthermore, it seemed that some American writers had not even studied in the university. "And all the leisurely aesthetes who feel themselves the contemporaries of Pericles, the pseudo-philosophers wound up in their metaphysical distinctions, the journalists who have taken on themselves the defense of the western world turn their backs on a people so obviously degenerate." [29]

Pintor's essay was highly subjective; it was not so much a literary criticism as a confession of faith. The America he had discovered was mythical and not geographical, and he was perfectly aware of this. The point was that, seen from a Europe in which the old values were collapsing on all sides, this myth of America was "the best and last hope of the earth" and America itself was the concrete and immediate incarnation of this hope. After the first enthusiasm of the Liberation wore off it was not fashionable among European intellectuals to speak of America in these terms, and if Pintor had lived he might have changed his mind himself. By 1960 the essay and the book that contained it were out of print, and even to Americans Pintor's enthusiasm seemed a little naïve. But his essay was less about America than it was about Europe, and he had understood this too. In the long historical view it was not American military force but the Myth of America that would change the face of Europe, and it would do this not because America was a "materialistic civilization" but because it offered a new and youthful set of ideas expressed in a fresh and revolutionary language. To Pintor, who had been both an army officer and a writer, the words that people made were more important than their weapons. In his conclusion he frankly admitted that his admiration for America was based on an imperfect knowledge. "In our words dedicated to America much may be ingenuous and inexact, much may refer to arguments extraneous to the historical phenomenon of the United States as it stands today. But this does not matter, because even if the continent did not exist our words would not lose their significance. This America has no need of Columbus, it is discovered within ourselves; it is the land to which we turn with the same hope and faith of the first immigrants, of whoever had decided to defend at the price of pains and error the dignity of the human condition." [30]

4 *"The Time Is Past in Which We Discovered America"*

In the years immediately after the war a remarkable resurgence in Italian fiction took place, led by Pavese and Vittorini and including a number of slightly younger writers: Vasco Pratolini, Giuseppe Berto, Elio Bartolini, Italo Calvino. This movement is sometimes called neorealism, but the term comes from the cinema and is not very satisfactory. It was realistic only in the sense that Sherwood Anderson and Hemingway were, and its real aim was to transcend realism and arrive at something beyond, Hemingway's "fifth dimension" or Vittorini's "something that will do for the novel what music does for the opera." It is true that this new writing dealt with reality, the Italian reality, with a greater accuracy and candor than any Italian writer had since Verga. It is also true that the movement was set off by the same factors as the school of neorealism in the cinema: the end of Fascist censorship and the reaction against a sterile academism. The new writing resembled the films of Roberto Rossellini and Vittorio De Sica in at least two other ways: it drew its data directly from life, and its language was vernacular and antiliterary. But a better term is needed for the writing than neorealism, if only to avoid calling two artistic movements by the same name. They were not the same thing in the first place because they had different aesthetic roots; the films were influenced by the French cinema and the writing was modeled primarily on American literature. Furthermore there was very little artistic connection between the writing and the films if only because they were separated geographically; the films came from Rome and the writers tended to gather in Turin and Milan. There was a "Roman school" of fiction, led by Moravia and Elsa Morante, but it did not have very much to do with the Pavese-Vittorini group. Although Moravia was the best-known Italian writer to most Americans, mainly because of the success of *La romana,* the really interesting things on the postwar Italian literary scene were happening in the north.

It is a mistake to regard this new Italian writing as a mere imitation of American literature, as some critics did immediately after the war. It was not; it was highly original and in many ways deeply Italian, even though there had been nothing like it in Italian literature before. Still there is no doubt that the American books they read under Fascism played an important part in the development of these new writers. Some of them had been followers of Pavese and Vittorini or had been sponsored by them; others had made the "discovery of America" by themselves and realized only after the war that they had taken part in a literary movement that had operated, so to speak, in the collective unconscious of their generation. In some, those who developed a little earlier, the influence was only slight. Vasco Pratolini was born in 1913 and so was only a little younger than Vittorini and Pavese. He had begun to publish in the early Forties: *Via de' Magazzini* in 1942 and *Le amiche* in 1943. The novel that first brought him popular success was *Cronache di poveri amanti* in 1947, published in English two years later as *A Tale of Poor Lovers.* Like the earlier *Via de' Magazzini* it was a kind of collective history of a working-class street in Florence; structurally it derived from the Balzac-Zola school of French naturalism. If it resembled the Americans at all it was in its style or poetic ambience: the half-sentimental, half-naturalistic mood of *Cannery Row* and *My Name Is Aram.*

Pratolini's *Mestiere da vagabondo* ("Vagabond by Trade"), also published in 1947, was more Hemingwayesque, mainly because it centered on a single autobiographical character. The tale "Lungo viaggio di natale" ("A Long Christmas Journey") in this volume is one of the finest pieces of writing to come out of Italy after the war. It resembles *Conversazione in Sicilia* and it also has the mood of the train trip to Spain in *The Sun Also Rises*. "The reading of Hemingway is like a childhood disease," Pratolini wrote a few years later. "Whoever has not gone through it remains a child. Hemingway was, for a number of writers of my generation, our Stendhal. Then we began to see that there was a little D'Annunzio in him. Then came the parting of the ways." [1]

In this same year of 1947 appeared the first novels of two other writers who were to go on to eminent literary reputations: Giuseppe Berto's *Il cielo è rosso* and Italo Calvino's *Il sentiero dei nidi di ragno*, the second launched with the help of a review by Pavese in *L'Unità*. Some of the others, those with less talent, bogged down in sterile imitation of the Americans and soon dropped out of sight. Of those who went on writing probably the most talented was Calvino, who passed out of the phase of his American influence, wrote several more novels in a more original vein, and eventually became an editor for Einaudi, occupying more or less the position held by Pavese during the Forties. In addition to Einaudi the new movement centered especially around two Milanese publishing houses, Bompiani and Mondadori. The Hemingway Prize for fiction, sponsored by Mondadori, served as an informal rallying point for the Americanisti from 1948 to 1955. Hemingway himself provided the funds for the prize out of his Italian royalties, and the jury included Vittorini and Fernanda Pivano, a translator and critic of American literature who a few years earlier had been a close friend of Pavese. The announced purpose of the prize was the encouragement of talented younger writers, but the fact was that by 1948 the best talents—Pratolini, Calvino, and their contemporaries—had already appeared. In practice the Premio Hemingway novels tended to be dominated by the American style and thin on originality. The model was not always Hemingway, however; Romualdo Romano's *Scirocco*, the 1949 winner, was a Sicilian pastoral in the manner of Pavese or Faulkner, and Sergio Maldini's *I sognatori* in 1952 was a novel of the Resistance more or less in the style of Steinbeck. The contest was abandoned after 1955, as much from a lack of promising candidates as from a lack of funds.

In 1954, about the time the Mondadori editors were losing their enthusiasm for secondhand Hemingway, the review *Galleria* sent a questionnaire to a set of younger writers about the influence of American literature on Italian writing in general and their own work in particular.[2] Of the fifteen writers who replied some were sympathetic to American literature and some hostile, but none of them denied that an influence had taken place. The most flatly anti-American was Pier Paolo Pasolini, a Marxist novelist who a few years later was to become a well-known screenwriter and director. "The influence was so weak, it seems to me, that it is impossible to say whether it was good or bad. Weak, I mean, in the case of the writers who count." Carlo Cassola's answer was another that seemed to be flavored by politics: "For us Europeans with such a dangerous literary tradition at our backs, the contact with American 'barbarism' could be nothing but helpful. However let us not forget another 'barbarism' even better than the American: the Russian." Most of the others who replied felt the influence had been beneficial, although sometimes they had reservations. "Saturated with European literature, especially the French, we sensed the need to turn to new sources, and for us the new was American literature" (Fortunato Seminara). "An influence that undoubtedly contributed to enlarging and enriching the horizon of Italian fiction" (Mario Pasi). Mario La Cava contributed a long and rambling essay analyzing the vogue of American literature as a social phenomenon rather than a literary influence, and arguing that it was based on a mistaken view of America—"a feeling of curiosity and love toward distant lands, lands that were thought to be happy because of their economic strength and their freedom of manners, lands that the cutting off of emigration and difficulties of travel under the Fascist regime had rendered even more attractive and fabulous." He admitted there had been an influence on certain authors, but he found Vittorini's *Il garofano rosso* his best novel precisely because it was the least American, and wondered whether the Italians had not taken over mainly the faults of their models instead of the merits.

Like many critics, Italian and otherwise, La Cava assumed that a foreign influence was something a writer had no control over and that warped what would otherwise have been his "natural" style. It was analogous to a disease that he picked up from the environment; the best thing was to be healthy and have no influences. This confusion was cleared up by Italo Calvino, who offered a statement that was honest and well-balanced without being obsequiously pro-American. As a critic and editor who was also a novelist he showed a much-needed insight into exactly what an influence was.

> For Italian literature these "grafts" have always been felicitous: provençal poetry, medieval romance, Walter Scott, French naturalism. The history of Italian literature is precisely a history of grafts. The important thing is to keep one eye on the books and the other eye on the reality around us and inside us. And to know how to choose the books (foreign or Italian, ancient or modern) which help us best to see this reality. Those who read the Americans during those twenty years in this spirit performed a useful function, and one that is still bearing fruit.

Many Italian critics, especially those who were hostile to America on political grounds, regarded the American influence as an accident of history or a condition forced on Italian culture by circumstances. But to Calvino the Italian part in the process had been active and not passive. They had gone to the American books deliberately, just as the fruit-grower deliberately grafts varieties onto his root stock. The plant is still rooted in the native soil and nourished from the same sources as before.

Grafting is a harmless agricultural process, always beneficial. The result, as Calvino pointed out, is fruit.

Only slightly before the *Galleria* symposium Calvino had published an article of his own in *Contemporaneo* that was a kind of farewell to Hemingway and a summary of what the Americans had meant for his whole generation. He took the opposite position from Pasolini, who had argued that the influence was the greatest on the writers who were the weakest. To Calvino it was the writers with the most talent who could safely absorb such an influence and make it their own. The better Italians who had undergone this literary apprenticeship had soon detected Hemingway's faults: the essentially romantic politics, the style that was always in danger of becoming mannered. For Calvino the weakest Hemingway was "The Snows of Kilimanjaro" and the best the Nick Adams stories. It was in his own early work that he admitted the greatest influence; although he did not mention the title he was talking about *Il sentiero dei nidi di ragno*. In 1947 Pavese had compared the hero of this novel to Jim Hawkins in *Treasure Island* and "the Nick in certain stories of Hemingway." [3] Now Pavese was dead, Hemingway had won the Nobel Prize, and Calvino was on his own. Ten years after his discovery of Hemingway he could judge his time of apprenticeship and find that the influence had been on the whole a positive one. " 'You couldn't do it, old man,' I could say to him, indulging for the last time in his style. 'You didn't succeed in becoming a *mauvais maître.*' " [4] In the school of world literature there were no bad teachers, only lazy pupils. They were the ones who, when they got bad marks, wrote "Teacher is dumb" on the walls.

By the time of the *Galleria* symposium, the two leading Americanisti of the Thirties, Vittorini and Pavese, were no longer active in the movement. To represent Vittorini in this issue, which was devoted entirely to American literature, the editors could find only a piece on Wilder dating from 1938. Pavese died in 1950, but as early as 1946 his growing hostility to American culture had been apparent. In the case of both writers the reasons for their change in attitude were mixed up with politics.

Even in the time of his enthusiasm for American literature Pavese had had Marxist associations; many of his friends in the Einaudi circle had been militant leftists and some were Communist Party members. Pavese had long political discussions with his friends and attended Party meetings without committing himself. At a time when America and the Soviet Union were allies and united in the anti-Fascist struggle Pavese, like most European leftists, saw no inconsistency in admiring both at the same time. After the war this situation changed. With the Cold War and the Truman Policy the whole European left underwent a process of gradual alienation from America, and Pavese went with it. Before the war and during it America had stood simply for anti-Fascism; after 1946 it seemed to Italian intellectuals to support the landowning class and the democratic right, those who were defending the privilege of the Church and advocating censorship of the arts. In theory Pavese's antagonism was only toward American foreign policy; in practice it extended to literature and American culture in general. The real reasons for his disenchantment went deeper than politics and involved his basic problem as a creative artist. For Pavese it was the Myth of America, particularly as embodied in Melville, that had brought the creative artist into being, and the myth was unable to survive the contact with reality that came with the Liberation. Like many Italians he had expected too much from America. In 1930 it had been a "breathing-hole to liberty"; in 1945 it was a flood of Coca-Cola, Spam, comic books, and gum-chewing soldiers. It was a time of crisis for Pavese, and he reacted to it by moving toward a solidarity with his friends in the PCI. After a period of indecision he finally became a Communist. By April, 1946, he was writing an essay entitled "Communism and the Intellectuals" advising his fellow writers to take out Party cards, and in 1947 he began a radio talk on Richard Wright with a sentence that summed up the whole disillusionment of his generation: "The time is past in which we discovered America." [5] It seemed to him now that since the war nothing had come across the Atlantic to fulfill the promise of those first books of the Thirties. When something came that seemed to touch the reader at his deepest and force him to a "furious re-examination" of his own convictions it turned out, like *Black Boy*, to date from 1937. A few months later, in an essay in *L'Unità*, he published his final declaration of independence.

> Now the times are changed and everything can be said, and in a certain sense everything has been said. So it happens that the years go by and more books come to us now from America than ever before, but today we open them and read them without excitement. There was a time when even a minor book from over there, even a mediocre film, stirred up and posed living questions, stripped away our complacency. Is it we who grow old? Or is this little liberty we have enough to distract us? The creative and narrative triumphs of the American twentieth century remain—Edgar Lee Masters, Anderson, Hemingway, and Faulkner have taken their place among the classics—but for us not even the long fast of the war years is enough to make us genuinely love what comes to us nowadays from over there. Sometimes it happens that we read a vivid book which provokes our imagination and speaks out to our conscience, and then we notice the date: prewar. In short, to be frank it seems that American culture has lost its mastery, that wise and innocent fury that thrust it to the forefront of the intellectual world. And one cannot help noting that this coincides with the end, or the suspension, of its struggle against Fascism.
>
> Now that the more brutal restrictions are at an end, we have come to understand that many lands today, in Europe and throughout the world, are laboratories where new forms and styles are created—that there is nothing to prevent anybody who wants to, no matter if he lives in an old convent, from saying a new word. But without a Fascism

> to oppose, without a progressive historical ideal to personify, even America—for all its skyscrapers and automobiles and soldiers—will no longer be in the vanguard of anybody's culture. Without an ideal and without a progressive struggle, it even runs the risk of surrendering itself to its own form of Fascism, though it be in the name of its best traditions.[6]

This needed saying. The America of the Bomb and the policy of massive retaliation was no longer the America of the New Deal, and the American writer of 1947 suffered from an obvious alienation from his culture, a lack of something to believe in. Even to many Americans the writing of the immediate postwar period was a disappointment. But Pavese's attitude was thoroughly subjective, as his attitude toward America had always been. In his mind American literature had always been associated with Anti-Fascism, and his own criticism and translation of American literature had been an implicit act of revolt against the Fascist regime. It was under these conditions that his personality as a writer was formed, and when there was no longer any Fascism to oppose he found himself faced with a creative vacuum. The question, "Now that Fascism has passed, what has America to say?" was really "What have I to say?" He was to write one more first-rate novel, *La luna e i falò*, in which he struggled to express in allegorical form his own experience of America and the part it had played in his formation. After he finished this in 1949, he wrote to a friend, "For a while—perhaps forever—I won't do anything else." [7] His diary for the same period is full of anguished fears for the future.

There were other reasons for this inability to write, some of them very personal and very deep. Pavese's creativity as a writer had always been closely connected with his private life and especially his relations with women, and these had never been very satisfactory. A long prewar affair with a woman identified by his biographer Davide Lajolo only as "the woman with the hoarse voice" had ended in betrayal and despair. There followed several minor and unsuccessful attempts at love. According to

Lajolo he proposed twice to Fernanda Pivano, who had been his student during a brief period of teaching in a Turin liceo, but she was "too young and too far from such thoughts to be able to answer either yes or no." [8] Opposite the title page of *Feria d'agosto* he set the dates of these two proposals, July 26, 1940 and July 10, 1945, with crosses after them to indicate the results. The climax of this long series of failures was his encounter in the last two years of his life with Constance Dawling, an American actress who had come to Italy to work in the films. Pavese's more serious critics have tended to treat this affair as a trivial incident in his life, but the relationship with Constance was an important one, and one that went very deep into his character and his nature as an artist. For the last time he was seeking to know and possess America. In the romance with Constance—and this is the only word to describe it—he was re-enacting the whole personal tragedy of his life and his "betrayal" by America, the America that had been his dream since his university days and before, from the time of his youthful infatuation with American movies. With Constance the Pavese who had sat through a thousand bad films in the Thirties now mingled with actors, drank whiskey in the grand hotels, and made the tour of the luxury resorts of northern Italy. For Constance he even wrote a love song that was a kind of parody of American blues, but a parody with an unmistakable emotion under the surface of the bad English.

> 'T was only a flirt
> you sure did know—
> some one was hurt
> long time ago.
>
> . . . .
>
> Some one has died
> long time ago—
> some one who tried
> but didn't know.[9]

One of the last comments he made on American literature was a remark in a letter to Lajolo at the end of 1949. "You know, they say Fitzgerald drank a lot and ended up half crazy. You can see that anyone who has something to say is destined to end this way." [10] His intuition was good; he was close to the same "crack-up" that Fitzgerald went through before he died. He separated from Constance, then in a brief period in 1950 she came back again. By this time he knew perfectly well that his relation to her, like his relation to America, was symbolic and mythical rather than physical, and yet he continued to be obsessed with the need for the physical woman. Like Swann in Proust's novel he went on trying to believe in the beloved object even after it had betrayed him, because the need was in himself and not in the object. "You don't kill yourself for the love of *a* woman," he wrote in his diary on March 25. "You kill yourself because a love, any love, reveals you in all your nakedness, poverty, defenselessness: nothing." And the next day he added, "Certainly in her there was not only herself, but all *my* past life, the unconscious preparation—America, the ascetic hesitation, the impatience with little things, my craft as a poet. She *is* poetry, in the most literal sense. How could I not have seen this?" [11] By this time he had left the Communist Party, since he no longer felt capable of the human solidarity that had led him to join five years before. Communism too had been a disappointment: the Czechoslovakian coup d'état, Stalinism, rumors of the forced labor camps. Pavese had always believed too much in things he idealized in his private world, and was embittered when they turned out to be imperfect. Probably the greatest torment was the thought that like Fitzgerald he had gone creatively sterile. The final entry in his diary was on August 18. "No words. An act. I will never write again." On August 26 he died by suicide in a Turin hotel room. His *La letteratura americana e altri saggi*, probably the most important book on American literature ever written by an Italian, was published posthumously in 1953.

Like Pavese, Vittorini drifted to the left after the war, and this led him into the same hostility toward American foreign policy. But he had never committed himself so totally either to

America or to Marxism as Pavese had, and in both cases the disappointment when it came was not so great. Vittorini was disillusioned by both but he never felt "betrayed." Probably this was because his politics was not involved with internal personal problems as Pavese's was, and because he never went through the same creative crack-up. Nothing he wrote after the war came up to the standard of *Conversazione in Sicilia,* which he had written in 1937–39, but he still wrote fiction (*Il Sempione strizza l'occhio al Fréjus, Le donne di Messina*). Meanwhile he became increasingly involved as a critic and editor. In 1945 he founded *Il Politecnico,* a cultural-political review with a Marxist flavor but one that frequently disagreed with Togliatti and the PCI. For this review in 1946 he turned to the job of editing his old *Americana* prefaces to make them into a serialized history of American literature, and ended by rewriting them completely. In contrast to what he had written in 1941 he now found the European element in American literature as important as its naive and "primeval" quality. "We see it elemental and new, even ingenuous at a certain stage, but not of unknown parentage. It is the daughter of parents only one of whom is unknown. The other is illustrious, a gentleman, and he has left his sign in the blood." [12] These were strange words for a Marxist, but it became increasingly clear that Vittorini was not an orthodox Marxist. Instead, he came to realize in his *Politecnico* period, he was a revolutionist in the sense that not only Lenin but Christ and Plato were revolutionists, and even the American patriots of 1776 as "bourgeois" as they may have been. It would be an exaggeration to call the *Politecnico* articles pro-American (the chapter on the Pilgrim Fathers is called "The Ferocious Priests") but they consistently treated America through its history as a revolutionary culture and therefore as a vigorous and progressive one. In the same period Vittorini was attacking the narrowness of Marxist criticism which refused, for example, to see any value in Hemingway or Kafka when Marx in his own time had seen value in Hölderlin, Heine, and Dickens—the "independent revolutionaries" of their time. By 1947 *Il Politecnico* was openly anti-Stalinist. In an open letter to Togliatti (January 1947) Vittorini reminded the Party Leader that Marx himself had warned that a world liberated from material need was always in danger of falling into cultural slavery. The essence of revolution was the "spirit of ascent," the spontaneous and creative progressivism of the individual thinker. It was this spirit that in 1947 was threatened by the automatism of Stalinist culture. "A society, even a classless one, in which man lacks this spirit and the questioning that comes from this spirit would be a society in which no new Marx, no new philosopher, no new poet, would have a reason to exist." [13]

Vittorini's interest in American literature continued through the Fifties; he wrote articles on Hemingway and Faulkner for the literary page of *La Stampa* and even made a new discovery: Nathanael West. But these articles were no longer the major essays of the Thirties, and now he often balanced Soviet literature against the American; in a 1951 *La Stampa* article he compared Steinbeck to Fadeyev. The Soviet Union and the United States had both conducted vast social experiments and broken the path to new literatures, but both had lost faith in their original ideas and fallen into a post-revolutionary conformism. Vittorini's criticism of America was similar to that of the American independent left, from F. O. Matthiessen to C. Wright Mills. His final parting from the American Dream came with the McCarthyism of the Fifties, but he was honest enough to point out that witch trials occurred in the Soviet Union too. By the time his *Diario in pubblico* was published in 1957 he had virtually ceased his activity as a critic of American literature. In a note prepared for the publication of this collection of short pieces and essays he confessed that he had expected the best American writing to come from "the John Fantes, the Jerre Mangiones, the Richard Wrights, the Carlos Bulosans, all the sons of the persecuted and humiliated races." [14] But none of these had progressed beyond the first cry of protest, or had seemed able to take the step from autobiography to literature. The impulse of the Thirties was exhausted, the new American legend had died in infancy. The best books to come out of America after the war were the work of writers of the older generation—*The Old Man and the Sea* and *The Fable.* Nelson Algren, Norman Mailer, Saul Bellow, Wright Morris, Truman Capote, Flannery O'Connor were "eccentrics." The future of American literature was more uncertain than it had been in 1938. It was probably no coincidence that the period in which he noted the decline of American writing, 1938–1939, was also the beginning of his own decline as a novelist. Like Pavese, he had begun his literary career with the discovery of America and was no longer able to write after he lost it.

There is even less comment in the later chapters of the *Diario in pubblico* on Soviet literature. In a long article on the Twentieth Party Congress he analyzed the hardening of Party apparatus that had taken place in the Soviet Union and concluded that the road to Fascism lay through socialism as well as through capitalism. During the Fifties he frequently returned to the theme of *littérature engagée.* He did not agree with Sartre that "engagement" meant that the artist should offer his services to a party or discernible historical movement. An artist was someone who was "engaged" in his own creative problem, and it was through this private creativity and not through political activity that he changed the world around him. It was in this sense that Dante and Giotto were "engaged" and had helped to transform their societies. The artist could not expect society—either socialist or capitalist—to be grateful for this, since as a revolutionist he was the natural enemy of all established orders. Vittorini had passed through Marx and ended up on the side of Thoreau and Ibsen. "The service that the writer renders to the community of men is by nature so delicate and complex that it may appear, at least initially, an antisocial activity. What the writer must therefore do is go on writing and publishing even if it results in his being considered an enemy of society. All other necessities are incidental compared to this." [15]

So far there had clearly been two distinct phases in the criticism of American literature in Italy. The first had begun in the time of Papini and Nencioni at the turn of the century and had continued into the Thirties with the criticism of Cecchi and Carlo Linati. These academic critics first brought American literature to the attention of the Italian public, but they were unequipped to deal with the new American writing produced after 1918. Their viewpoint was essentially a nineteenth-century one, and their view of American literature, while often sympathetic, was not very different from that of American critics of the era of William Dean Howells. They admired the "barbarism" of Melville in the way the Romantics had admired Ossian, that is from the cloistered security of their studies. In general they failed to appreciate the importance of the vernacular revolution in American literature led by Stephen Crane, Hemingway, and the naturalists of the Thirties. This was the situation through the time of Cecchi's *Scrittori inglesi e americani* in 1935. The second phase was the clandestine movement led by Pavese and Vittorini, which reached its climax during the war and ended definitely with Pavese's death in 1950. The Italians who took part in this movement were mostly writers, and their interest in American literature was personal and aesthetic rather than scholarly. After Pavese and Vittorini came the third phase, that of the scholars.

A link between the second and third phases was provided by Fernanda Pivano. As a schoolgirl in the early Thirties she had been Pavese's pupil at the Liceo D'Azeglio in Turin, and it was Pavese who first introduced her to American literature. According to her own account, when Pavese came back from his exile in Calabria she asked him to explain the difference between English and American literature, and for an answer he gave her books to read: *Moby Dick, Leaves of Grass, A Farewell to Arms, Spoon River Anthology.* She spent a year working on a university thesis on Whitman, but her professors "suddenly decided that a well-brought-up young lady should not interest herself in a subject so scabrous." [16] Instead she was allowed to write a thesis on *Moby Dick.* When this was accepted by her committee in 1941 a Fascist newspaper deplored that certain Italian young people abandoned their own classics to concern themselves with such "plutodemocratic Judeo-Masonic literature," but nobody actually came around to arrest her and she was encouraged to bring out her translation of *Spoon River Anthology*, which she had made several years before. A shortened version of this was submitted to Einaudi with Pavese's recommendation, and the publisher applied to the censor for permission to print it. Pavese was probably joking when he told Fernanda that Einaudi had requested permission for an "Antologia di S. River" and that the censors had granted it under the impression it was a collection of poetry by a Catholic saint, presumably a South American. It was more likely that the permission was granted through sheer bureaucratic confusion. The first edition of the book was seized by police order, then the cover was changed and it was allowed to circulate. "*Spoon River* came out in the middle of the war and Pavese brought me the first copy in a café where we used to meet wrapped up to the nose so nobody would recognize us," she remembered later. "I don't know whether my heart was pounding more from emotion or from fear." [17] This was the beginning of a distinguished career as a critic and translator of American literature. In 1949 Einaudi published a more complete version of her *Spoon River* which became the standard edition of Masters in Italy. She went on to translate Fenimore Cooper, Sherwood Anderson, Gertrude Stein, Hemingway, and Faulkner. From 1948 to 1955 she served on the judging committee for the Hemingway Prize. Her essay "Il sud di Faulkner," originally written as a preface to the Mondadori edition of *Intruder in the Dust* in 1952, was one of the first scholarly studies of Faulkner's fiction in postwar Italy. In 1961 her pieces on American literature were collected in *La balena bianca e altri miti*, which won the Soroptimist Prize for the following year. By this time there was no doubt of her position as an accepted authority on American literature, the "scabrous subject" her professors had refused to let her study in 1940.

One of Fernanda Pivano's most influential articles, the essay on Gertrude Stein, appeared in a 1952 number of *Pensiero Critico* devoted entirely to American literature. She also contributed to the American-literature issue of *Galleria* in 1954 with an essay on Sherwood Anderson, called "America: sogno in dimensione." Several other literary reviews, including *Aut-Aut* and *Nuovi Argomenti*, devoted special issues to American literature in the Fifties. These new reviews were typical of the magazines that had come to dominate literary criticism in Italy, and along with it criticism of American writing. *Solaria* and *Letteratura*, the typical literary reviews of the Thirties, were edited mainly by poets and writers. They resembled the American little magazines of the same period; they were strong on enthusiasm and weak on scholarship, and they tended to be hostile toward academic circles. The new reviews of the Fifties were edited by people with a scholarly background and were often connected with universities, like the *Kenyon Review* or the *Sewanee Review* in America. Fernanda Pivano was a university-trained scholar and an indefatigable researcher; her models as a critic were Malcolm Cowley and Edmund Wilson. Many of the new generation of critics were members of university faculties. Before the war American studies had been almost nonexistent in Italian universities. If American literature was studied at all it was as an appendage to English literature—Linati's well-known book was called *Scrittori anglo-americani d'oggi* and Cecchi's *Scrittori inglesi e americani*. Professors were suspicious of students who wanted to work in American literature; it was a vaguely raffish subject, like Zen or beat poetry in America in the Fifties. Through the Pavese-Vittorini period American literature remained the province of novelists, translators, and journalists. By 1950 this situation had changed. As the nonacademic intellectuals—the novelists and journalists—developed an anti-American strain the universities moved into the field and became the real centers of activity in American studies. In 1930 a young Italian who was interested in American literature would have gone to Florence and become a Solarian; in 1960 he went to the university.

Not only was there a new wave of students but there was a new generation of professors, many of them as well qualified in American literature as their counterparts in the United States. By 1960 these scholarly Americanisti had set up institutes or centers of American studies in half a dozen Italian universities, most prominently Rome, Bologna, and Milan. Some of the older generation were still around. Mario Praz, who had begun between the wars as a specialist in English literature and the author of the influential *La carne, la morte, e il diavolo nella letteratura romantica* (1930; translated as *The Romantic Agony*), was the first Italian to publish an article on Hemingway, on the Terza Pagina of *La Stampa* in June, 1929. He continued to write on English and American literature after 1945 and, from his position at the University of Rome, served as a kind of Grand Old Man of Anglo-Saxon studies. The third edition of his *Antologia della letteratura inglese e scelta di scrittori americani* (the American reader is perhaps permitted to wonder why the English have "literature" and America has only "writers") appeared in 1955. Praz was perhaps even more important as a teacher; many of the younger Americanisti after 1950 had been his disciples or students. Carlo Izzo, a Venetian who settled in the late Fifties in a chair at the University of Bologna, won an equally admirable reputation as a translator and anthologist. As a critic of American literature, and American culture in general, Izzo was a good deal more sophisticated than anyone who had written in the Thirties. He agreed with Pavese that the main gift of America to Europe was its "pensive barbarism," its poetry of the primitive and its intimacy with the soil, but he also emphasized the part that Europe had played in the formation of American culture. In fact Izzo regarded the whole course of American literature as a process of alienation from European civilization followed by a reconciliation—an idea he shared with many American scholars and historians. "In its origins America was a flight from so-called civilization; hardly had the Atlantic coast created its own civilization than the most impatient took flight again toward the west; arriving at the sea and being unable to flee any longer, some of them turned back to Europe. But the most recent rebels appear, it seems to me, to turn at least in form back to Whitman, and thus continue the 'escape'—no longer possible in the horizontal sense—in the vertical sense. In this they repudiate the mass stretched out over the surface of the land in order to find freedom in a realm of their own, suspended between earth and heaven—or hell." [18]

By 1964 the number of competent younger Americanisti in the universities was so great as to make it impossible to list them all. Agostino Lombardo, who taught at the University of Rome and later at Milan, was one of the most prominent. He was one of several who were American-trained; he began his academic career as a Fulbright scholar at Yale and returned to the United States again in 1963 on a grant from the American Council of Learned Societies. In addition to his many articles and monographs, he produced two influential books on American literature, *Realismo e simbolismo* (1957) and *La ricerca del vero* (1961), the latter dedicated to his old professor Mario Praz. Lombardo's work as an editor was equally important; from 1956 he edited the annual *Studi Americani*, which served as a rallying point for the university Americanisti and published a good deal of their best writing, and he also functioned as editor of the Biblioteca di Studi Americani, a series of book-length works by university scholars which by 1963 had reached nine volumes. Glauco Cambon, also a former Fulbright scholar (Columbia, 1951–52), was the first to discuss Hart Crane at length in Italy, in a 1956 article and later in his *Tematica e sviluppo della poesia americana* (1960; issued by the Indiana University Press as *The Inclusive Flame*, 1963). In addition to publishing a long list of articles, many of them in *Studi Americani*, Cambon translated Faulkner's *Absalom, Absalom!* with an important preface (1954) and taught and wrote at American universities, including Michigan and Rutgers. A third former Fulbright scholar was Sergio Perosa, who became interested in the unpublished Fitzgerald papers in the Princeton library when he was still a student and went on to write one of the best scholarly books on Fitzgerald in Italian or English (*L'arte di F. Scott Fitzgerald*, Biblioteca di Studi Americani, 1961). After his return from Princeton he held university positions at Venice and Trieste and translated a versatile selection of American authors including James and Melville. Biancamaria Tedeschini

Lalli, at the University of Rome, specialized in the nineteenth century, wrote books on Thoreau and Emily Dickinson, and published frequently in *Studi Americani.*

Virtually all the others among the new generation of university Americanisti contributed articles to *Studi Americani.* Two of the most prolific were Nemi D'Agostino, who published on James, Faulkner, and Fitzgerald, and Elémire Zolla, who contributed studies of Cabell, Melville, Djuna Barnes, and Emily Dickinson. Zolla also wrote two first-rate essay collections, *Volgarità e dolore* (1959) and *L'eclisse dell'intellettuale* (1961), as well as a curious Proustian-Joycean novel, *Cecilia o la disattenzione,* whose heroine lives in Turin but reads *Vogue* and once studied at Yale (which in fact admits females to its graduate school). Alfredo Rizzardi, who taught at the University of Urbino in the late Fifties, distinguished himself mainly as a translator, and of the most difficult American poets—Ezra Pound, Wallace Stevens. Finally, Vito Amoruso was the author of an important and perceptive essay, "Cecchi, Vittorini, and American Literature," in *Studi Americani* (1960). These and the generation of younger scholars like them were competent, well informed, and virtually bilingual, and even American scholars could profit by reading their work. It would hardly be fair to compare them with Pavese, who had different inclinations and different talents, but at least their command of the facts was more impressive.

In short, by 1950 there was no doubt that the time was past when the Italians had discovered America. The question now was whether Pavese had said the last word in 1947 when he asserted that America was "no longer in the vanguard of anybody's culture." The new critics of the Fifties and Sixties examined this death sentence and found it premature. In a 1954 article in *Aut-Aut,* Claudio Gorlier argued that Pavese's statement was simply "a typical manifestation of the consequences of a naïve discovery, glamorous and exaggerated, comprehensible in the particular years when it took place, but certainly not later in a postwar period in which there was no lack of occasion for a broader and more detailed approach to the subject." [19]

Pavese was not a scholar but a poet. He had read American literature enthusiastically but rather unsystematically, seizing on what he needed for himself as though he were picking nuts out of a fruitcake. The Italian scholars of the new generation worked like crime-lab technicians, examining the fruitcake with tweezers and microscope. The things the Italians of 1930 had to learn painstakingly and half-clandestinely from their books the students of 1960 could acquire at firsthand, either in American universities or from Fulbright professors in Italy. The ones who went to Yale or Princeton came back with American accents, collections of Bechet records, and a thorough grounding in American scholarship. If they were not as fervent about American literature as Pavese, they were also not as naïve. It was no longer possible to sum up America as "pensive" and "barbaric" and American literature as an elemental cry in the wilderness. They had read Whitman, and they still read him, but now they read Eliot, Cummings, and Wallace Stevens too. "Blue jeans do not suit Mr. Prufrock," a young Italian novelist concluded in 1959.[20]

TWO

Legend to Literature

5 *Guareschi: America or Castor Oil?*

The writer in Italy under Fascism had three alternatives. The first was to write what the regime wanted, if he could manage to figure out what this was. Not many were successful at this, and the ones who were did not make any major contribution to world literature. The second was to ignore the regime and go on writing what he would have otherwise, that is an honest portrayal of his society and his own relation to it. The writers who tried to do this usually ended up not writing, or at least not being published. Vittorini's *Il garofano rosso* was censored and the review *Solaria* which had printed it was suppressed, and other writers like Pavese were banished to primitive towns in Calabria. Those who dealt more directly with political questions often ended like Leone Ginzburg, who died in a Fascist prison. The Italian censorship of the Thirties was not as efficient as the German, but it worked well enough to interfere seriously with any honest creativity. The situation was worst for novelists and less crucial for painters, composers, and poets. But it was a problem for all of them, and in many cases it brought their artistic output to a standstill.

The third alternative was to turn away from a direct encounter with the problem and write some form of escapism. This of course required special talents and was not an alternative open to every writer. For a Vittorini who felt the presence of "abstract furies" in every newspaper headline, or a Pavese whose relation to his material was intensely serious and intensely personal, it was an impossibility. If such writers indulged in levity at all it generally took the form of irony, and the irony of writers who feel politically oppressed tends to be barbed and rather obvious, even to the opaque mentality of a censor. Escapism requires something else, a flair for improbable whimsy in the manner of that produced in America, perhaps, by Bemelmans or Joseph Wechsberg or in England by G. K. Chesterton. Giovanni Guareschi is, in fact, a kind of an Italian Chesterton, even to his politics and his religion. The difference is that where Chesterton wrote in a free society, Guareschi was obliged during the early part of his career to write in a climate of censorship. By confining himself to light whimsy and avoiding any real confrontation of this situation, he managed to publish three books under Fascism before he emerged in his true light as a political satirist with his *Don Camillo* sketches after the war.

Guareschi is hardly an author on the same level of importance as Vittorini or Pavese. *Don Camillo*—and all of his work—lies in the area somewhere between *feuilleton* journalism and popular fantasy. Much of it is contrived and all of it has the hackneyed quality of writing produced to meet a deadline or fill up a given space. (The *Don Camillo* material was originally written in episodes for the weekly *Candido*.) But for the literary historian, or the historian of culture, such material can have a value it does not have for the literary critic. It reveals undercurrents, social tendencies, popular attitudes in the way even a schoolgirl's essay on America can, or a letter from an American emigrant to his relatives in Italy. Guareschi is at least a cut above the schoolgirl or the emigrant. He has never been regarded as important by Italian critics, scholars, and writers, although part of this can be ascribed to his politics, which please nobody, not even the Catholics and Monarchists. The American who goes to Italy, hears Italian writers talked about, and finally inquires, "And Guareschi?" will be told with a curious tight-jawed contempt, "Non esiste, Guareschi doesn't exist." But the very fact that such large masses of the unlettered, or semi-lettered, public read him makes him a social phenomenon of a certain importance. And for the student of the American Myth in Italy he has another kind of importance. Escapism is fantasy, fantasy leads to myth. Although Guareschi never particularly admired America, although he was not influenced by American literature stylistically as Pavese and Vittorini were, he expresses something no other Italian writer expresses so well: the Myth of America in the Italian popular consciousness as it existed on the eve of the Second World War around 1938.

Naturally, escapism itself can be a form of political protest in that it is an implicit indication of the writer's refusal, or inability, to deal with the world around him realistically. In this sense even Guareschi's mock-autobiography *La scoperta di Milano* (1941), a kind of babes-in-toyland fable of newlyweds challenging fortune in the big city, is a political satire although a very innocuous one. Often he seems to be poking fun at the austerity of the Abyssinian War period; one of the more whimsical bits concerns a plucked chicken named Francesco who is put into a pan of water on the stove and left until he feels uncomfortable, and his bath water served as a "light broth." To the ordinary reader Francesco was simply a comment on petit-bourgeois manners rather than on Fascist economics, if in fact this is what Guareschi intended. His second novel *Il destino si chiama Clotilde* ("Destiny Is Called Clotilde," 1942) is escapism of a different kind. Although Guareschi had never been out of Italy when he wrote it, it takes place for the most part in America, or rather in a land by this name which bears about as much relation to the real America as Alice's looking-glass land does to the real England. But the Red Queen is after all only Victoria, that cross old lady who was annoyed when Carroll presented her with a book on higher mathematics. Or is she? The question arises as to just what extent a lightweight satire of this kind can be taken as a political allegory, either overt or (more likely in the case of Lewis Carroll) subconscious. The danger of overinterpretation is always particularly present in the case of books that were not meant to be serious. And yet Freud has demonstrated that humor may be more serious than it intends. The critic is faced with a double danger, that of being pompous (seeing what is not there) and that of being dense (not seeing what is under the surface). Guareschi himself explained that the intention of *Il destino si chiama Clotilde* was merely to "cheer up the reader a little." Leaving aside the political comment implied in this—why should the reader of 1942 need cheering up?—it is possible to read even this light novel as a kind of fable, that is a story that says more than it seems to.

Il destino si chiama Clotilde was published during the war but was evidently conceived earlier, in the period 1938–1939. Guareschi at this time was a journalist who had come from a small town near Parma a few years earlier to become a humorist and feature writer for a Milan daily. He knew no English and had never visited America, and claimed in later years not even to have read those two ubiquitous travel books of the Thirties, Soldati's *America primo amore* and Cecchi's *America amara.* His information about America was derived almost entirely from motion pictures and from an odd volume he happened to have in his library, Dario Papa and Ferdinando Fontana's *New York,* published in Milan in 1884 and intended mainly for Italians who had relatives in the United States. With this dusty tome at his elbow, he set out to write a novel about America. What resulted was an implausible farrago that might have been written by Lewis Carroll if the author of *Alice in Wonderland* had been an amateur of American films, and if he had not been so primly Victorian.

The hero or anti-hero of the novel is Filimario Dublé, the son of wealthy parents who lives with his widowed mother in an elegant house in Nevaslippe, an imaginary city vaguely resembling Monaco or some resort on the Italian Riviera. Guareschi is careful not to mention the names of any real European countries and the characters throughout evidently speak some kind of Esperanto; there is never any language problem in America or anywhere else. As an additional precaution the epoque is 1885, that of the Papa and Fontana book. The first chapter is actually a prologue which begins somewhat earlier. At the age of six Filimario, or Fil, is requested by his mother to drink a glass of castor oil. He refuses. She informs him he cannot eat until he does. He fasts. After three days he goes to live with an uncle who detests his mother, and remains there until the age of twenty-seven. He comes home then, but at the door he is met by his mother with the glass of castor oil. He says, "No, Mamma"; she closes the door and he goes away again. His mother shortly dies, leaving a will specifying that he can claim his inheritance only when he drinks the castor oil, the original glass of which is held by a notary in a safe. This brings us to 1885, when Fil becomes involved with a wealthy Nevaslippian heiress, Clotilde Troll. Clotilde, who is secretly in love with him, spirits him aboard her yacht, and through a complicated sets of adventures he finds his way to America.

It is apparent at this point that there is more to Fil's stubbornness than mere whim. To Americans castor oil is only a mildly unpleasant laxative suitable for children, now obsolete. To the Italians of 1938, it had become something else, a symbol of political oppression administered through a semi-legalized violence. The tradition had begun even before 1923; the liberal or "subversive," cornered by Fascists often in a public street, was invited to drink castor oil under the threat of a beating, and afterwards usually beaten anyhow. To the Fascists it was a kind of joke, to the victims not quite so funny. It was probably preferable to what happened to liberals and leftists in Germany in the same period, but hardly pleasant, and above all humiliating. It is possible to be dignified while being burned at the stake, but not after drinking castor oil. The alternative was to abandon one's heritage as an Italian, to go underground, to "go to America" either figuratively or literally as some like Gaetano Salvemini did. This is the choice that faces Fil. In order to stay in his native land and claim his heritage he must drink the castor oil forced on him by the dominant authority, his mother. If he is to avoid the castor oil he must become, quite literally in his case, an émigré. For Guareschi as for the rest of his generation there was only one place to which you could emigrate, and so Fil goes to America.

This is not to say that America as an alternative is always an ideal one, and some of Fil's adventures are uncomfortable if not downright unpleasant. Aboard Clotilde's yacht he is taken with two companions, Settembre Nort and Pio Pis, to the vaguely West Indian island of Bess. There he gets involved with a gang of opium smugglers led by the beautiful American girl Ketty Blimont. When her boat, the *Jeannette,* is searched by the customs patrol the opium is found in the baggage of the three Nevaslippians; the American girl has tricked them. They are taken to jail in New York where they are confronted by a dignified gentleman who inquires with the utmost politeness, "Are you ready to confess spontaneously your real identity, which is certainly not that appearing in your documents, or would you prefer doing so after an interrogation by third degree?" [1] The three Nevaslippians, having no other papers than their own, stay in jail. Later the Dignified Gentleman explains to his assistant why he cannot allow the foreigners to go free—the press demands a conviction, and in America the courts are at the mercy of the mob in the street. Guareschi is not a great admirer of democracy; his own political sympathies are monarchist and conservative. The Dignified Gentleman goes on to a topical allusion evidently extracted from Papa and Fontana's *New York.* "The Reverend Beker [Henry Ward Beecher] is thrice famous in the republic: first because he is the brother of [the authoress of] *Uncle Tom's Cabin,* second because he seduced the wife of the Reverend Tilton, third because he is a great orator. Well, you and I would become in twenty minutes more famous than he is." [2] They are spared this notoriety when Fil and his friends are released into the custody of Clotilde Troll, or rather climb out the window of the jail rather than fall into her hands. When Fil reaches the street outside he finds himself in a kind of stage set of Old New York, drawn partly from Papa and Fontana and partly from emigrant lore. "He entered the metropolis the evening of June 7 of the year 1885. The bluish flames of thousands of gas lamps lighted one by one in the houses, in the streets, in the shops. People crowded along the sidewalks piled with goods. Seas of heads along the sidewalks of every street, and between the two rivers of humanity another river of omnibuses, trams, carriages, and carts. Horses, horses; whips cracked, bells jingled. Overhead smoke, sparks, and the clanking of the 'Elevated,' the aerial steam trams." [3] On the whole it is an accurate description; even many modern New Yorkers do not know that the Elevated ran by steam in the late nineteenth century. But it is hard to know what to make of the "great advertising wagons" in which ladies in evening gowns could be seen sitting in armchairs and conversing with elegant gentlemen. Perhaps Guareschi has the carriages on Fifth Avenue a little confused with department store windows. The crowds of newsboys shouting headlines are authentic, as is the old-fashioned fire engine drawn by galloping horses and spouting splendid plumes of steam. But there are other vignettes that show a more squalid side of the city, the New York of O. Henry and Stephen Crane—a crying woman, a tattered and drunken "loffer" (loafer?) taunted by a crowd of youths. Back in Italy, we are reminded, Mussolini had cleared the loffers off the streets. Viewed from the Milan of 1938 New York resembles the decadent plutocracy of Fascist propaganda: teeming, colorful, and under the surface corrupt.

It is this squalor which now faces Fil and his companions. Without money and without friends, they are more or less in the position of the traditional Italian immigrant, forced to earn their living by brute labor and at the mercy of every cop. Bedding down in the park, Fil remembers the M. Bertrand who had slept in the Bois de Boulogne and later enjoyed the hospitality of Mme. de Staël, and who had assured his hostess there was no comparison between a marble bench and a featherbed. "Even admitting that the benches of the New World are softer than those of the Bois de Boulogne, it can be understood that our estimable gentlemen, when they awoke in the morning, could not help sharing M. Bertrand's opinion of benches." [4]

• • •

They are saved by a traditional Italian talent, that of pleasing the fairer sex, especially Anglo-Saxon. From Casanova through Valentino the legend of the Italian lover is invincible. Applying to an employment agency for work "suitable to European gentlemen," the three are hired out as professional escorts for parties given by New York society ladies. At this they are devastatingly successful. One of the ladies, Mrs. Thompson, asks Fil to demonstrate how he can "make a compliment." His skill is so effective that she soon flings herself into his arms moaning words of surrender. Recovering, she advises him to "moderate himself a little" in order to avoid scandal. Thompson, incidentally, is one of the few Anglo-Saxon names which Guareschi spells correctly, probably because it was the name of a street in lower Manhattan where Italians settled around the turn of the century, a street better known in some parts of Italy than it was to many New Yorkers. Fil "moderates himself" a little, but Mrs. Thompson is only the first of his amatory conquests, and the beginning of his wild success in New York society. His exploits are made even easier by two typical American customs, cocktails (a slight anachronism, although the word is found in James) and facile divorce. Bored amid the "damned cocktails," he distracts himself by making love to the wife of the wealthy banker Babbith (Guareschi has read at least one American novel). After ten minutes the lady assures him she is ready to get a divorce the next day. Fil escapes with difficulty, but this is not the last incident of its kind. It is really not his fault; the fact is that at the sight of him all American women, even those who have previously disapproved of divorce, are ready to pass bag and baggage into the enemy camp, with cries of "We were blind! Now we finally see the necessity of this legal device!"

In short *Il destino si chiama Clotilde* is a fairly amusing handbook of Italian stereotypes about America. The ways of justice are as corrupt as those of love, although somewhat less pleasant. Italians have never had a high opinion of American justice; in *America amara* in 1938 Cecchi portrayed Italian immigrants in New York as hard-working and honest, faithful to the European tradition of frugality and patient saving, but "intimidated by a capricious legislation." [5] The convolutions of the law and legal procedure in any country are more or less capricious, and they always seem more so to foreigners. Americans in Italy can never understand why hotels are allowed to quote one price and then charge 20 percent more, or why when their car is robbed in broad daylight in a piazza all the witnesses in a nearby café seem to have gone blind and the police shrug their shoulders. Fil's encounter with the American law are frequent and unfortunate. Several times he narrowly escapes some violent legal fate and is saved only by recourse to a certain Smitson, an undefeatable criminal lawyer resembling Clarence Darrow or Jerry Giesler. The services of this cynical genius are available only to the rich; he costs a fortune, but he never loses a case. Luckily, Fil is in funds by this time; otherwise he might have languished in Sing Sing for an undetermined period. America is a fine country in which to be rich, provided you like "damned cocktails," champagne, and society ladies.

Fil does not marry either Mrs. Babbith or the smuggler-girl Ketty. At the end of his adventures he goes back to Nevaslippe and marries Clotilde, who even persuades him to drink the castor oil which meanwhile has turned rancid in the safe. "In the end it was not so bad," he admits, "and I believe it might even be good for me. Perhaps my mother was right." [6] Exile really solves nothing, and the bitter medicine of one's native land is preferable to damned cocktails among the skyscrapers. Guareschi's notion of how to deal with Fascism was to make yourself inconspicuous and wait it out, if necessary even drinking the castor oil. He is like that timid anti-hero of Brecht who, challenged by a bully with "Will you serve me?" said nothing, waited on his enemy hand and foot, gave up his bed and slept on the floor, and years later when the unwelcome guest finally died, whitewashed the whole house and shouted "No!" In this way Brecht himself managed to stay alive under Nazis and Stalinists and ended up the manager of a prosperous theatre in East Berlin. For Guareschi too the medicine was "not so bad after all." He fought in the war and managed not to get killed, and when he found himself in a German internment camp in 1944 he used the spare time to write a book called *La favola di Natale* ("The Christmas Fable"). This is probably the only book of humor ever written in a concentration camp.

In spite of the fables and Ruritanian romances of his early period, Guareschi was not basically an escapist. This became clear after the war, when in the new freedom of an uncensored Italy he turned to the style that made him famous, a kind of whimsical *littérature engagée*. In 1945 he founded *Candido*, a weekly humor magazine with a political-satirical slant, and the following year this magazine published the first of the *Don Camillo* sketches. Here he finally found his true vein as an anti-Communist humorist. It was a peculiarity of his talent that he was able to make Peppone, the Communist mayor of the *Don Camillo* sketches, seem both totally human and completely wrong-headed. Whatever the literary merit of these pieces, and the truth is that they were rather slight, they were "engaged" enough for the B.B.C. to broadcast some of them behind the Iron Curtain in the Russian and Bulgarian languages. Collected in volume in 1948, they were translated into twenty-eight languages, including Vietnamese, and transcribed in Braille; over eight hundred thousand copies were sold in France alone. Having demolished international Communism, Guareschi turned his attention to the Christian Democratic government in Italy. In 1954, while he was still under a suspended sentence for libeling former President Luigi Einaudi, he was charged with another political libel against Alcide de Gasperi. After a tumultuous and well-publicized trial in which he succeeded in making the future of freedom of the press seem to coincide with that of *Candido*, he was sentenced to an eight-month prison term. At this point, having gone to jail for his ideas, he had become about as engaged as a writer can get without being shot. But at least the democracy he mistrusted enabled him to write about what he chose and attack his enemies openly, and he never wrote about America again after he was free to write about Italy. The *Don Camillo* sketches were about people he actually knew and about his own soil, the Emilian countryside near Parma. Asked if he would serve, he had waited a long time and then shouted "No!" Ten years after the war he had become a unique phenomenon on the Italian literary scene, the only Catholic and conservative writer who was read by large masses of people. Meanwhile he had left Milan and gone back to live in the country of Don Camillo, at Roncole Parmense on the banks of the Po. With the royalties and screen rights from *Don Camillo* he had plenty of money to travel in America now if he liked, but he had never been very much interested in traveling.

6 *Silone: Emigration as the Opiate of the People*

For over a century the name of America has had an extraordinary power among the Italian poor, the power of a legend that has little to do with the real geographical America and is basically unaffected by surface political attitudes. The Italian worker or peasant may very likely vote Communist, but he has no secret reverie of emigrating to Russia. He associates the Soviet Union with work and America with easy wealth; "workers" live in one, millionaires in the other. If he has a little education and reads the newspapers he knows this is not really so. But he still half-believes in the reverie, just as he still half-believes in San Giuseppe and San Gennaro after he has read in *L'Unità* that religion is the opiate of the people. He needs this America for the same reason he needs religion, because it is a consoling glimpse of bliss that compensates him for the hardness of his existence. In the same way the ancient Greeks dreamed of another kind of escape from their earthly existence and invented the myth of Dedalus, who built wings and flew through the air. But they knew this was not really possible, so they also invented the myth of Icarus, who flew too high and crashed. Icarus really failed not because the sun melted his wings—this was a metaphor—but because the dream was too good to be true. America, the America of the Italian peasant, was too good to be true too. Therefore, as in the Greek myth, there are two sides to the legend. In the Dedalus-myth of America the peasant saves his money, embarks on a ship and lands in America, where he quickly becomes rich. Then he comes back to his native village with his pockets full of dollars to buy the church a new clock and live a life of ease: the "millionaire," the Americano. The return to the village is an indispensable part of the legend. The fact that some Italians actually did this—went to America, got rich, and came back to their native towns—does not affect the legendary quality of the story. In the subconscious of the Italian poor this America is a reverie of revenge against their "betters:" the rich, the landowners, the government.

There is also an Icarus-myth of America, and this too is based on a reality, a bitter one. Sometimes the flimsy wings melted and the hero crashed. The typical Italian emigrant came to America believing he would go on doing the same work he did in his native town, except that the work would no longer be hard and would quickly make him rich. An expectation like this is too much to ask of any country. In America he had to work hard too, perhaps even harder than in Italy, and he made a bitter discovery: he was a member of a racial minority, a wop. His boss exploited him and American women, the blonde movie-princesses of his reveries, were unattainable. The new technology was complicated and confusing, and for some emigrants the handicap of language was overwhelming. In Italy they had been poor, but at least they had been poor in their own land. In every village in Italy there were some who had come back, not millionaires but bitter and broke. For them America was the land where Italians were wops, the land of Sacco and Vanzetti. The Italian poor knew both of these legends and believed in them both at the same time, in different parts of their mind. The Dedalus-America explained to them why their own lives were so hard, and the Icarus-America explained why they didn't go there.

This whole pattern is reflected frequently in the Italian literature of the last fifty years. Both the "American uncle," the fabulous relative who sends money from Philadelphia, and the Americano, the returned emigrant, are familiar figures in modern Italian fiction. Usually these stories are not written by emigrants; some of them are the work of writers who have visited America, others of writers who stayed in Italy and came into contact with emigration folklore in popular culture. The great novel of Italian emigration, something that would express for the Italian emigrant what Rölvaag's *Giants in the Earth* did for the Scandinavian, has not yet been written. Probably the reason is that the emigration legend in Italy is essentially a peasant folklore, nourished and kept alive by people who do not write books. The Italians who came to America before 1939 were mainly poor and illiterate. If they had a little education or a little money they stayed home—*Chi sta bene non si muove,* he who is well off doesn't move, says an Italian proverb. Those who came to America often made money, and their children went to school. But by the time the children were old enough to write books they had become Americans and lost touch with the experience of their parents. Pietro Di Donato was born in America and *Christ in Concrete* is an American novel; besides it is marred by stylistic tricks and too angry to be an honest portrayal of either the Italian emigrants or the America they came to. The ideal novel on this subject would be one written by an Italian writer of great talent who had personally undergone the experience of emigration. Soldati might have written such a book but his "attempt at emigration" failed; instead he went back home and wrote first *America primo amore* and then *Le lettere da Capri,* a novel about Americans in Italy. It was a good novel, but there were already plenty of these written by Americans, from *The Marble Faun* through *A Farewell to Arms* to *The Roman Spring of Mrs. Stone.* The Americans who "discovered" Italy were mainly intellectuals and writers, expatriates who had a foot in both cultures and could write about Italy without losing their viewpoint as Americans. Their experience of Europe was essentially a literary one, from Hawthorne to

Tennessee Williams, and they wrote books about it as naturally as a hen lays eggs. The immigrants lacked the background to see their experience in literary terms, and in a sense they belonged to neither culture. They quickly lost their contact with the body of tradition they left behind them and they rarely succeeded in becoming Americanized enough in the first generation to lose their sense of bewilderment. Sometimes, quite literally, they forgot the Italian language before they had learned to speak English properly. Under these conditions it was not surprising if they did not write books about their experience. The Italians who wrote about emigration were therefore mainly intellectuals who picked up the folklore at second hand: Pavese, Carlo Levi, Silone. They were often leftist in politics, and this influenced the picture they showed. But basically their America was the same one the peasants believed in: half a dreamland of easy wealth, half a place of bitter disappointment.

Ignazio Silone had been one of the original founders of the Italian Communist Party in 1921. In 1930 he left the Party after a profound intellectual crisis, and he spent most of the Fascist period and the war years in Switzerland. His primary interest was always politics, and he began to write fiction only because he had nothing else to do in exile and no other way of earning his living. Because of his apostasy from the Communist Party he had little contact with the anti-Fascists who stayed in Italy, and in Switzerland he was cut off from the important literary movements that took place in Italy in the Thirties. For this reason he did not share in the discovery of American literature that had such an important effect on Pavese and Vittorini. His position as an exile gave him an independence the others did not have, but it also isolated him from the experience of his generation and made him, in a sense, a more international author than an Italian one. At the same time he had a deep emotional attachment to his native Abruzzi, the rugged mountain region east of Rome; it is the setting of all his important fiction, and he never wrote effectively about anything else than this region and its people. In exile he was possessed by the memory of his native soil, and out of this nostalgia came the power and bitterness of his novels. In this way Fascism, by forcing him into exile, perhaps had an even greater effect on him than it did on the writers who stayed in Italy.

Fontamara was written in Davos in 1930, in the middle of his crisis over leaving the PCI. In many respects it is a typical Marxist novel, and one of the more interesting ones. The central characters are a group of peasants in the Abruzzi mountains whose water rights are stolen by the local Fascist landowners in league with a mysterious capitalist referred to only as the Impresario, who is evidently backed by the city banks. The action takes place entirely in the Abruzzi, and there are no Americans in the novel. But to these peasants, among the most poverty-stricken and exploited in Italy, the word America has the power of a fetish; it stands simply for the opposite of hunger. It is a part of their private vocabulary of values and has nothing to do with the real United States. In their opinion the one who has really "discovered America" is the Impresario. He has come from nowhere, he acquires wealth invisibly and effortlessly, and he is gradually squeezing the country dry; sooner or later everything falls into his hands. "The peasants have to cross the sea to find America, but this robber has found it here," they say of him. This refrain is repeated in the conversation of the peasants until it turns into a kind of chant:

> "The Impresario has discovered America right here, that's the truth."
>
> "America?" the others answered. "America is far away and doesn't look like this."
>
> "America is everywhere," the Impresario told those who referred the argument to him. "It's everywhere, you just have to know how to look for it." [1]

There were some who said the Impresario had sold his soul to the devil, but in any case it was clear he had found a way to turn the thorns into gold. "America is work," he tells them. But it is work only for the others. The Impresario himself does nothing and yet he gets rich. The peasants find this logical; if the

Impresario had to work for the money it would not be America.

At least in *Fontamara* Silone treats this Dream of Emigration with a kind of wry sympathy. Since he is on the side of the peasants he sees it as they do, and it is not America that is out of joint but Italy. Some of the Fontamaresi, the luckier ones, have made the voyage across the Atlantic, and after years of dogged work in the United States or Argentina or Brazil they come back with a little money which they soon lose cultivating the dry and sterile earth. Their only mistake was to come back. After a while they fall back into the old lethargy, "holding like a memory of lost paradise the image of life glimpsed across the sea." [2] As a monument to the Dream they leave their tombs which can be seen in the local cemetery; they never become rich enough to own a house or live a better life, but at least their dollars buy them a grave as fine as those of the gentry. Like most of Silone's work *Fontamara* is a tragedy, but a tragedy written by a satirist. The peasants lose their fight against the landowners, and without water they face starvation. For a while the children who play in the piazza of Fontamara are unaware of the disaster. They have their own Myth of America; the game they play is cowboys and Indians, and since it would not be seemly for the sheriff to go on foot the little girls take turns serving as his horse.

By the time he wrote the two Pietro Spina novels, *Pane e vino* (*Bread and Wine*, 1937) *Il seme sotto la neve* (*The Seed Beneath The Snow*, 1940), Silone's attitude toward America had changed a little. These two novels are slightly more optimistic about the Italian situation and about human nature in general. Silone was still a Marxist, but now a religious element entered, a kind of private and heretical Christian mysticism. "If education creates in us a religious dimension, it goes on living no matter what our relations are with the Church," [3] he told an interviewer in later years. In *Pane e vino* Pietro Spina enters Italy disguised as a priest, and his inspiration comes from the saintly Don Benedetto, a kind of modern-day St. Francis who takes the side of the poor against the wealthy and powerful. As a Marxist—even a mystical Marxist—Silone now saw some possibility that men could improve their condition and build a new society through their own efforts. The only hope for Italy was some kind of revolution, either inward or outward. Silone had no reason to be hostile to America and if anything was friendly toward it; in 1938 the United States was the main hope of anti-Fascists all over the world, especially those like Silone who had repudiated the Soviet Union. But the United States was one thing and the Dream of Emigration was another. This reverie of easy wealth was merely another opiate; like religion it consoled the poor for their wretchedness instead of encouraging them to do something about it. As long as the Abruzzi peasant dreamed—futilely— that some day he might emigrate to America, he would never do anything practical to improve his own condition. To a Marxist this kind of escapist reverie was illusionistic and anti-revolutionary, and to the Silone who was deeply rooted in the Abruzzi the idea of emigration was a betrayal of the native soil. In the Pietro Spina novels he is more critical of the Dream of America and more sarcastic about the peasants who have gone across the Atlantic and come back penniless. There is no more talk now about "the lost paradise glimpsed across the sea."

The typical Americano in *Pane e vino* is the old man Sciatàp, who is first seen beating his donkey to impress on it that its name is Garibaldi. It later transpires that his own christening had resembled that of his donkey. In his youth he had gone to America to work for a fellow countryman, one Carlo Campanella, who sold coal and ice on Mulberry Street in New York City. But in America, Carlo Campanella had become Mr. Charles Little-Bell, an arrogant boss who treated his employee like a beast of burden. At the least complaint Mr. Little-Bell would lose his temper and shout "Shut up!" When the emigrant came back to the town of Pietrasecca this was the only English phrase he knew, and he used it on every possible occasion. If his wife opened her mouth, he would shout "Sha-tap!" and kick her. This phrase, rendered into Italian as Sciatàp, passed into the local dialect. "It was all the English that was known at Pietrasecca, the solitary example of a modern, foreign culture grafted on the ancient culture of the peasants."[4] It is this same Sciatàp, in *Il seme sotto la neve*, who first hides the hero Pietro Spina and then later tries to sell him to the Fascists, a plan he does not carry out only because the officials to whom he goes are having a party and give him vinegar to drink as a joke. This incident is significant because Sciatàp is obviously intended to stand as a representative of America or of the peasant notion of America in this novel, just as the Impresario is all the America there is in *Fontamara*. What these two characters, Sciatàp and the Impresario, have in common is a vulgar and cynical materialism. In all three novels the "Americani" are contrasted to other characters—Berardo Viola in *Fontamara*, Don Benedetto and Pietro Spina in *Pane e vino* and *Il seme sotto la neve*—who represent a hope of "spiritual" Italy, a future society of socialism and human brotherhood. Pietro Spina's companion in the months when he hides in a stable is the peasant boy Infante, whom everybody has treated as an idiot because he is deaf and dumb. Infante stands for illiterate peasant Italy; he is simple-minded on the surface but underneath there is something to be awakened. Spina tries to tell him about the Soviet Union, but he succeeds only in teaching him the meaning of the word companion: *cum pane*, "cumpagnia letizia." This is the message that the Italian intellectual and the Italian peasant end by sharing. But the two, like Berardo in *Fontamara*, are destined to be betrayed, and the characters who betray them are the ones who are connected with the name of America. Not only does Sciatàp try to sell Spina to the Fascists, but Spina's final downfall is specifically caused by another returned emigrant, Giustino. This pattern extends through the three novels and seems too consistent to be accidental.

America is involved in *Pane e vino* in another way, in connection with the hysteria over the Abyssinian War. When the war is announced the orator Zabaglione makes a speech to rally the peasants to the cause, a speech that is a parody of provincial rhetoric but one that might have been made by Mussolini himself. "Who was it who brought culture and civilization to the whole Mediterranean and to all known Africa? . . .

Who brought culture and civilization to the whole of Europe, even to the misty shores of England, and built towns and cities where savages had grubbed for food with wild hogs and deer? . . . Tell me again, I beg you, who discovered America?"

The crowd, on signal, roars, "We! we!"

But Zabaglione reminds them that the fruits were enjoyed by others. By this time the peasants are ready to conquer not only Africa but America as well. There are shouts of "To London!" "To New York!" "To California!" Sciatàp, who wants revenge on Mr. Charles Little-Bell, adds, "To Forty-Second Street!"

They all shout this too, but then somebody asks, "What is Forty-Second Street?" Sciatàp tells them it is the entertainment quarter for the rich, where beautiful women can be found by the thousands, all perfumed. Then he starts to explain to his son what he should do when he gets to America. "Now you listen to me. Don't forget what I tell you. If the government decides to send the soldiers with the death ray to New York, just you step forward and volunteer. Tell the government that your father has been there and has a lot of old scores to settle. Well, when you disembark at Battery Place, turn to the right and ask for Mulberry Street. When you get there ask for Mr. Samuel's old-clothes shop. He's a Polish Jew who talks Neapolitan. . . . He knows where there's good food and where there's good drink and where the rich people live. It's a big city, and if you don't want to lose your way about, go and see him." [5]

Everybody but the orator has forgotten about Abyssinia. Soon a troupe of drunken peasants around a wine cask are singing an emigration song:

> Trenta giorni di barca a vapore
> E nella Merica siamo rivati. . . .[6]

"After thirty days in the steamship, we got to La Merica." This is America as opiate of the people; with the spell of this single word the Fascist orator manipulates them like puppets. Meanwhile Pietro Spina, disguised as the priest Don Paolo, says to the cowherd who walks with him on the edge of the village,

"War has begun, the war of the bank. The war will be fought by the Italian peasants against the peasants of Abyssinia." [7]

Pane e vino was originally published in English in 1937 and in Italian in 1938. This first Italian edition printed in Switzerland is today a rare book. After the war Silone set about systematically rewriting the fiction of his exile period, from *Fontamara* through *Pane e vino* to *Il seme sotto la neve*. In the Fifties and Sixties these novels began appearing in new versions published by Mondadori in Italian and Atheneum in English. In 1961 Silone told an English interviewer, "I have now rewritten *Fontamara* and *Bread and Wine*, and I am working on *The Seed Beneath the Snow* which is turning out to be twice as long as the original. Actually it repels me so to re-read one of my own books because I find so many faults in it. Yet that is the reason I feel compelled to keep correcting and trying to improve it. . . . I believe an author's first book is an expression of his attitude to life. After that, each year he lives should give greater depth, subtler refractions, to his understanding of life. Isn't it right that he should try to pass on to his book that same growth?" [8] Many writers feel this way—Vittorini felt the same about his early novel *Il garofano rosso*—but most of them write new novels instead of setting out on the tedious task of rewriting the old ones. Whether or not the idea was a felicitous one, Silone's revisions provide some interesting comparisons. In 1955, eighteen years after the original writing of *Pane e vino*, Mondadori issued the new Italian version under the title *Vino e pane*. There are some significant differences between these two versions of the novel. The most important change is that the Mondadori edition deletes the murder of Don Benedetto with the poisoned sacramental wine, an incident which suggested symbolically that the Church was "poisoned at its source." This detail might have made the novel censorable in Italy under a Christian Democrat government, and besides Silone was not as anticlerical, or more precisely anti-Church, in 1955 as he was in 1937. Most of the other changes involve deletion of the more bawdy satire and emphasis of the serious political content. Silone cut out the description of the three clumps of bushes in Pietrasecca where peasants, landowners, and women traditionally went to relieve themselves—a tradition violated only at the time of the so-called Red Peril when the peasants used the bush properly belonging to the gentry. Along with other passages of satire he deleted several references to America. In the 1937 version there is a cairn of stones near Pietrasecca to mark the spot where an emigrant, coming back from America to find his wife had been unfaithful, killed her lover with a razor. In the Mondadori version this passage is missing. But it is part of a guided tour of Pietrasecca by the carter Magascià which consists of one such horror after another, and probably it was cut out because it was redundant rather than because it involved an Americano. Another deletion is the passage which tells the story of the half-witted boy Americo, whose father emigrated to America, sent money to build a house which fell down in the earthquake of 1915, and was finally killed by an automobile. The boy, who looks like "a toothless little old man," is the son of this emigrant and of a particularly superstitious and ignorant woman named Matalena; he is therefore a kind of by-product of emigration. Silone evidently had something in mind when he named him Americo, but at least as a symbol of the New World he cannot be accused of cynical materialism. He is as simple-minded as Infante but without Infante's saintliness. When he is sent to the store for a kilo of salt, he "would get up, walk ten paces, stop, start picking one nostril, then the other, and suddenly burst into tears." [9] All this was deleted in 1955. Sometimes a passage is left almost intact and only the reference to America is removed. One of the more effective pieces of political satire is the scene in which the whole population of the surrounding countryside comes to town to hear the declaration of war on Abyssinia, and the schoolmistress explains to them how they are to comport themselves, when to sing and when to shout. But Sciatàp loses patience: "Leave us alone! We're not children. I've been to America." [10] In the 1955 version this is attributed to another peasant, who says only, "Leave us alone . . . we're not children." [11]

It is not clear why Silone went through the novel deliberately removing these references to America. Perhaps his early sarcasm now seemed to him flippant, or perhaps his experience of the war and the Liberation had changed his ideas about America. It is one of the ironies of his career that his novels have been more popular in America and Britain than in Italy, where he is considered mainly a political writer. Part of this was due to his exile; his novels were published in English before they were in Italian, and by the time the Italian public discovered them the political situation they dealt with was a thing of the past. Silone was accused of writing about things he had never seen; for example when the Abyssinian War broke out in 1935 he was in Switzerland. Finally, he was on bad terms with the PCI and there was a consistent campaign against him in the Party press. A writer who tries to make his way in the Italian literary world with the Communists attacking him on one side and the Catholic conservatives on the other is under a certain handicap. Silone never won a major literary prize in the years when prizes were being handed out on all sides to writers of less importance. By 1954, when he set out to revise *Pane e vino,* his work was seldom mentioned by Italian critics and many younger Italians had never read him. Meanwhile in America he was widely read and intelligently criticized; for example R. W. B. Lewis devoted a long chapter to him in *The Picaresque Saint* in 1958, a better study of Silone than anything done in Italy. His American royalties continued to roll in, part of them from popular paperback editions. This situation probably influenced him to be a little less sarcastic about America than he had been before the war. The peasants in *Fontamara* were not altogether wrong, and it seemed that America had a mysterious way of turning thorns into gold.

7 *Emigration Continued: Levi, Alvaro, and Others*

Like Silone, the Carlo Levi of the period of *Cristo si è fermato a Eboli* is an intellectual who writes about peasants, from the outside but with sympathy. There are other parallels between the two writers. Silone was physically exiled from Italy in the time when he developed as a writer, and in the same period Levi as a Jew was psychologically "exiled" in his race. Fascism before 1938 was not violently anti-Semitic, but it was enough so to give Levi a feeling of being an outsider. Neither Silone nor Levi began as a writer; Levi was a physician and painter. The final parallel is that both Silone and Levi began writing as the result of their political misfortunes. Levi was a member of the Einaudi anti-Fascist circle in Turin and he was in frequent trouble with the police all through the Thirties. He was arrested in 1933 and again in 1934. Finally, in the general purge of the Einaudi group in 1935 he was jailed for the third time and then exiled—the technical term was *mandato al confino*—to the small town of Grassano in southern Italy. After a few weeks his orders were changed and he was transferred to the even smaller town of Gagliano, which was little more than a village. Both towns were in Lucania on the instep of the Italian boot, the poorest and most depressed corner of Italy. Here for the first time Levi felt free from the atmosphere of racial prejudice; he was among people so ignorant they did not know what a Jew was. The peasants told him, "We're not Christians, we're not human beings, simply beasts of burden." [1] Among these impoverished peasants and shepherds he lived for a year, doctoring a little when he could find the medicine, painting, and walking over the barren hills. Out of this experience he wrote *Cristo si è fermato a Eboli* (*Christ Stopped at Eboli*), which was published by Einaudi after the war in 1945. The American translation two years later was the first postwar book out of Italy to become a best seller; through an accident of Fascist police procedure the small town of Gagliano became as familiar to many Americans as Venice or Florence. But America was already a name well known to the inhabitants of Gagliano, even before Levi went there.

In his politics Levi was, and still is, a typical Italian leftist. After 1948 he was a leader among the intellectuals who opposed NATO, the American military bases, and the whole tendency of American foreign policy. The difference between Silone and Levi is that Levi has no spiritual pretensions and is therefore not basically hostile to American materialism. For this reason he has more sympathy with the peasant desire to emigrate, and is even sympathetic to America itself as a symbol of prosperity and material progress. His exile gave him a chance to observe the legend of America in one of its strongest and most deeply rooted forms. In Lucania, as in all of the Italian south, emigration had been so common as to leave some districts practically depopulated. When Levi went to Gagliano in 1935 it had twelve hundred inhabitants, and there were two thousand emigrants from Gagliano in America. A few had come back; the only houses in Gagliano that had second stories, balconies, and brass doorknobs belonged to these Americani. The town's only motor vehicle, a decrepit old Fiat, was owned by another returned emigrant, a mechanic who had bought the car with the savings he had brought back from New York. The others gazed on this wealth dumbly, knowing that it was something they could never attain; under the new Fascist laws there was no hope of emigrating. To these illiterate peasants Rome meant very little, only a place that sent tax collectors and carabinieri. "Not Rome or Naples but New York would be the real capital of the peasants of Lucania, if ever these men without a country could have a capital. And it is their capital, in the only way it can be for them, in a mythological way. As a place to work it has no particular meaning for them; the ones who go there live in America as they would live anywhere else, like animals harnessed to a wagon, and it doesn't matter which road they pull it on. But as a paradise, heavenly Jerusalem, it is so sacred as to be untouchable; a man can only gaze at it, even when he is there on the spot, without becoming any real part of it." [2]

In three months the returned Americani forgot their English and became the same peasants they were before, "like stones which a stream has washed over for a long time but which dry out under the first warm rays of the sun." [3] Some came back intending to stay only for a summer, to visit their relatives and show off their new-found wealth. But one was offered a piece of land at a bargain price, another met a girl and decided to marry her, and soon their re-entry permits had expired. The land they bought with their American money was stones and clay, and the harvest brought barely enough to pay the taxes. Many of these emigrants had come back in 1929, frightened by the stock-market crash and deluded by Fascist propaganda which promised work and security for all back in Italy. Some of them tried to keep up the trades they had learned in America, but there was no demand for locksmiths and watchmakers in a village with few doors and no clocks. Over the mirror of the barber, who had left a prosperous shop in New York, were photographs of Roosevelt and American movie actresses. The Gagliano tailor, an excellent craftsman, measured Levi for a suit in inches by the American system. He could always tell these Americani of 1929 by their whipped-dog expressions and their gold teeth. "Damn 1929 and those who made me come back!" [4] swore the tailor.

In a slightly larger town of Grassano, where Levi spent the

first few weeks of his exile, there was one emigrant who had achieved the Dream down to the last detail. He had not only gold teeth but a gold tie pin, watch chain, cigarette case, and cuff links. All day long he sat in front of his house in a panama hat, watching the people go by. He had made a fortune in America as a businessman, but he came back to Grassano every three or four years to show off his dollars and his few words of bad English. This man was a living parody of American robber-baron capitalism. He explained to Levi that he might have stayed in Grassano and "built the place up" with his capital, but it would be effort wasted, and besides there was more to be done in America. At the first news of the war with Abyssinia he packed his bags and left. His America was a vulgar and materialistic dream that remained vulgar and materialistic even after it was fulfilled. Like Silone, Levi shows the successful American immigrant as even more corrupted than those who fail. His man from Grassano is the Mr. Charles Little-Bell of *Pane e vino* back in the old country for a visit.

After 1929 only a few emigrated to America from Lucania and only a few came back. The towns like Gagliano were split in two, half their population on one side of the ocean and half on the other. Many women had been left behind without any hope now of regaining their husbands in America. The mail that arrived in Gagliano came largely from America. The relatives overseas sent not only money but material goods, a continual stream of packages: food, tools, knives, razors, all the gadgets of everyday use. Life in Gagliano was entirely American in tools and measurement; the peasants spoke of pounds and inches rather than kilograms and centimeters. The women wove on primitive looms but they cut their thread with scissors from Pittsburgh. "They had no prejudices against these modern instruments, nor did they see any contradiction between them and their ancient customs. They took willingly whatever came to them from New York, just as they would have taken willingly whatever came from Rome. But from Rome came nothing. Nothing had ever come but the tax collector and the speeches over the radio." [5]

Levi is a kind of writer found more often in Europe than in America. Basically he is a journalist and his material is factual, but he treats it in a novelistic style and he has a novelist's insight and flair for character. With this combination of qualities he manages to be both objective and personally involved in his material at the same time. He records without rancor and almost with a kind of ironic sympathy the fact that Gagliano had become a cultural colony of America. As an anti-Fascist he associates himself with the peasant attitude, and since this is confused and ambivalent his own feeling about the facts he is describing is ambiguous. He has more detachment than Silone, who was too emotionally involved in the Abruzzi to sympathize with peasants who emigrated from it, and more objectivity than writers like Cecchi who saw emigration as somehow a slight on Italian national honor. His attitude did not change very much even after the war when his politics became more anti-American. In 1951 he wrote a humorous and on the whole sympathetic account of the visit of Mayor Vincent Impellitteri of New York to his native town in Sicily, a piece of reportage he later reprinted in the essay collection *Le parole sono pietre.* As in *Cristo si è fermato a Eboli* he manages to put himself in the peasants' point of view and see America as they see it: a dream of the unattainable that compensates for the hopelessness of their daily lives. Impellitteri as a mythological figure is the Dream incarnate: the native son who became *il Sindaco d'America,* the King of Heaven. In the village of Isnello the boys who run after the Mayor's Pontiac in the street cry, "*Toccamo 'a macchina,* touch the car, this way we'll go to America." [6] Perhaps Levi felt like running after the car himself; at least he makes the reader want to. This is honest journalism even if it does not put Italy in a very good light. Levi has too much detachment and too much irony to become impassioned about national honor, even if the nationalists had not tacitly excluded him from their circle on account of his race. But if the journalist Levi is objective, the novelist Levi is still an Italian. In spite of his Jewishness and his Turin urbanity, the peasants of Gagliano are his people and the soil of Lucania is his soil, and America is not. In *Cristo si è fermato a Eboli* the peasants he admires are those who stayed in Gagliano and somehow stuck it out. In spite of poverty, hardship, and sickness some did, and perhaps they fulfilled themselves in a way those who went off to America did not. Levi agrees with Guareschi, with Silone, and with practically every other Italian writer that emigration is not a permanent answer to any problem, either personal or social. The Pittsburgh scissors are good, life in America is good, but the price you pay is too high. The price is to be uprooted from your native soil and lose the source of strength you drew from the earth. Even the shiny bathrooms are not worth selling your immortal soul for. A returned emigrant in *Cristo si è fermato a Eboli* tells the story of a group of Italians in New York who used to leave the city on weekends in search of a bit of green earth. When they reached the open country, they would all let down their trousers under a tree and—what joy! "We felt like boys again, as if we were back in Grassano; we were happy; we laughed and we breathed the air of our homeland. And when we had finished we shouted together: 'Viva l'Italia!' The words came straight from our hearts." [7]

When they wrote about this legend of emigration, neither Silone nor Levi had been to the United States. One Italian writer who had was Livia De Stefani; the American scenes in her novel *Passione di Rosa* (*Passion of Rosa*, 1958) are based on a long visit to America two years earlier, most of it spent in Los Angeles. As a tourist she was thoroughly feminine; instead of researching systematically for her novel she spent her time in California quite simply, acquiring the feeling of America and observing normal American life. *Passione di Rosa* communicates the experience of being an Italian in America, the flavor of America as it seems to an Italian, in a way few other books do. The other pole of the novel is Sicily. Livia De Stefani was born in Palermo and she is deeply rooted in the region where her best books are set, the Sicilian coast between Palermo and Trapani. This part of Sicily, which is also the locale of her earlier novel *La vigna di uve nere* (*Black Grapes*), resembles California even to the orange trees and the climate. Part of the interest of *Passione di Rosa* turns on this geographical resemblance: The two regions are physically alike, and yet their people and customs are totally different. This difference in the two societies and the effect it has on a young Sicilian emigrant is one of the themes of the novel.

The central character is a girl who never leaves Sicily: Rosa, almost a child when the action begins, dark, simple, passionate, her whole being devoted with a primitive ferocity to the man she loves. Rosa is a character out of Verga; in fact De Stefani is clearly a follower of the great Sicilian regionalist not only in her setting but in style and psychological viewpoint. She differs from Verga mainly in that she lacks his sociological and folkloristic dimension and is more intuitive and feminine. This does not prevent her from having certain preconceived notions about society. As a Sicilian woman but an emancipated one—one who went away to Rome to compete equally with men in a world of men—she has a deep-seated hostility to the Sicilian sexual order in which women are relegated to cooking men's meals and serving their pleasure in bed. In this attitude, as well as in certain aspects of her style, she resembles Katherine Mansfield. In *Passione di Rosa* this theme is expressed in the conflict between Rosa and her husband Ruggero, and later in the novel it is also developed as an aspect of the contrast between Sicily and America. Here the possibilities of the geographical polarity of the novel became apparent: where Sicily and California differ most is in their sexual conventions.

In this pattern Rosa stands for Sicilian tradition in its most primitive form. When the novel opens she is only fifteen. She has just come back to the small town of Altofonte from her schooling in a convent, and by the fountain in the piazza she meets Ruggero, a youth only a little older. But he is experienced and she is naïve; her convent training has left her totally unprepared for dealing with men or for the realities of marriage. Ruggero is quite literally the first man she has ever talked to. She falls completely and irrationally in love with him, and this passion dominates her for the rest of her life. Ruggero is an unfortunate choice; he is selfish and lazy, and he is already the lover of Gianna Morra, a married woman and former teacher who is amusing herself with him because she is bored with her own life. At first Rosa is too innocent to notice these faults and even when she realizes them they make no difference; her love for Ruggero is the traditional blind submission of the Sicilian woman to her mate. Ruggero accepts this "passion" and even marries Rosa because Gianna points out to him that she will be a convenient screen for their own relations. A week after the marriage Ruggero has gone back to his old habits, leaving his bride every night and staying out until the small hours of the morning. One night Rosa in a fit of childish spite locks him out of the house, he fires a pistol at her, and the bullet lodges in her breast. This incident plays an important part in the plot. Not only does it later bring about the climax of the novel, but the bullet Rosa carries in her breast becomes a symbol of the joy and pain of her love for Ruggero. He persuades her not to be treated by a doctor, who would report the incident to the police. The weeks of her convalescence, when Ruggero is close at hand by her bedside, are the finest in Rosa's life. But Ruggero grows restive; his ideal is not love but independence, or rather irresponsibility. It seems to him that these two women, Gianna and Rosa, between them claim his whole life. His idea of escape is the traditional one; he decides to emigrate to America.

De Stefani has already established the Myth of America as part of the folklore of her characters. To Rosa's mother, the very word has the unsubstantial and ecstatic ring of "in Paradise"; to her father America is the land of the pictures in the Sunday supplements where old men of eighty make babies and take baths in the sea. Most of the emigrants from Altofonte had gone to California; the climate was the same as Sicily and Hollywood was there, gold mines, and petroleum so rich that if you made a hole with a screwdriver it spouted up out of the ground. The girls in California were the ones in the illustrated magazines, "marvelous girls with their own automobiles, all you had to do was whistle and they were in your arms, happy and insouciant." Ruggero's whole life has been a search for what this picture-magazine America represents: easy wealth without working, facile love without responsibility. His father, who is more hard-headed and realistic than Rosa's, approves his plan of emigration, but his notion of America is a different one. "Good idea . . . you'll learn to work seriously. There, if you don't produce you'll never see dollars even in a picture. But whatever happens to you, it'll be better than here." [8]

The first America Ruggero discovers is his father's, the one where you have to work. In Orange County near Los Angeles he gets a job stamping fruit in a packing house. After a few days he sends a letter to Rosa with his first impressions of California. He is living with two companions in a house trailer and eats meat and eggs every day, but it doesn't fill you up like a good dish of pasta. Everybody has a car in California, even the Negroes and the children who go to school, and Los Angeles is a hundred times bigger than Palermo. Near Los Angeles is *Ollivud*—this is the way it is really pronounced, but "here they say everything one way and then they write it in Turkish." [9] He tells Rosa he is doing fine except that the work is boring and you can never get rich at it, because even though they pay you four dollars a day everything costs more in America. He includes a picture of himself sitting at the wheel of an automobile which belongs to another emigrant. It is obvious that Ruggero is not going to be packing oranges much longer.

He very quickly finds something better. In a Los Angeles billiard parlor he meets the Mexican dope-peddler Pedro Mora, and he is soon working for him smuggling narcotics from Tijuana. This life is almost too easy to be true; there are false passports, stolen Cadillacs, free meals in a Greek restaurant—Pedro arranges for everything. On one of the trips to Mexico Ruggero meets Molly, a silky blonde who got her start in life as a Strawberry Ice Cream Queen. She is one of the girls out of the picture magazines he used to read in Sicily; she has "breasts that didn't need a brassiere and legs like a dancer," her fingernails are lacquered, and she is always laughing, even when she makes love. This is the way Ruggero has always

Giulio Einaudi Editore

P.I.P. photo by Elio Sorci

Italian Information Center

P.I.P. photo by Elio Sorci

1 Cesare Pavese

2 Elio Vittorini

3 Alberto Moravia

4 Emilio Cecchi

Mario Soldati

5 *Mario Soldati*

Italian Information Center

6 *Carlo Levi*

7 *Giuseppe Berto*

P.I.P. photo by Elio Sorci

Wide World Photo

8 Ignazio Silone

Giorgio Soavi

9 Giorgio Soavi

10 Fernanda Pivano

E. Sottsass, Jr.

Italian Information Center

11 Corrado Alvaro

12 *Livia De Stefani*

13 *Luigi Squarzina*

P.I.P. photo by Elio Sorci

P.I.P. photo by Elio Sorci

thought women should be. After he meets Molly he stops writing letters to Rosa.

These two women are the two poles of his life, as Sicily and California are the two poles of the novel. Rosa is not Sicily, or at least not all of Sicily, but she is Sicily as it seems to Ruggero. Likewise Molly is the incarnation of a certain kind of America, again as seen by Ruggero: fast cars, rootless pleasures, easy sex. When he decides to marry Molly (he has put Rosa so completely out of his mind that he hardly thinks of it as bigamy) he takes her to Las Vegas across the "desert of Walt Disney," in a fast car like the ones in the movies. When they come back to California they rent a house near Santa Monica and settle down like two newlyweds in *Life* magazine. De Stefani's picture of life in America is detailed, honest, and by no means naïve, even though it is seen through the somewhat limited eyes of Ruggero. The house is set in a lawn with geraniums around it and there are easy chairs in the back yard. To Ruggero it is a "villetta," finer than those the rich in Sicily have for their vacations by the seaside. Molly ecstatically opens and shuts the refrigerator to make the light go on, and Ruggero pushes the button to start the furnace even though it is the middle of summer. The marvels of the house are endless. De Stefani is obliged to resort to footnotes to explain two of its features, the deep-freeze and the disposal ("sucks up, grinds, and dissolves all refuse, including glass and crockery").[10] The only thing that is not out of the idyll in *Life* is Ruggero's job. This is from the American crime films with Humphrey Bogart and Edward G. Robinson. His two or three trips a month to Mexico bring him all the money he needs. In five years, he learns, he can become an American citizen. He has discovered his America, the easy life where machines do all the work.

But Pedro is part of the "machine," and the one thing Ruggero still resents is his dependence on his Mexican boss. To go in business for himself he begins organizing illegal poker games in the house in Santa Monica; he is on his way to becoming a model Sicilian-American gangster. But meanwhile he has forgotten the passion of Rosa, and it is this that finally destroys him. When his letters stop coming Rosa waits for long anguished months, and finally she applies to the American Consul to try to find some trace of her husband. A whole bureaucratic machinery is set in motion; the Los Angeles police find Ruggero and raid the poker game in Santa Monica. When he is arrested the whole dream vanishes: the house, Molly and the child she has just borne, the easy money and the fast cars. In a downtown jail he finds himself in a cell with a Chinaman, a mulatto, and a homosexual with peroxided hair. It is not clear how Livia De Stefani found out so much about the inside of jails in Los Angeles. She makes only a few mistakes; Ruggero is taken to "the white tower of the Town Hall" although the county jail is in the Hall of Justice and not in the City Hall, which does however have a white tower. She is also convincingly accurate about the Liberty ship on which Ruggero is deported back to Italy as an undesirable alien. There is a writer (male) on this ship who is traveling third class to collect material for a novel, and perhaps this is a disguised self-portrait. The writer has more money in his baggage than he seems to need, and the temptation is too much for Ruggero. At all costs he must get back to America, clandestinely if necessary, and for this he needs money. He is easily trapped in the theft, and when he lands in Palermo he is taken off in handcuffs to the Ucciardone prison. This De Stefani describes in even more convincing detail than the county jail in Los Angeles. There are two prisons in the novel, just as there are two women, and they are symmetrical opposites. When Ruggero asks for a lawyer he is told he is not in America now, and ordered to shut his mouth. It is the end of the Dream, and for Rosa who has waited for him through the long months it is the end of her life. Everything comes out: the silky blonde girl in America, the bigamy, even the early relations with Gianna. Now the symbol of Ruggero's hatred, the bullet still lodged in her breast, comes forth and kills her; she dies of a hemorrhage on the Palermo pavement.

As a novelist Livia De Stefani is objective about both Sicily and California. It is obvious that she is personally attached to both; in a 1959 letter she called California "an enchanting memory" and recalled the blue sea and the orange ranches, "these places so similar in their beauty to Sicily." [11] But in the novel the two settings are seen only as they seem to the fictional characters, especially to Ruggero. Ruggero's father was right about America; it is a good place to go, better than Sicily if you are poor, but if you don't work there "you'll never see dollars even in a picture." Ruggero's dream is too facile and too vulgar to last for long; he has the mentality of a petty criminal and not the Al Capone he imagines himself, and he is destined from the beginning to end up behind bars. Molly, who stands for America, is a bad influence in his life, but the fault is his and not hers. She remains in the end what she was in the beginning, a Strawberry Ice Cream Queen, as innocent as a large doll. Rosa, who stands for Sicily, is a sympathetic character but she is fated like Ruggero to be unhappy because her values are confused; she is a victim of an antiquated and irrational sexual folklore. De Stefani is for the emancipation of women, but in a special way: freedom not only from social restrictions but from the myth that love is everything in a woman's life. Molly, as "free" as she is, has not reached this ideal either. Even though she is emancipated in the social and political sense—"American" emancipation—she is treated by others simply as a love object and accepts this rôle herself. She is rootless in a way that is typically American; she seems to have no family or past and comes from no particular place. She is simply the beautiful doll of the popular songs, made for having fun and not hampered by any visible morals: "Molly thank heaven was no Quaker." For De Stefani the ideal woman is neither Rosa nor Molly but something else. And, since these two women are in a sense symbols of their culture, the implication is that the ideal country is neither Sicily nor California but somewhere else, a place that perhaps does not exist. De Stefani does not explain what this country would be like. The novel asks questions about America and about Sicily without providing the answers. But it is clear that there is no paradise on earth, and that Ruggero's father is right. America as Dream lasts only as long as it remains a dream; at the first contact with reality it dies. The one who still has her America at the end of the novel is Rosa's mother, who never went there. As for Rosa herself her America is Ruggero, and this dream too is shattered when she finds out what it really is.

Some interesting if minor treatments of emigration are found in Italian short stories. The short story tends to simplify the conflict of a situation more than the novel, and for this reason it often presents things simply and clearly where they would be complicated and obscured in a longer work of fiction. "Tristan" and "Tonio Kröger" show Mann's view of the artist more clearly and obviously than *Doktor Faustus,* although with less subtlety and richness. Corrado Alvaro's story "Il rubino" ("The Ruby") is simple in this way; it turns around a single symbol that illuminates the contrast between the emigrant's America and the Italy he comes back to. Like most of Alvaro's fiction the story is a curious mixture of realism and fantasy. It starts like a tale from *The Thousand and One Nights*—in a taxi in "a metropolis of North America" an Indian prince loses a ruby as big as a nut. The search of the police is in vain, because the ruby has already been pocketed by the next occupant of the taxi, an Italian immigrant on his way back to his home in southern Italy. The immigrant has no notion of the value of the stone, and since he is illiterate he does not read newspapers. He barely knows how to shut the door of the taxi because it is the first time he has ever been in a car. He imagines the ruby is some kind of a good-luck piece and takes it back to his Italian village along with his other possessions: an imitation-leather suitcase, a dozen fountain pens, a few scraps of linoleum and other objects *per far figura,* to make a showing and boast of the wealth he has acquired in America. He plans to sell the pens to his fellow villagers, forgetting that they are all illiterate and that there are only half a dozen people in the village who know how to write. This is the reward of his five years of expatriation: a suitcase full of junk, the detritus of a vulgar materialism.

The things he brings back are worthless and not adapted to

European needs. He has also found a real treasure in America, but he does not know what this is and is unaware of its value. He senses vaguely that it is a *portafortuna*, a good-luck piece, but just how it brings good luck or how to turn it into wealth he has no idea. He takes an infantile pleasure in touching it. "It was one of those useless objects that stay with us a lifetime, that no one manages to get rid of, that finally become the companions of a lifetime and even of whole generations. Many important things are lost, even well hidden and locked up, but these objects are never lost, and sometimes we think about them." [12] After many years he ends with a feeling that it is the most valuable thing he has brought from America, but he never understands what it is. The American shoes he brings back wear out on the feet of his wife, the linoleum is given to "important families," nobody wants the fountain pens. Sometimes he takes out the American newspaper he has brought back and looks at it again, remembering the gold-tipped cigarettes, the girls, the phonographs, the life of the downtown streets where he "sometimes ventured." As for the pink crystal, he gives it to his son, who uses it to play a kind of marble game for which the other boys use nuts. There is one other glass marble in the village, but the son thinks his is finer because it came from America and because it is pink. "As he watched this thing which his boy used as a toy the father often thought of his illusions in the days when he had traveled around the world, and how the world seemed to him full of precious lost things which lucky people found. For this reason he had always felt around wherever he was, under the mattress on the steamship, behind the leather seat on the bus, but he had never found anything. Yes, just one time, he had found five dollars on the street and he always remembered it, that day it rained." [13]

This story was published under Fascism, in the volume *Gente in Aspromonte* in 1930. Its America is pure fantasy. In some ways it resembles Guareschi's *Il destino si chiama Clotilde*; in both Guareschi and Alvaro the American setting is deliberately unreal, and both perhaps unconsciously reflect certain Fascist attitudes toward the decadent plutocracy. (The rich have jewels and the immigrants are poor, the Prince was on his way to a dubious hotel with a companion when he lost the ruby in the taxi, but "excluded that the person with whom he was traveling could be considered responsible for the loss." [14]) Alvaro's story has the curious abstract quality that is often found in Italian writing, even the good writing, under Fascist censorship. But it differs from Guareschi's novel in that the major part of it, the Italian part, is realistic and honest about peasant culture and about the view of America held by the Italian poor. *Gente in Aspromonte* was one of the first books to show the southern Italian peasant as he really was, ignorant and illiterate, reduced to an animal existence by his poverty.

When the book was awarded the La Stampa Prize in 1932 it was attacked violently by the Fascist press, and the controversy that resulted was so bitter that the prize was not offered again. If Alvaro had been a little more explicit about America and the Italian peasant, the book would probably have been suppressed outright. Levi's *Cristo si è fermato a Eboli,* which presented a similar view of the peasant and his ideas about America, was not published until 1945. But Levi's style was factual, documentary, vulnerable to censorship, where Alvaro's was suggestive and metaphorical. His symbol hangs vaguely in the air at the end, still only half explained. What is the real treasure of America? Whatever it is, it is not something you find behind the seat on a bus.

After the war it was possible to be more specific. But this allusive and suggestive style, the "soft-focus technique" that Italian writers had learned under censorship in the Thirties, had its influence on postwar writing. Language that appears to be talking about one thing but is really talking about something else is useful for several purposes. Prisoners can use it to talk in the presence of their guardians, and poets can use it for the possibility of richness that lies in ambiguity. The tendency toward multiple meaning and half-statement is found in all of Pavese's fiction, in Vittorini's *Conversazione in Sicilia,* in Alvaro and the other writers who learned to write under Fascism; it was one of the results of the atmosphere of censorship. The effect went so deeply that it is apparent even in the new generation of writers who began publishing after the war. Giuseppe Cassieri's "L'Ospite americano" ("The American Guest"), an emigration story published in *Il Messaggero* in 1962, resembles Alvaro's story written more than thirty years before, not only in its theme but in its style and treatment of symbol. The main difference is that Cassieri avoids outright fantasy and writes only about what he has seen firsthand; his story is set entirely in Italy. Mr. Scarabei, an emigrant who has lived in America for over half a century, comes back to his native Umbrian town to dedicate a pair of bell towers restored and provided with new bells by the emigrant colony in New York. Greeted by the whole population of the town as a prodigal son and hero, he makes a conventional speech protesting that he is neither Garibaldi nor Franklin, only a country boy who has had good luck in the New World, and that he owes what success he has had to the democracy of his adopted country. One of the bolder voices in the crowd shouts, "Viva il nostro Tonino!" and he tells them humbly, "I am your Tonino in spite of all." [15]

But he soon perceives that he is not any more, and it is around this realization that the story turns. Where Alvaro's story uses the single symbol of the ruby, Cassieri uses a double image to convey the difference between the two cultures. Mr. Scarabei's boyhood friend Vincenzo is a beekeeper and a leading authority on the problems of apiculture. After the banquet he tells Mr. Scarabei some interesting facts about bees. They are extraordinarily efficient insects and their society is highly organized. The queen lays as many as three thousand eggs a day. Her union with the male drone takes place in the air; the drone dies afterward and the queen returns to the hive. Vincenzo has even found in his researches that the queen is chosen democratically. It is not hard to see in his description of bee-society an analogy of America as the Italian often sees it: the efficient production, the high degree of organization, the cold love which takes place "in the air" with a mate selected at random, even the matriarchal implications of the male who is cast aside as a corpse after he is used. "We can learn much from these useful insects," Vincenzo tells his friend. "They are so well organized that the human race would do well to imitate them. It is because I live in close contact with the bees that I have such a great admiration for America." There is no irony in Vincenzo's tone and his admiration is sincere. The one who is perturbed by the analogy is Mr. Scarabei.

That night he cannot sleep. Perhaps it is the heavy Italian food, or perhaps it is something else. Finally he realizes it is the bells that are keeping him awake. Not only do the two bells in the new towers ring every quarter hour, but the bells in all the sixteen surrounding villages are set to ring in harmony with them. Sixteen bells, four times an hour, echo from one side of the valley to the other. But wasn't this what he and the other Americans wanted to give to their native town? The bells are harmonious but their very harmony makes him nervous. After fifty-six years, he concludes, you can't come back. He had grown accustomed to the beehive pace of New York, the hurried efficiency, the noise, until he hardly noticed it, but he had grown out of tune with the traditional and melodic harmony of the bells. Something had profoundly changed in him, "to the point of looking and not seeing, seeing and not remembering." In short he had become an American, uprooted and restless in spite of his wealth, anxious to go back to the beehive where he will be a part of the mass. His name is the Italian word for an insect, a beetle. As for the beekeeper Vincenzo, the story does not explain what he thinks of the bells, but perhaps he is the one who should have gone to America. Or perhaps if he had emigrated to America like Mr. Scarabei he would not admire bees so much.

Another of Cassieri's Terza Pagina stories involving emigration was "Posta di New Jersey" ("Mail from New Jersey"), published by *Il Messaggero* in the same autumn of 1962. This was the first piece of Italian fiction to deal with a new kind of emigration: the transplanting of professionals and intellectuals to America in the period after the Second World War, when entry permits were available mainly to Italians with special qualifications. The social class is different but the human problems of emigration are the same. Old organisms cannot be transplanted; young ones can, but they lose something in the process and in the new soil they become new plants. Signor Antonio, evidently a state employee or minor functionary, has emigrated to America thirteen years before with his wife and two daughters. He leaves behind a third daughter, Fiorella, whose husband Eugenio is a professor although not a very successful one. For thirteen years Eugenio in his "simple and dreamy mind" has cherished the idea of following his wife's parents to America, where the shock of dislocation will be cushioned by the presence of relatives. Eugenio is no pioneer. He is essentially a dreamer, and his idea of America is not very different from the traditional dream of the Italian peasant. He imagines it as a place where you can live without working, in his case by giving prepared lectures on the mission of Italianità to Italo-Americans, who will pay richly for the privilege of hearing their mother-culture flattered. For three years Eugenio and his wife have been "sitting on the packed bags of their hope," waiting for word to embark for the New World.

Then comes the letter from New Jersey. The dream is shattered; the father-in-law announces his imminent return to Italy, and describes what life in America is really like. A flat monotonous country, either too hot or too cold depending on the season, and nothing to do but go to work and come home again at night. No theatres, at least not for the parents who have never learned English properly, and no cafés, only squalid beer parlors where people sit and get drunk. Perhaps, Antonio concludes, he and his wife have "antiquated sentiments." The daughters, who came to America as children and married Americans, will stay with their husbands. For them it was not so difficult to learn the new ways and pleasures, the restless American way of being happy. They mastered everything, even the American slang and songs. "Yes, Bice and Cesira dress well as you have seen, but there is nowhere to wear their dresses. Trenton is terribly provincial. They do a queer thing sometimes: they dress and put on their makeup until they look as though they are ready for an opera at the Metropolitan, then they go out and pose for snapshots by their shrubbery, by their Cadillacs. What else is there to do after you have used up your enthusiasm for automobile rides on those magnificent roads, as wide as rivers, that lead through a landscape without savor, without mountains, without surprise?" [16] The color cameras, the American machines, he tells his Italian children, are "not the instruments but the very end of their happiness." Antonio, in spite of his culture and his social position, has been no happier in American than Silone's peasants.

Emigration is not a panacea; even when it solves the economic problem it creates others. To Cassieri successful emigration is possible only for a very few, those who are temperamentally rootless, adjustable, and energetic; in short those who are "Americans" by nature. Bice and Cesira will go on taking snapshots of each other and their husbands in front of their Cadillacs. This is a way of being happy, the ephemeral and uncontemplative American way. But for Antonio who was too old America was an exile; and for Eugenio who stayed behind it was a dangerous narcotic, a reverie in which he forgot his own mediocrity and wasted his life in fruitless dreaming. Cassieri wrote about emigration without personally experiencing it (he had never been to America when he wrote the two stories), but what he says about it is sound, and it is essentially what every other Italian writer has said from Silone to Livia De Stefani. In the pattern of emigration there are three kinds of Italians: those who only dream and never go, those who emigrate successfully (Dedalus), and those who fail at emigration (Icarus). Antonio is probably right to come back to Italy. But he is wrong in imagining that you can recapture your happiness by going back to the place where you lived it. When he comes back he will find that he has changed and Italy has too. In the last paragraph of his letter he reminds his daughter of the good days before the war when they used to put the family in the old Lancia on Sunday and go to Velletri or Fiumicino for a picnic. What Antonio does not grasp is that in his absence Italy has "Americanized" until it is not very different from New Jersey, at least not as much as he remembered. In 1949 when he left Italy Fiumicino was a quiet fishing town; by 1962 it was the site of an international airport where the jet airliners from London and New York landed in an endless stream. On a Sunday the highway to Fiumicino or Velletri was clogged with shiny new automobiles, and many Romans preferred not to fight the traffic; they stayed home and watched television. This kind of "progress" is not American; it is an inevitable development of industrialism which happened to come to America earlier, and many Americans deplored it as much as Antonio. And even if this had not happened, even if Italy had not "Americanized," it is not very likely that Antonio would be any happier there than he was in New Jersey. Emigration is like a transplantation or a surgical operation; something is removed, the roots that connect the emigrant to his own soil. Operations like this are irreversible. That was the point of Cassieri's other story, "L'Ospite americano." Antonio can come back, but now he will be half an American in Italy as he was half an Italian in America. Emigration is a leap in the dark. If the emigrant makes it, if he manages to put down new roots in the foreign soil, he will probably live a fuller life in America than he did in Italy. If he doesn't make it there is not much point in coming back.

8 "*Liberation*"

The psychological conditions of war are not the sort that encourage a clear use of language, and this is particularly true of modern wars. In practice war means to bomb cities, kill human beings, and destroy crops, but radio announcers and statesmen do not like to describe it in these terms. Times of war are therefore particularly rich in euphemisms: "pacification," "greater East Asia co-prosperity sphere," "the final solution of the Jewish problem." The Korean War, which was comparable to the American Civil War in the amount of men and matériel involved, was not a war at all but a "police action." Such slogans may be reassuring to well-dressed people sitting in warm rooms listening to radios, but they do not have much effect on soldiers, bombed-out civilians, or others who have had first-hand experience of war. After the air raids of 1943, the Fascists wrote on the ruins of Naples, "The fewer houses, the more honor." A statement like this could not fail to provoke irony among the Neapolitans, a race whose view of life is somewhat ironic anyhow. After every new raid they walked through the rubble repeating to each other, "*Che onore,* what an honor."

After a while the term passed over to personal misfortunes: "I broke my leg. *Che onore.*"

To anyone who took a personal part in the Second World War the same ironic connotations were attached to the terms "liberation" and "fraternize." They were part of the special vocabulary of that war, as "lousy" and "I'll tell the cockeyed world" were of the war of 1914–1918. "Fraternize" equaled a well-known four-letter verb, and "liberate" was simply theft, or worse. It did not take the American draftee of 1943 very long to learn what it meant to liberate a chicken or fraternize with a fraulein. When the Colonel in Hemingway's *Across the River and into the Trees* goes duck-shooting on the Venetian lagoon he senses a certain antagonism on the part of the boatman, who seems to resent his uniform. Then it is explained to him that the boatman was "a bit over-liberated"; when the Moroccans came through they had raped his wife and daughter. This was the way the Japanese army "liberated" Manila from the Americans.

Italy entered the Second World War as an ally of Germany, and came out of it a "co-belligerent" of America and Britain. This in itself caused a certain confusion of language. By 1944 many Italians were not quite sure what the words "enemy" and "friend" meant. But after incidents like the massacre of the Ardeatine Caves (March 24, 1944) and the extermination of almost two thousand inhabitants of the town of Marzabotto (September 28–30, 1944) they knew they wanted the Germans out of Italy. The military and political struggle that took place in Italy from 1943 to 1945 is commonly called the Liberation with a capital L by Italian historians as well as British and American, and the term is used here more legitimately than it usually is. The two years began with Italy occupied by the Nazis, and they ended with free elections and a constitutional government. The freeing of the country was carried out partly by the Italians themselves, and after the farce of the Greek campaign and the defeat in Africa it was one of the finer pages in Italian military history. The Liberation started with the "four days of Naples" in September, 1943, when the Neapolitans rose up spontaneously and threw bedsteads, bathtubs, and heirlooms out the windows on the heads of the Wehrmacht, and it ended with the civil war in Piedmont and Emilia when the partisans operated at division strength with air support and radio communications. It was a time of agonizing human conflicts and uncertainties. While the Allied advance from Salerno to Milan was systematically destroying Italian cities and causing casualties among civilians, the Italians were asked by the Allied radio to believe that this was the work of friends who were coming to liberate them. Most of them did believe this, and some of them even risked their lives to help the Allied forces destroy their own homes. The partisans were not always popular; every partisan action resulted in the shooting of hostages and other reprisals that left bitterness and grief in the civilian population. Some even accepted this as necessary if Italy was going to be freed. But the Liberation was a time of trauma for Italy, and one that left its mark very deeply in the national subconscious. The confusion, the uncertainty, and the heroism of this time are reflected in the books that were written about it. There are a number of novels about the Resistance and Liberation, some of them good ones and some not so good, but they all have in common a quality not found in mere war reporting: a quality of having been written out of a profound national experience.

There is a difference between the Italian and American fiction about the Second World War. *From Here to Eternity* and *The Naked and the Dead* were good novels, not as good as *The Red Badge of Courage* perhaps, but they had their own kind of sincerity and internal integrity. They shared one important quality with Crane's novel: they were written to "explain" war to non-soldiers. Crane's Civil War novel, of course, was written for another generation who had not known the war personally. This was the last war fought on American soil. For the majority of American readers the First and Second World Wars were something they had not experienced and therefore something that had to be reported to them by people who had experienced it. It was essentially a literature of exoticism, an account of certain strange and terrible things that had happened in foreign countries. Even if the strange and terrible things sometimes happened to Americans this did not basically affect this quality of foreignness. One of Hemingway's best war stories is actually called "In Another Country," another one "A Way You'll Never Be." For the Italian reader of 1945 a war novel was something different, an account of something that had happened to him personally and had affected him deeply and traumatically in ways even he himself did not fully realize. His own emotions toward the war and the Resistance became inevitably mixed up with his reading, just as the writer's emotions toward these things had been involved in the writing. The Italian attitude toward the war is a mixture of incompatible opposites: a wounded military vanity, admiration for the partisans, an inferiority complex over the enormous material and technical superiority of the Allies, the sympathy for America left by a century of emigration, a resentment for the bombed cities and ruined monuments. Some Italians felt a vague guilt over the fact that Italy had made a separate peace in 1943 and Germany had fought to the end. The American soldiers were nice boys and their pockets were full of money, but the Italian male with his traditional sense of sexual honor could not forget the girls who sold themselves for chocolates and nylons, the wives and daughters who were "liberated" by the Moroccans. Finally there was the disenchantment that came from disappointed hope. The Liberation had been looked forward to as an event that would solve all problems, that would bring absolute political freedom and the end of hunger and injustice. No mere military operation could come up to these expectations. In 1945 the playwright Guglielmo Giannini complained, "The Fascists deprived the Italians of their freedom, but no one yet has restored it to them." [1] As it happened Giannini was a neo-Fascist, but many other Italians, those who had risked their lives in the Resistance, felt the same way. The objection was a natural one; if there was no freedom then what was meant by "Liberation"? What it seemed to mean was that the Allies collected the partisans' guns and promised to hold an election later. The historical event carried with it a burden of inevitable disappointment, like all events from which too much is expected. By the time the elections were actually held, in 1946, the attitudes had already been formed.

The literature of the Resistance and Liberation is similar in many ways to the literature of emigration, especially in its ambivalence toward America and what it represents. There is one important difference: where the emigrants were mainly unlettered people who were unable to express their own legend, the Liberation involved large numbers of intellectuals and writers who had a firsthand body of material to convert to fiction. No first-rate novel has yet been written by an emigrant; there are half a dozen good novels about the Resistance and Liberation. Many of these do not particularly involve America or the Allied part in the war. In fact this is a pattern that is interesting in itself; especially in the books written before 1950 there is a curious impression that it is all about another war in which the partisans liberated Italy without any help from the Allies. The reasons for this were first of all political. The typical postwar Italian writer inclined toward the left, particularly if he had been involved in the Resistance, and he shared the more or less official anti-Americanism of other European leftists. Often this did not affect his admiration for America in senses other than the political, but it did warp his view of just how the Liberation had taken place. But the attitude went deeper than politics; it was part of the whole psychological pattern of inferiority and resentment that resulted from the Italian experience in the war. Italy had always prided itself on its tradition and cultural maturity, and had regarded American culture as vigorous but raw and gauche. Now it seemed that these Huckleberry Finns had conquered Europe; many Italians had the humiliating feeling of having been liberated by children. The Americans seemed to combine technical mastery with an incredible naïveté. One of the few hearty laughs the Italians enjoyed in the terrible winter of 1943–44 was hearing Fiorello La Guardia open a radio address to the crown prince of Italy by remarking, in a heavy American accent, "Tonight I would like to speak to Prince Umberto as I would to any Italian boy." When the American soldiers arrived the whole legend that had been forming for over a century collided with an immediate and banal reality. The generation that fought in the Resistance was the one that had grown up on cowboy films and read *Moby Dick* clandestinely in the Thirties, but it was one thing to believe in the America of Whitman and Melville and it was another thing to see the Pensive Barbarians sitting in a jeep in an Italian piazza, eating Spam and reading comic books. These enormous youths with their crew cuts and their cheerful faces were the final reality of a myth: it was the end of Douglas Fairbanks, Tarzan, Ahab, and all the other personifications of Chateaubriand's noble savage.

Italian writers were not ready to deal with this disenchantment for some time, and the first books to come out of the war were curiously reticent about the Allied part in the Liberation. In Vittorini's *Uomini e no* ("Men and Not-Men," 1945), a novel of the Resistance set in Milan in the winter of 1944, there is no mention of the Allied landings in the south, no hint that anyone except the partisans is fighting the Germans, no suggestion that the English and Americans are on the same side as the protagonist N–2 and his companions. Only once is there a reference to the air raids of the summer before: "The sun glittered on the rubble of '43."[2] Vittorini had a personal reason to remember those raids, since his own house with all his books and papers was destroyed in them. He makes another reference to the same raids in the "Autobiografia in tempo di guerra" published in *Il Politecnico* and later reprinted in his *Diario in pubblico*. In the sketch "Milano come Madrid" the anti-Fascist prisoners in the Hall of Justice argue about the raid while the bombs fall:

> One of us said that he hated "them." And who? The enemies of our enemies?
>
> "They're our real enemies," Gubbio shouted.
>
> "They're Americans," said somebody else. "Are the Americans our enemies?"
>
> "They're the Fascists," yelled Gubbio. Was it the Fascists who were destroying Milan?
>
> "Let's understand each other," said Molina.

> "We do understand each other," said Gubbio. "I said it's the Fascists. It's the Fascists. It's the Nazis." [3]

If there is any confusion here it is the confusion of a man whose house has just been destroyed by the "enemies of his enemies." Gubbio seems to be trying to convince himself as much as the others. No amount of argument could change the fact that the Americans were destroying Milan, while the anti-Fascists were helpless to do anything about it and could only listen to the bombs fall. This mental conflict is one that many Italians felt, and Vittorini as an honest writer simply records it. But neither here nor anywhere else in his fiction does he come to grips with the obvious reality: that without the Allies there would have been no Resistance and no Liberation.

None of the other Italian novels about the Resistance—and there are half a dozen or so good ones—has very much to say about the Allied part in the war. Oddly enough there is not even one good novel written by an Italian soldier who had taken part in the war as a member of the regular armed forces. The nearest thing to it is Giuseppe Berto's *Il cielo è rosso* (*The Sky Is Red*), which is about the war in Italy in 1943–44 but was actually written in a prison camp in Texas. This novel has more to say about America and Americans than any other Italian book to come out of the war, and for an obvious reason: Berto had more firsthand contact with the American army than any other Italian writer. Born in the town of Mogliano Veneto near Treviso in 1914, he was trained as an army officer and served both in the Abyssinian War and the North African campaign of 1941–1943. When the Italian army surrendered in Tunisia he was captured and spent thirty months in a prisoner-of-war camp near Hereford, Texas. The war was a profound experience for Berto, and one that dominates his writing even into the Sixties. His autobiographical *Guerra in camicia nera* ("War in a Black Shirt") in 1955 was a remarkable diary of his North African experiences with the Italian army, ending with his capture. Berto is perfectly candid about his ingenuity in escaping the worst part of this disastrous campaign. When the confused retreat began from Libya into Tunisia he found a convenient oasis from the war in the town of Gabès, where most of the population was French. Here, under the pretense of gathering supplies for his battalion, he spent several brief "vacations" which in any well-organized army would be considered desertion. His account of his relations with the French population in Tunisia is interesting because it is an ironic foreshadowing of the situation of the American soldiers in Italy as he later described it in *Il cielo è rosso*. When he first came to Gabès he found many women and children and few men; they had all gone off to join the Free French forces who were fighting the Italians. It was therefore "comprehensible," as he remarked, that the population should regard his uniform with a certain diffidence. The next time, he decided, he would bring the children candy. They were shy at first, but finally they flocked around him like the pigeons in Piazza San Marco. He made friends with the seven-year-old Martine, who was thin with two enormous black eyes and a small voice. For Martine he brought more gifts on his next trip, not only candy but meat and bread. She took him to her house and he met her family: a mother, an aunt, and a grandmother. "They accepted the meat and the bread with dignity, without thanking me excessively, and suddenly I was disappointed; I had wanted something in exchange for these things, something at least equal to them." [4] Martine was too young to understand the significance of his uniform, but the women were distant if not actually hostile. It was hard for the young officer, full of good will, to understand that women could not be friendly to soldiers who were killing their husbands and sons. "I don't think I'll go back to that house the next time," he concluded in his diary. The campaign was almost over anyhow. The Tunisian front collapsed and Berto joined the other stragglers who were waiting on the beach at Cape Bon for a ship to take them back to Italy. But the Italian Dunkerque was not very well organized and the ship never came; instead he was captured and ended up in Texas.

When he arrived at the prison camp in 1943 Berto was already a graduate in letters from the University of Padua, and off and on he had nourished a vague ambition to write. In an article in *Il Libraio*, a Longanesi advertising brochure, in 1946 he explained how he happened to write *Il cielo è rosso*. "I am convinced that if I hadn't ended up in a concentration camp I would never have succeeded in writing a novel. But I found myself with an indefinite series of days to fill up, and there was no doubt in my mind how to fill them up. My first concern, as soon as I arrived at the camp where I would be permanently, was to build myself a table. I went around collecting the pieces of wood that were scattered over the compound and built a table out of them. I pounded in the nails with a piece of iron from the stove. Then I began writing a novel." [5] This first attempt was written on a roll of toilet paper in lieu of any better material, and the "intellectual exponents" of the camp judged it worth saving. But Berto threw it away and started over. This time he wrote a story which appeared in a prison magazine (one copy, hand-written) published by the PW's. It was not a very good story, but in the same magazine there was another piece of fiction that seemed to him remarkable. He went to find the other prisoner and talked to him. Where had he learned to write like that? "You should read the Americans," the other prisoner told him.

There was not very much to read in the prison camp; occasionally YMCA workers brought around Italo-American books in bad Italian and a few old magazines. In back copies of *Esquire* he found "The Snows of Kilimanjaro" and "The Short Happy Life of Francis Macomber." By the terms of the Geneva Convention he received a few dollars a month to spend in the canteen, and in this way he bought a few other books; one that he remembered later was Steinbeck's *The Red Pony*. This reading was all the background in American literature he had when he began to write *Il cielo è rosso*. Probably it made a greater impression on him than it would have otherwise because there was nothing else to read in Compound Number 4 of the prison camp in Hereford, Texas.

Berto later described this thirty months in the prison camp as the most unhappy period of his life. Probably these special conditions made him more hostile to America than he would have been if he had stayed in Italy, or if he had not been captured. By 1944 many Italians had begun to think of the Americans as liberators, but the soldiers with automatic rifles who stood guard in the prison compound were not anybody's liberators. Even in late 1945, when the war in Italy was over and Italians were greeting the Americans with open arms, the hostility between PW's and guards continued. "We were still at war with the Americans, our own private war, out of our pride and our punctilio. And we were right, because the Americans were at war with us in the same way, and they didn't even have the excuse of being prisoners." [6]

It was under these conditions, practically with the rifles of the guards pointed at him, that he conceived his first two books. When he wrote *Il cielo è rosso* and *Le opere di Dio* he was still a Fascist; in fact he was confined in a special section of the camp set aside for officers who refused to sign a "co-belligerency agreement" after the armistice of September, 1943. He took the manuscripts back to Italy with him in 1946, and *Il cielo è rosso* was published the following year by Longanesi. It was an immediate success; it won the Premio Firenze in 1948 and established Berto as one of the most important younger writers to come out of the war. The novel is set in an Italian city which is never named but is obviously Treviso; Berto had lived in Treviso as a child and gone to school there, and perhaps for this reason most of the characters are children and adolescents. The period covered is from 1943 to the fall of 1944, approximately the time when Berto was writing the novel in Texas. Treviso, a minor industrial center, suffered particularly from Allied air raids; on Good Friday of 1944 nearly half the town was destroyed by American bombers, and this was only the first major raid of a series. Berto learned about these air raids by reading *Life* and by talking to prisoners who arrived at the camp in 1944. He did not get a very clear picture of what was happening in Italy, and *Life* like other American publications tended to exaggerate the damage for propagandistic purposes. What he did understand was that his own country was being systematically destroyed, by the same people who were standing guard outside his barbed-wire fence with rifles. Considering all this his description of the raids in *Il cielo è rosso* is remarkably free from hatred. He describes them with a curious ambivalence, half as an Italian and half with the detached mentality of the American flyers who are intent on their technical tasks. The section that describes the first air raid ends in a kind of meditation on the responsibility for what has happened. "For a certain time the enemy will not be able to make use of the station, the railroad tracks, perhaps the bridge if it was hit. And if to do this they have produced a sum of human suffering that nothing, not even the greatest good on earth, can ever cancel, this has no importance for them. They don't think about it, and it is not their fault, because of the universal evil." [7]

This concept of universal evil underlies Berto's whole thinking about the war and the causes that brought it about. It is reflected in the title of the collection of stories that came out of the same period, *Le opere di Dio* (*The Works of God*). The officer who wore a black shirt in Africa is not ready to blame the war on the Italians and lacks the real evidence for blaming it on the Americans. It is easier to blame it on "Dio," a vague and undefined Divinity. In *Il cielo è rosso* the American aviators who have bombed the Italian town, concentrating on their instruments, fly on under the stars. "And the stars fly too; they fly at fantastic speed toward the places where these men belong, in another part of the earth. In only a few hours the stars that are now over their heads will be above Kentucky, Missouri, California. And each of these men who have destroyed houses and human creatures can still think lovingly of other houses and other human creatures." [8]

This is taken from the early part of the novel, where Berto's point of view is still panoramic and Olympian. Later, after the Liberation and the arrival of the American troops, the style shifts to the typical Italian neorealism of the postwar period, in Berto's case formed partly on the examples of the American writing he had read in the prison camp. In the *Galleria* forum in 1954 Berto admitted his debt particularly to Steinbeck, Melville, Faulkner, and Hemingway. In his early work the influence of Hemingway is most obvious. At its best his Hemingwayism is almost as good as *A Farewell to Arms*; at its worst it descends to parody.

> The corporal and Bill looked towards the group of people in the piazza. There were probably seventy or eighty of them now, and the shadow of the school building was lengthening steadily toward them.
>
> "But when are they going to send us home?" said Bill.
>
> "Don't think about it, Bill," said the corporal. "It's worse if you think about it."
>
> "We ought to go, now that it's over," said Bill. "Why don't they send us?"
>
> "It's no good thinking about it," said the corporal.[9]

This is nothing more than a sophomoric imitation of the famous ending of "The Killers," which Berto had possibly read before the war; it was one of the few Hemingway stories translated into Italian in the Thirties. The resemblance extends not only to the refrain ("Well," said George in Hemingway's story, "you'd better not think about it") but to the alternation of imagistic description with short terse dialogue and to the building of effect through the echoing of key phrases. Berto is over his head in trying to write from the point of view of American soldiers, and it is here that his Hemingwayism is the flattest. When the style is assimilated and converted to Italian characters he is better. After the death of the girl Giulia the reactions of her lover Daniele are described in a passage which resembles the similar scene in *A Farewell to Arms*—which Berto says he had not read in 1944—but which has a keen and particular emotion of its own.

> He walked slowly up and down in the hallway. Carla was still sitting on the doorstep, and she didn't turn her head when she heard him walk. He had no desire to go to her right away. He had no desire to do anything. He leaned against the wall waiting for some thought to come, but

> nothing came, probably because his stomach hurt him, and all he could think about was the pain in his stomach. He went into Carla's room. He looked at himself in the mirror. On the table there was a basin full of water. He put one hand in the water and held it there for some time. Then he passed his hand over his hair, and put it back in the water, and then passed it over his hair again, and went on doing this until his hair was wet. Then he turned away from the table and went out, and sat down on the doorstep next to Carla. "Have you got a cigarette, Carla?" he asked.[10]

In the same way Frederick Henry moves somnambulistically through banal actions as he tries to forget that Catherine is dying. "I ate the ham and eggs and drank the beer. The ham and eggs were in a round dish—the ham underneath and the eggs on top. It was very hot and at the first mouthful I had to take a drink of beer to cool my mouth. I was hungry and I asked the waiter for another order. I drank several glasses of beer. I was not thinking at all but read the paper of the man opposite me." [11] Both the narrator and the reader are constantly aware of Catherine in the hospital, but the emotions never come to the surface. Instead they are concealed in the banal mechanical motions which the narrator forces himself to carry out with a kind of rigidly willed automatism. The two passages, Hemingway's and Berto's, succeed in a difficult thing: communicating a high state of emotion without ever mentioning the emotion itself. At the end of the restaurant scene Frederick reports simply, "I walked through the rain up to the hospital," in the same voice in which Daniele asks for a cigarette.

Berto's most successful characters are those closest to his own psychology. For this reason the Italian-American soldier Roy is somewhat more convincing than the Anglo-Saxon American soldiers in *Il cielo è rosso.* In one early scene when Daniele tries to beg gloves from two American soldiers, Roy and a non-Italian corporal, the corporal curses the boy and refuses to give him anything. But Roy says, "If I had two pairs of gloves I'd give him one." Finally the corporal, complaining, "The hell with him. These people would take the shirt off your back if they could," reaches into his pocket and throws the boy a pair of woolen gloves.[12] This is typical of the difference between Americans and Italian-Americans. Roy is more immediately compassionate; the corporal is callous on the surface but underneath it good-hearted. From ten thousand feet in the air the Americans drop the bombs and are oblivious to the suffering they cause, but when they are face to face with the Italians they see them as human beings and try to alleviate their suffering, although they often put on a hard-boiled manner to cover up their softness. In a story published fifteen years later, one of Berto's characters says, "If men could look in each other's faces they would never make war." [13]

It is not easy to be generous without being hated; Berto had already found this out in Tunisia. In a later chaper of *Il cielo è rosso* some American soldiers, including an Italian-American cook named Appiano, get permission from their officers to give leftover food to Italians out of a garbage can. But this causes a riot in which a woman is hurt. Berto had seen pictures of this kind of "American aid" in *Life*. The only one who emerges content from this incident is Daniele; in the confusion someone gives him bread and cans of food which he hides under his shirt. As he leaves the camp he smiles because the sentry is "smiling enigmatically" and pretending not to see the food under the shirt. A little later Daniele goes to work for the Americans, and when the unit is transferred he is offered a chance to go away with the soldiers. He almost accepts, but he decides to stay out of his love for Giulia, and by implication his loyalty to his own people. In spite of their power and generosity the Americans are no permanent answer to Italian misery and suffering. Their mana is that of foreigners; whatever it is that makes them strong seems to evaporate in the hands of the Italians. "There are so many things I don't understand," says the young Tullio. "Because if you take these American soldiers one by one, there's nothing you can say against them. There are good ones and bad ones, like all the other people in the world. Maybe there are even more good ones than bad ones, and they help us whenever they can. But it doesn't do any good. Our lives get worse and worse, and they don't solve any of our problems, even if they do give candy to children." [14] Giving candy to children, of course, will not permanently correct an economic collapse. Marshall Plan tractors might, but this came later. Berto's Italians expect too much from the Americans, more than any mere army could give. They waited for the Liberation as though it were the Second Coming, and instead of the Messiah there were soldiers who passed out food in garbage cans. Who is to blame? The stars? "There will always be wars," argues the old man who serves as a kind of spokesman for Berto. "As long as one people is unjustly treated, or thinks it is unjustly treated, sooner or later there will be a war, unless the other people are willing to remedy the injustice. But that would be expecting too much from human beings. Nobody will give what he has to somebody else, just out of love of justice. This will never happen in the world." [15] It is true that it would have been expecting too much from the French in 1940 that they should give Nice to the Italians out of the goodness of their hearts. Or that the Abyssinians should have voluntarily offered their country to Italy in 1935 to remedy the "injustice" of the Treaty of Versailles. One of the basic realities that Berto never faces up to is that Italy got into the war in the first place through a series of cynical aggressions: the Abyssinian War, the Albanian-Greek campaign, the invasion of southern France. Berto did not start the war himself, even if he did wear a black shirt. But in spite of his philosophizing about injustice he never explains just how it did start. Furthermore he never mentions the Resistance and the Allied support of the partisans—for the excellent reason that when he wrote the novel he didn't know about them. The chronology of *Il cielo è rosso* as it relates to the actual events of history is curious. It was written in 1944, and when he wrote it, Berto thought the war would end that year. Actually it lasted a year longer than he expected. His view of the Liberation is therefore totally unreal. Most of all, he failed to grasp the implications of what happened on September 8, 1943: the Badoglio government signed an armistice with the Allies, the Nazis seized control in Italy and began arresting hostages, and the Italian people—or a large proportion of them—began to regard the Germans as their enemies and the Allies as their friends. All this he comprehended when he came back to Italy in 1946, but he let the novel stand. *Il cielo è rosso* is therefore less a history of actual events than a document of Berto's emotions toward the war as it seemed to him in the prison camp in Texas. The attitude of the Italians in the novel is quite simple: somehow the war started, the Americans came and bombed everything and destroyed the crops, therefore it is up to them to feed the population. For this the Italians are "grateful but with dignity," like the French women in Tunisia. After all who could be grateful for food out of a garbage can?

It is impossible for the conqueror to be loved; at the best he can hope not to be hated. At this the Americans did better than the Germans, who started out as Italy's allies. The real meaning that lies underneath *Il cielo è rosso* is one Berto never gets to: The world is out of joint, and those who wore black shirts must accept at least part of the responsibility for making it that way. To the Berto of 1944 all the responsibility belongs to the victors. Perhaps he was more influenced than he realized by the psychology of the prisoner of war; once he lays down his arms the prisoner falls into a passivity in which all the problems are his captor's. "And so," the old man in the novel concludes, "a soldier who gives candy to children, or a major who tries to govern a town with humanity and justice, does no good at all. They are not the ones who count. They come and go, and others come who may be good or bad, and what they do has no great importance, because they are all carrying out things that are decided by people we never even see; many times we don't even know who they are. . . . Perhaps we don't deserve a better fate. But they ought to feel the responsibility they take on themselves by conquering other people. I don't mean the killing and the destruction, which may be necessary in war. But disorder, famine, moral ruin—these are things for which they ought to provide some remedy." [16]

It is not hard to guess what Berto meant by "moral ruin." In American magazines he had seen pictures of Italian girls fraternizing with American soldiers in Sicily; for example in the *Life* of August 23, 1943, one of the issues that circulated in the camp, an old Italian knelt down to shine the shoes of an American soldier while another soldier, his arm around a girl, waited in line.[17] For the PW's this was even more bitter than the bombings; while they were in prison their own sisters and fiancées were betraying them. This was simply the result of a military situation and nobody in particular was to blame, either the girls or the Americans. A "moral ruin" is something that is easily felt but difficult to pin down, and even more difficult to correct. In any case the American army was not intended or equipped to correct other people's moral ruin. But the old man's implied indictment of America, even if it is not very logical, is human and understandable. It has its own logic, the logic of rationalization. In the face of an inexplicable defeat the human tendency is to blame anyone, preferably someone near at hand, rather than admit one's own mistakes. In the same way the American right preferred to blame "pinks," professors, and liberals for the defeats in China and elsewhere rather than examine the real historical and economic reasons for the success of Marxism. In spite of the sham Hemingway *Il cielo è rosso* succeeds in being a good novel; the characters are real and the events are described movingly and convincingly. But it is perhaps even more valuable when it is read as a psychoanalysis of Italy's Liberation trauma, the complicated and inconsistent set of emotions that Italians had toward the Americans who had "liberated" them by destroying their houses and killing Italian soldiers. Berto was uniquely qualified to write such a book, qualified in a way that no other Italian writer was. He was an Italian and wrote from an Italian point of view, but he had lived among Americans for two and a half years and he could imagine what it was like to be an American. In Tunisia he had been part of an occupying army, he had given candy to children, and he had been hated. In writing *Il cielo è rosso* he had worked out his own thinking about these things. At the end of the novel he comes back to the abstract-essay style again for a final comment. "Little by little people understood. It was no longer a war to be endured, it was a war that had been lost. In spite of everything that had been said, they had to realize now that the war had been lost. And they alone had to support the weight of this defeat, a weight too heavy for a poor people, in a country devastated and sterilized by war." [18] In 1944, in the prison camp in Texas, this is the way it seemed to Berto. When he came back to Italy and saw what had really happened the truth was hard to accept. It was not the war; the war was as he had imagined it. It was the politics, the way the best part of the Italian character had turned in revulsion against Fascism, the way a new Myth of America had taken root in the Italian consciousness. He saw that his politics had been wrong and he swung over to the left; he became a socialist. But this didn't solve the problem; the problem was inside him. The problem was that everything he had held out for, everything he had refused to betray, in those long thirty months in prison had been wrong. Finally he stopped writing. He was sick, and he went into psychoanalysis. When he came out he was a different person, and a different writer. He did not repudiate his earlier work—he let the words stand as he had written them in the prison camp in 1944—but his new work was different. *Un po' di successo* ("A Little Success"), published by Longanesi in 1963, is a collection of stories ranging back as far as the Texas days but many of them later, dating from the period of his psychoanalysis. The later ones are often humorous, of a particular fantastic and exuberant kind of humor seldom found in Italian literature. In a 1963 article in *La Fiera Letteraria*, written on the occasion of the death of his friend Giuseppe Marotta, Berto analyzed the three-way connection between neurosis, physical illness, and humor, and concluded that for Marotta as for himself "humor is the essence of writing, because without humor there is no other way of escaping from the neurosis and anxiety that would otherwise condemn us to impotence." [19] One of the stories in *Un po' di successo*, "Fatima," may very well be the funniest novella since Boccaccio. Another one, "Zia Bess, in memoriam," is the most preposterous and perhaps the most entertaining version yet of an Italian myth, the legend of the American Uncle. It takes place in a Venetian town resembling Berto's own Mogliano Veneto. The narrator's father is a returned emigrant who, according to his own story, was once a prospector in the Klondike. Although some of his anecdotes are dubious, it is clear that he did succeed during his years abroad in making friends with one Aunt Bess, who lived in "Wichita Falls, Texas, U.S.A." This American adventure so impressed him that he named his children Tom, Mike (the narrator), Johnny, and Peggy, and fondly cherished the nostalgia of these youthful years the rest of his life. It takes the children some time to realize that Aunt Bess had not been an aunt at all but "someone with whom our father had taken up" during his glorious American adventure. In any case Aunt Bess serves as an ideal personification of the Myth of the American Uncle converted to the female sex—remote, mysterious, fabulously rich, a focus for all the suppressed longings and aspirations of the family. Every Christmas she sends a package of gifts from Wichita Falls. The children imagine her as "some kind of *vamp alla western,* the kind that dances and shows her thighs through a slit in her skirt, singing huskily as she slinks from table to table plucking men's billfolds while they devour her with their eyes, the kind that finally, when her handsome bandit arrives, shoots out all the lights in the saloon with her six-shooter." [20]

Then comes Fascism. The father, who has always been a talkative ne'er-do-well, turns into a minor Fascist official. After the war, disaster. The father runs away and the children are left to their own resources. (Berto's psychoanalyst would perhaps point out that Fascism had been a father-figure to him, and that after the war he was shattered by the loss of this psychic authority.) Amid the confusion of the Liberation it is the daughter Peggy who saves the family. She disappears in the direction of the city and comes back with one American soldier after another, an endless succession of Joes and Jimmys and Bobs. With them comes a constant stream of chocolate, American cigarettes, and cans marked "Meat & Vegetables." But this kind of "Liberation" is too good to last. Peggy goes off to the nearby city with a sergeant named Harry, and the boys are left faced with hunger again.

> Broken by adversity, weakened by hunger and the desire for smoking, we passed long hours in silence, looking at each other with sighs from time to time, with all the weight of our misery on top of us. It was from one such siege of meditation that one day a long-forgotten name suddenly emerged: Aunt Bess. Aunt Bess could save us; in fact more precisely she *ought* to save us, and not only because if it hadn't been for the imbecility of our father, we might well have been her children. It was her duty to save us also because she, for better or worse, had won the war, and so it was up to her in a way to remedy the damage the war had caused. We decided to write her a letter invoking her aid.[21]

The wait for help is rather long, but eventually a package arrives from Wichita Falls. There is a letter on top, and underneath a cellophane bag tied with a red, white, and blue ribbon. The letter is in English and none of the boys can read it. They decide that the contents of the bag, an amorphous gray substance, was probably intended for the preparation of soup. It is not very appetizing, but they eat it anyhow, since it comes from America. Then Sister Peggy comes home, having had a "misunderstanding" with her American, and they show her the letter. It is not from Aunt Bess at all; Aunt Bess has passed on, and the letter is from her friend Alice Smith. "She left instructions that her body should be cremated and the ashes sent to you," the friend explains tactfully. "With this package I am carrying out her will." [22] At the end of the story the boys, their faces gray, are rushing in the direction of the churchyard.

The treatment of the American Myth and the Liberation in this story is simply a parody of the attitudes in *Il cielo è rosso*. (Compare "It was her duty to save us . . . because she, for better or worse, had won the war," with "They ought to feel the responsibility they take on themselves by conquering other people.") Berto had come a long way, so far that he was able to view his mental state of 1944 with irony, even to treat it farcically. This does not mean that his later view of America is not a serious one, or that his treatment of the Myth is unsound. On the contrary it is extraordinarily consistent with what other Italian writers have said about America, emigration, and the Liberation, and with what he himself had said—perhaps only half understanding it—in *Il cielo è rosso*. The father in this story plays the role of the typical emigrant, the one who returns to Italy without ever understanding the America where he had failed to take root. From the beginning his attraction to America was simply a lust for wealth. Quite literally he was a gold-hunter. In Wichita Falls Aunt Bess offered him something more valuable—affection, comradeship, perhaps matrimony—but this was not what he had come to America to find, and he went back to Italy. Like many returned emigrants he became a super-patriot, extolling the virtues of everything Italian—in his case a Fascist orator. But the subconscious nostalgia remains; he gave his children American names. At the end of the story America—Aunt Bess—offers these children a gift more valuable than they are aware, one so precious they do not even recognize it for what it is: her very essence, which she wishes to bequeath to the Italian soil. But the boys regard America simply as the eternal source of chocolate, cigarettes, and canned goods. Aunt Bess's ashes are a mysterious symbol like the ruby in Alvaro's story, even if here the symbol is treated somewhat farcically. Whatever the true gift that America offers Europe may be, it is something more essential, more precious, than chocolate and cigarettes. But the Italians treat this gift exactly as they have always done with things that come from America: they eat it. If there is anyone in this story who understands America a little better it is the sister Peggy. Not only does she take the trouble to learn English, but she gives love to the Americans and receives love from them in return; if love is the proper word for it. And the irony is that she is the one who gets the chocolate and the cigarettes. "We must love one another or die," says Auden.

• • •

Mario Tobino's *Il clandestino* (hard to translate, but perhaps "The Underground" is the closest that English can come) was published in 1962 and won the Strega Prize for the same year; it was one of the biggest best sellers in Italian publishing history up to its time. It was also the first Italian novel to deal candidly and fully with the Allied help to the Resistance and the whole English and American part in the Italian campaign. The reasons were fairly obvious. By 1962 Italians were beginning to get over their inferiority complex about the war and were ready to look at it more objectively, and Tobino was a psychiatrist who was especially trained to see through his own complexes and others. As an example of its more relaxed attitude, this novel along with Berto's "Zia Bess" was one of the first Italian works of fiction about the war to involve humor. When the invalid can joke about his ailment he is already on the road to recovery.

Il clandestino is not basically a war novel. Tobino was not a professional novelist and stylistically it is old-fashioned and almost Victorian; psychologically it is a study of the way people behave when they are faced with the anguishing choice between collaboration and resistance. The setting is Medusa, a seacoast town modeled on Tobino's native Viareggio. The characters are intellectuals, professionals, an admiral, and a few workers and fishermen from the port who band together in a rather confused underground group in the fall of 1943. The anti-Fascists are not shown as uniformly heroic and their motives are examined with a clinical perception. One of them, Lorenzino, is a devotee of American movies; for him the underground is "a cinema without film," "an American adventure." His previous life has been rather ineffectual, and in the underground he imagines himself rising to the level of the heroes he has seen on the screen. This unreal view of the war does not prevent him from behaving heroically when the time comes. As a psychologist, Tobino knows that conscious actions are often prepared for in the pre-enactment of fantasy. The fact that an image of war, or an image of America, is unrealistic does not mean that it is invalid or ineffectual or that it cannot have positive and concrete effects. In Lorenzino's case it leads him to fight to the end and then die like a movie hero, killing himself when he is wounded in order not to be a burden on his comrades.

One of the realities often ignored by earlier novels is that the whole partisan movement in Italy was armed and provisioned by the Allies, often by airdrop. In Tobino's novel the whole plot turns on the effort to get into contact with the Allies and to plan and carry out these airdrops. Finally two contacts are established, one through a secret agent who is parachuted by the British and the other through the young schoolteacher Rosa, who passes the German lines and makes her way to the American command in the south. The two Allied armies are shown as markedly different. The British are efficient but impersonal and rather cold; they are interested in the Italian Resistance only as it serves their own ends. They are suspicious of underground groups until they are sure of their authenticity. When they are finally convinced, they are generous but not altruistic. When the secret agent, an Italian who had emigrated to Scotland before the war, is asked by his father why he is serving as a spy, he says, "For money. They pay me well." [23] As it happens this is exactly the right answer to make to the father; he is a peasant and this is the only reason he would be a spy.

America stands at the opposite pole from this detached Machiavellianism. For the schoolteacher Rosa and her friends it is less a country than a legend, a tremulous complex of emotions. As Lorenzino tells Rosa of the plan to send her through the German lines he tries to keep his face impassive, but he feels "something like a breath of joy that came from the name America." [24] Rosa, a rather placid and sedentary girl, carries out her dangerous mission without hesitation and without a sign of fear. When she comes back from the south the others embrace her and feel an odd lump under her dress; it is an American radio transmitter, which fits around her like a belt. Laughing, with theatrical gestures, she tells them her adventures. She hid among the peasants until the American line passed over her, then the soldiers took her to the Italian-American intelligence officer Joe Frosine. Joe, as Rosa is calling him five minutes after she has met him, is the American Legend in flesh and blood.

"We understood each other immediately," she tells them breathlessly. "It's fine working with them. You don't waste time, it's as though you'd always known each other."

"But what are they like, the Americans?" Lorenzino asks her several times, like a child who wants to hear the details of a fairy tale again.

"Didn't I tell you? We agreed right away. I felt like a schoolgirl again. Imagine, I might have been a spy and they believed me immediately. They're right, if you don't believe in people you can't get anything done. . . . Joe understands everything. He's extraordinary."

Rosa manages to be enthusiastic even when she describes the destruction the Americans cause as they fight their way north. It was simply the American way of doing things, the technique of total efficiency, and it couldn't be any other way. It didn't matter anyhow because probably the Americans would pay for it all later. "They're as rich as lords. They make war calmly. Before they get here they'll destroy everything in Italy."

"Why?"

"Because they bomb everything flat first and when they get there everything is safe. I saw it twice, passing through the lines. There were no more Germans and they never even came close to them."

"Why didn't they come close to them?"

"I don't know. They don't want to die."

"They're realists."

"They have another way of looking at things." [25]

Tobino sets all this down absolutely without irony. In the heat of enthusiasm it all seems glorious to the Italians, and twenty years later there is no rancor in the novelist who recounts it. Probably the Italian mentality, more than the German or the English, is sympathetic toward the anti-heroes who "don't want to die" and "have another way of looking at things," the rich children who can afford to knock everything down as they come so they won't hurt themselves making war. In the popular mythology, Germans in uniform were fanatics and the English had ice water in their veins. The Americans, like the Italians, knew when to be afraid. It was not a question of cowardice to Tobino; both Italians and Americans showed great courage when courage was necessary. But there was no point in attacking a house with your bare hands when you had a machine to knock it down with. The machine was made in U.S.A. and it was a pleasure to watch, even when it was knocking down your house. Tobino had fought in the Resistance himself, and he knew what he was talking about. This is the way it seemed to him in 1962.

9 *The Moon and the Bonfires*

It is curious that Cesare Pavese never seems to have considered the idea of emigrating to America, or at least he never mentions the possibility in his diaries and letters which cover a period of over twenty years and discuss matters even more intimate and crucial. In many ways emigration would have been the logical solution to his personal problem. He felt alienated and restless in Italian culture, and from the time of his first poems America had always represented for him a new start, a return to the primitive and genuine. Naturally there were practical difficulties in the way of such a solution. As a well-known anti-Fascist in the Thirties he would not have been allowed to leave the country, and later he was involved in the intricate personal and political problems that were to lead to his suicide. It is not very likely that he would have emigrated even if it had been possible; there were deeper and more personal reasons under the obvious practical ones that would have prevented it. But even if he never considered it as a personal possibility, the idea of emigration is always under the surface in Pavese's writing. In the beginning it was his hope, and toward the end it became his sin. "I say unto you that whoever looks on a woman to lust after her has already committed adultery in his heart."

The first poem of *Lavorare stanca,* written as early as 1931, is about this myth of emigration. The poem is called "I mari del sud" ("The South Seas"), it describes an emigrant who really existed: a cousin who came back to Pavese's Piedmontese village after twenty years of wandering over the world and climbed the hills with the boy who was to become a poet. But in the poem the real cousin is euhemerized into myth. When Pavese first read this poem to his Turin university friends it seemed "Homeric" to Massimo Mila, and Pavese himself consciously associated the cousin with Odysseus.[1] The returned emigrant is "a giant clad in white who moved calmly, his face tanned, taciturn."[2] His homecoming ends ignominiously; instead of bending the bow and slaying the suitors he buys a cement garage with red gasoline pumps in front, and soon loses his money. But before, on the hillside walks, he tells the boy stories to match those in the *Odyssey.* One dream in particular had stayed in his blood, the sight of a whale seen from the deck of a Dutch fishing boat: "He had seen the great fins soaring in the sun, had seen the whales fleeing in a foam of blood."[3] It was a time when Pavese was steeped in Melville; his translation of *Moby Dick* appeared the following year.

This poem, Pavese's first except for the immature work he later rejected, is closely linked thematically to the last book he wrote, the novel *La luna e i falò* (*The Moon and the Bonfires*). Both the poem and the novel are about an emigration that failed. In both cases the emigrant is not an intellectual like Pavese but a peasant, a native of the Langhe hills where Pavese was born but which he left at an early age to go to Turin. Both the poem and the novel seem to have occupied a special place in Pavese's own view of his work. Of the poem and the images in it he said later, "I literally discovered myself in those remote persons and things."[4] About the novel he wrote to the critic Mario Camerino that it was the work he had carried longest in himself and the one he took the most pleasure in writing. *La luna e i falò* was written in three months of intense activity in the fall of 1949 and published early the following year. The time of the action is about that of the period of writing, or a little earlier. It is important to establish when the action of the novel takes place, because there is a sense in which it is a chronologically precise allegory of Pavese's own life. The emigrant, who narrates his own story, is never named; as a boy he is called Anguilla or Eel because of his skinniness, and the nickname is one that would have fitted Pavese at the same age. His second important characteristic is his bastardy. He is an illegitimate child who is raised in a foundling hospital in Alessandria and later farmed out to a family of peasants who receive a small subsidy for keeping him. When he is old enough to work—ten or twelve—he is sent to the nearby farm of La Mora, first as a kitchen-boy and later as a laborer. Shortly after his military service he leaves for America, where he stays for about twenty years. All this is narrated in flashback; the novel opens with his return to the Piedmontese village, which through allusions to the war and the Resistance can be dated as 1948. The narrator therefore emigrated about the time that Pavese himself "discovered America," that is, around 1928–1930 when he began to read and translate American literature and wrote his thesis on Whitman. The return of the emigrant twenty years later coincides approximately with the writing of the novel itself. This was a critical period in Pavese's creative life, the time when he turned back to his rural Piedmont material after the Dolce Vita settings of *Il diavolo sulle colline* and *Tra donne sole*. The only quality of the narrator that Pavese did not share was his bastardy, and this is comparable to Pavese's own rootlessness and sense of alienation in Italian culture. When all these things are put together it is possible to read *La luna e i falò* as a projection of Pavese's own personal emigration reverie, an account of *what would have happened* if he had gone to America physically at the time he merely discovered it in a literary and symbolic sense. The disillusionment of the returned emigrant is therefore not only that of a physical disappointment in America; in a deeper sense it is an expression of Pavese's own relation to the myth of America and his pessimism when the events of the postwar period made him see things in a different light. In 1947 he wrote the bitter essay "Ieri e oggi," in which he concluded that America had "lost its mastery" and was "no longer in the vanguard of anybody's culture." It was certainly not in the vanguard of Pavese's culture as it had been in 1931.

Actually Pavese had two different and contradictory images of America, even in the time when his admiration for American culture was total. One was the traditional America of the emigrant legend, a land of opportunity and easy riches; or in a less crassly material sense, an outer and wider world with greater possibilities of self-fulfillment for the individual. It is of this wider world that the Cousin of the South Seas speaks when he says, "You who live in Turin . . . but you are right, life is lived somewhere else than in the country."[5] The word "country" here is *paese,* which means countryside in the sense of the French *pays* but also village or home town, the Santo Stefano Belbo where Pavese was born. For Pavese the opposite of *paese* was the Turin where he went away to study and discover the outer world; for the cousin it was the South Seas. In relation to *paese* America too is a kind of super-Turin. But in another way America itself is *paese.* This was the America that Pavese had discovered in his books, the America of the Pensive Barbarians, the mythic soil of Whitman, Sherwood Anderson, and *Spoon River Anthology.* It was the example of these writers that had led Pavese to the search for his own native soil, the search that had ended in the rediscovery of Santo Stefano Belbo and the writing of *Paesi tuoi* and *La luna e i falò.* "For Anderson the whole modern world is a contrast between country and city, frankness and empty pretense, nature and little men. How much this idea relates to us too, I don't need to say," he wrote in 1931.[6] The title of his first published novel was borrowed from a peasant proverb: *Donne e buoi dei paesi tuoi,* women and oxen from your own village. Pavese's whole personal tragedy is bound up in his proverb: his sexual failure, his search for a place to belong, his eventual collapse as a writer. If he had ever found "a woman from his village," if he had ever found a village that wanted him and accepted him, the final catastrophe might have been averted. But Santo Stefano Belbo was never really his, he had lost any roots he had once had there, just as he had never totally taken root in the intellectual life of Turin. Instead he committed his whole sexual happiness into the hands of an American actress with blond hair, and when this failed him he was through as a writer too.

The stylistic influence of American writers is less apparent in *La luna e i falò* than it was in the earlier *Paesi tuoi*. There are occasional passages that fall into the cadence of Hemingway or Anderson, like the beginning of the second chapter which resembles the opening of *A Farewell to Arms*: "That summer I stayed at the Hotel dell'Angelo, in the piazza of the town, where nobody knew me any more, I had grown up so much. I didn't know anybody in the town either; in my time I used to come there only now and then, I lived on the roads, along the river, in the barnyard. The town is higher up in the valley, the water of the Belbo goes by the church a half an hour before it widens under my hills." [7] But the novel relates to America in a more important sense: It is the only fiction Pavese wrote that deals with the physical America and is set partly in the United States. Considering that Pavese never visited America the details of the setting are strikingly accurate, so much so that it is a little baffling where he got them. His biographer Davide Lajolo believes they came mostly from American films, some of which he sat through five or six times until he knew regions, places, even local accents by heart. He would go willingly even to bad films if they showed him some aspect of America he didn't know, or one that interested him. Other details he had known since his childhood from the stories of emigrants who had come back to Santo Stefano Belbo and the other towns of the Langhe. Lajolo has explained, "His town and my own were places that had always given many emigrants to America, many. And these emigrants, almost all of them poor peasants who often worked as dishwashers over there, came back and recounted the life of an authentic America, in their memories a good place, even a fabulous one. Pavese not only listened to their stories, but since he had always felt himself an emigrant from his peasant village he had thought of America as a goal from the time of his childhood." [8] A third source was his encounter with the American actress Constance Dawling, which preoccupied him almost entirely in the time just before he wrote the novel. The dedication of *La luna e i falò* was "For C," and the epigraph that followed it was the phrase Melville underlined in his copy of *Lear*: "Ripeness is all." From Constance he picked up habits, mannerisms, characterization, scraps of American idiom, the whole mood and ambience of American sexual life. The encounter was a traumatic one, and one that helped prepare the way for his suicide, but it was also the natural and inevitable climax of his lifelong fascination with American films. A year before meeting Constance he had written in his diary: "An old dream. To be in the country with a beautiful woman—Greer Garson or Lana Turner—and live a simple and perverse life." [9] *Country, simple, perverse*: these three words might sum up his image of America in 1930 as in 1950.

It was in this emotional state, at a time when he was consciously seeking a return to the earth and immediately after his encounter with Constance Dawling, that he wrote *La luna e i falò*. It was a time when he strongly felt that the important part of his life was past, and the whole tone is retrospective. It begins at the end, with the return of the emigrant to the Piedmontese village. "Here they've got it in their heads that I've come back to buy a house, and they call me the Americano and show off their daughters to me." [10] But he is staying at the hotel and is not sure he wants to buy a house; he is afflicted with a sense of his own rootlessness. In the weeks that follow he finds his old friend Nuto the musician and carpenter and seeks out the traces of his childhood in the Langhe hills: the farm of La Mora where he worked as an orphan boy, the piazza of the country town where he used to go to the fair in the fall. But he has lost his intimacy with the countryside, or perhaps it was an intimacy he never had in the way that Nuto has it. Coming from a wider world, he feels only the detached skepticism of the traveler for the two peasant superstitions that provide the title of the novel: the moon which governs the time of planting and the time of graftings, the bonfires which the peasants burn on

St. John's Night to "wake up the earth." Nuto believes in these things, Nuto who had a father and was born in the *paese*, but the narrator's birth is recorded only in the foundling home and he doesn't belong here. Then where does he belong? Now he remembers that even as a boy he wanted nothing but to go away, to follow the railroad to the sea, to Genoa and beyond to America. "The good thing about America is that they're all bastards," [11] he tells Nuto. It was for this, he realizes, that he had instinctively drifted toward the country where nobody has any roots, not even those who are born there. This is the second symbolic use of the moon in the novel: America is "like the moon," there is nothing there, only a surrealistic lunar landscape. Pavese's America is erotic but fleshless, cinematographic; love is the disembodied love of the movies in which the figures who meet and embrace are made out of shadows. It is one of the paradoxes of the novel that Pavese is more autobiographical in his descriptions of America, where he had never been, than in the scenes set in his native Langhe. Under the surface of the narrative he is retelling the story of his own encounter with Constance, and in a broader sense his whole emotional relation to America from the time he was a university student in Turin. In the novel the artificial "American" atmosphere of his months with Constance becomes the real geographical America. In the California town of El Cerrito the narrator works in a café with a girl named Nora, and imagines taking her out in the hills at night as he would in the hills of the Langhe. But even if Nora had let herself be rolled in the grass it would not have made any important difference to anyone. The automobiles would still roar down the valley with their headlights blazing toward the city, along the highway that never ended. "I understood in the dark, in that odor of garden and pines, that those stars were not mine, that like Nora and the customers in the café they made me afraid. The fried eggs, the good pay, the oranges as big as melons, were nothing, they were like the crickets and the croaking of the frogs. Was it worth the trouble to have come? Where could I go now? Jump from the pier?" [12]

This is not only a projection of how Pavese would have felt

if he had emigrated to America; it is also an implied and perhaps only half-conscious comment on the years he had spent in his inward "emigration" in American literature, the crucial years of his career and the years when he had formed himself as an artist. Now he understood that, just as the stars over California were not the narrator's stars, American literature was not his literature. It was good (like the fried eggs and the oranges) but it was not his. This was why in *La luna e i falò* he had come back to the rural Piedmont setting of *Paesi tuoi,* in the hope of recapturing something essential about himself that would give him an identity as an artist and as a human being. But like his own protagonist, he came back too late. The narrator is "the Americano" to the peasants in the countryside, and Pavese had been a critic and translator of American literature too long to be able to free himself from this rôle. Like his own character, he knew what it meant to be uprooted.

The narrator never rolled on the grass with Nora. In America love is made in bed, in anonymous rooms. He understood after a while that the others, the Americans, wanted as he did to throw themselves on the grass and "own a piece of land as big as a woman." There was plenty of land, enough for all. But it was a land without bonfires, a lunar landscape; the Americans moved around so much that they had lost touch with the earth and no longer knew where they belonged any more. "At Fresno where I lived I went to bed with many women, one of them I almost married, and I never found out where they had their father and mother and their land." [13] Rosanne, the second of the two American women who are described in detail, is a schoolteacher "who came from who knows where," somewhere in the middle west. She had come to California originally to get into the movies, and would not say what had happened, only that it had been "a hell of a time" (in English). Nora had only been a passing desire to roll in the grass, but Rosanne he hopes to marry. After a while he realizes why this is: It is because she is "illegitimate" too. She has no past, no scruples, and no passions except the single one of succeeding in Hollywood. When he asks her why she goes to bed with him she laughs and tells him that he is after all a man. Or, as she remarks, "Put it the other way around, you come with me because I'm a girl." [14] She is not stupid, she knows what she wants, and she has her own kind of self-discipline; she never drinks because "your looks are your only free advertising." She is ready to work to help the narrator open an Italian restaurant ("a fancy place, you know") where she will be seen by somebody who will put her picture in the newspaper. Her femininity is essentially narcissistic; she is always rubbing cream into her face and combing her blond hair. She is a woman to go with the landscape, a moonling. Or more precisely, a minor motion-picture actress. The autobiographical part of all this is obvious.

But it is not because she is using him as a means to an end that the narrator decides not to marry her. It is precisely because she is a character on the moon, and he knows that wherever it is that he belongs he does not belong there. When she asks him why he doesn't become an American he tells her it is because he is not—"because I'm a wop." This, like a good deal of the dialogue with Rosanne, is in English. "I often thought what race of children would have come out of us two—out of those smooth hard flanks, out of that blond belly nourished on milk and orange juice, and out of me, out of my thick blood. Both of us came from nobody knew where, and the only way to find out who we were, what we really had in our blood, would be that." [15] But he knew that all he would make would be another bastard, an American son. In spite of all this he cannot bring himself to leave Rosanne; for all her hardness and her superficiality, she still pleases him "like the taste of certain mornings, like touching the cool fruit in the Italian roadside stands." [16] In the end it is she who leaves him, depriving him of even this last dignity. She goes back to Santa Monica, but he never sees her picture in the Sunday supplements. Once a postcard comes, asking him for money. After that he never hears from her again.

One other night the narrator remembers from his twenty years in America. It was in 1940 or 1941, the time when Italy was in the war and America was not yet, and he had left California and wandered off across the desert with the vague idea of going to Mexico. The chapter that describes this trip gives a curious and in many ways precise picture of the American southwest. One afternoon the truck he is driving breaks down and he spends the night in the open, in "a gray expanse of thorny sand and rises that were not hills." Nearby are railroad tracks and a line of telegraph poles, then nothing. Across this wilderness two or three cars a day pass, and for the rest it belongs to the rattlesnakes, centipedes, and coyotes (if this is what he means by wild dogs). When it grows dark, really dark, he turns on the dash lights of the truck and remembers the things that have happened in this country: the bones found on the desert, the bandits, the travelers who died of sunstroke. It was easy to understand why there was a time when people killed each other in this country, where nobody touched the earth except to stay lying on it. The pioneers too were *déracinés*; a few of them died and left their blood on the sand, and the others moved on. The thin thread of the railroad and the highway were all they had left. The adjective that recurs in Pavese's description of America is "uninhabitable." For a long time the only human beings who pass are a family of Mexicans, going to look for seasonal work near San Bernardino. "And these too, I thought, where did they have their home? Was it possible to be born and live in the country like this?" [17] The Mexicans, he thinks, had no need to pass through the foundling home in Alessandria; they were born orphans and dispossessed. Like Cecchi and other Italian writers, Pavese in his bitterness for America makes exception for the minorities, the Mexicans, the Italians, the Armenians of Saroyan. If the Mexicans were rootless it was not their fault; it was the world that had come to drive them out of the house with its hunger and its railroads, with revolutions and petroleum. In addition to Melville, Pavese had also read Dos Passos and Upton Sinclair.

The Mexicans are the only human beings the narrator meets in the desert of centipedes and coyotes. Later that night a train goes by, but this has nothing to do with humanity. It begins with a sound like a horse along the tracks, then the headlight appears, then something that fills the whole plain with din and sparks. The train, he realizes, was what he had been waiting for, but when it finally comes it comes as an intrusion; even in the desert the mechanical America of noise and hard steel will not leave him alone. When he finally falls asleep it is to be awakened by the coyotes at dawn. "There was a pinkish light, I got out chilled and stiff; through the low clouds pushed a slice of moon that looked like a knife-cut dripping blood on the plain. I stood watching it for a while. It made me really terrified." [18]

America is the moon and the Piedmont hills are the land of bonfires. But in this case what is the significance of the peasants' lunar superstitions? It is clear that the moon of the title has two meanings, which at least on the surface have little to do with each other. The first sense is the moon of peasant magic. "You have to believe in the moon," says Nuto. "Try to cut a pine in the full moon, the worms will eat it. A wine-vat should be washed in the new moon. Even the grafts won't catch if you don't make them in the first days of the moon." [19] The other sense of the moon is sterility. Earlier, in the California café, the narrator has complained that there is no good wine in America: "There's nothing. It's like the moon." [20] There is a temptation to try to find some connection between these two symbols, moon as dark agricultural magic and moon as America-sterility. Through his narrator Pavese is writing consciously from a peasant point of view, and possibly the peasants sense that, like the moon, America has a power over their lives in some way they do not fully understand. America at the time the novel was conceived, 1948–1949, literally had the power of sustenance and death over the Piedmontese peasant as it did over the rest of Europe. On the one hand it offered the Marshall Plan, on the other hand the Bomb. But probably this is too ingenious; it is doubtful whether Pavese himself had any intention of connecting his two moon symbols in this way. The most that can be said is that the moon is important to the narrator as it is to the novel, and that in both symbolic functions it has a power that eludes rational analysis. In the Piedmont scenes the moon is always connected with Nuto, who performs the function of a kind of magus or sage in the novel. He is uneducated and has seldom gone beyond the hills of the Langhe, but he possesses a power of seeing into the heart of things that the narrator for all his travels still lacks. Nuto is the knower and also the charmer. This is apparently connected in some way to his trade as a musician and maker of musical instruments. "If I knew how to play like you I wouldn't have gone to America," [21] the narrator tells him. His instrument is the clarinet, the nearest modern equivalent to the Dionysian pipe, and he plays mainly for rural fairs, which are of course agricultural festivals. It is Nuto who has instructed the boy in the mysteries of physical love twenty years before, and it is Nuto now who interprets the violent events of the Resistance which took place while the narrator was away in America. These events have both a political and a sexual significance, as will be seen presently. On the subject of lunar folklore he is quite unmoved by the narrator's taunts that he is superstitious. "Nuto told me quite calmly that superstitions were only things that did harm, and if anybody used the moon and the bonfires to rob the peasants and keep them in the dark, then he would be the ignoramus and they ought to shoot him in the piazza. But before I could talk about it I would have to become a country boy again." [22]

This is exactly what the narrator cannot do. He has been away too long, and like the Americans he has lost touch with the earth. And even if he could recover his childhood it would not do any good, because while he was away the *paese* he is looking for has changed. Here the political thread of the novel becomes entangled with the sexual. Through the experiences of Fascism and the war Italy has been first sick, then insane, then tortured. It has been transformed by events in which he took no part, particularly the Resistance and the trauma this caused to the whole national consciousness. He begins to understand this when he finds out what happened to the three sisters who lived on the farm of La Mora where he was a kitchen-boy, and especially to the youngest sister Santa.

La Mora was a prosperous farm with a large staff of servants and hired hands; its owner Sor Matteo was one of the wealthiest landowners in the region. Sor Matteo himself is countrified, but a relative is a countess. His daughters play the piano and wear fine dresses, and are courted by officers and lawyers. It is these daughters who first disturb the adolescent boy's erotic thoughts, and he falls in love with each of them in turn, or with all of them at once. At first it baffles him that "all women are made in the same way" [23] and that Irene and Silvia, the two elder daughters, run after men like peasant girls. It is Nuto who explains to him that blood is red everywhere, whether you live in a cave or a palace. In spite of their fine airs and piano-playing these three girls are associated thematically with the land; their father is a farmer and they grow up among the vines and bonfires. They belong to the Dionysian part of the novel, and as such they are the diametric opposite of the moon-woman Rosanne. Where Rosanne is rootless they are attached to the *paese,* where she is cynical they are innocent, where she is indifferent and calculating they are passionate and impulsive. Rosanne is complicated in that she is simultaneously cold and promiscuous ("I go with you because you're a man"). The sisters are complicated in exactly the opposite way; they have an ingenuous and even saintly innocence (the youngest is called Santa or Santina) but in the end they are destroyed by their passions, which spring out suddenly and willfully. They follow the pattern of Faulkner's Temple Drake: first innocent, then violated, then depraved. This pattern becomes clear only at the end of the novel, and it is only then that the erotic contrast between Italy and America is seen in its full clarity.

The key to this pattern is Santina, the most innocent and in the end the most depraved. The elder sisters show signs of corruption earlier and both end badly; Silvia rides over the countryside on motorcycles with men and finally dies of an illegitimate pregnancy, and Irene, sick and sullen from jealousy, marries a worthless husband who beats her. But Santina at first seems untouchable. She was still a child when the narrator went away to America. At Irene's wedding it was Santina who was the most beautiful in her silk dress; "she was only six but she looked as though she were the bride." [24] Shortly after this the narrator goes off to his military service and then to America. He stays for twenty years and has his adventures with Nora and Rosanne, then he comes back. Although he does not fully realize it he has come back instinctively seeking Santina. He never inquires directly about her, but he remarks to Nuto once that he can't get the daughters of Sor Matteo out of his head. "Never mind Silvia, she died at home. But Irene with that good-for-nothing. . . . And Santina, I wonder how Santina died?"

For an answer Nuto suggests that they climb the hill above the town of Gaminella, as the boy did with the Cousin of the South Seas in Pavese's first poem. There, at the scene of Santina's death, he tells the whole story. Santina, who seemed the best of the sisters, turned out to be the worst. She went to school and became a teacher, but with the air of not knowing what to do with herself. When the war started she was seen going around with Fascists; she drank too much and went on midnight motor trips with them in their cars. It was common knowledge that she went to bed with the militia officers and the secretary of the local Fascio. When she passed Nuto in the street she avoided his eyes. In 1943 when the partisan war began she was afraid, or had an attack of conscience. She offered to serve as a spy for the partisans, but by this time she was too corrupt even to do that. After she had betrayed both sides she was caught by the partisans and shot. Nuto was there when she was sentenced, in a white summer dress instead of the soldier's trousers she usually wore. When Nuto caught her glance she "made a face like a child" as though it were not important, but outside she tried to run away. When it was over, the partisans sensed that they could not simply cover her with earth and leave her that way, in her white dress. Instead they cut the dried grapevines and piled them around her, and poured on gasoline and set it afire. "By noon there was nothing but ashes. Last year you could still see the mark, like the bed of a bonfire." [25]

This symbolism seems rather heavy-handed when it is summarized in this way, but it is more natural when it is told in

Nuto's offhand and laconic manner. Like Faulkner, Pavese is saved from obviousness by his style. The last word of the novel is "bonfire" in the description of Santina's end. Santina, who has seemed a minor character earlier, now emerges as the key figure in the novel. The contrast between Santina and Rosanne stands not only for the contrast between *paese* and city but also for the difference between Italy and America. In this sense the pattern of the novel recapitulates Pavese's whole developing attitude toward America from 1928 to 1948. In those twenty years, the years of the narrator's emigration, Pavese "discovered America," came to know it intimately through its books and through its women, and finally understood that its stars were not his own. Turning back at that point to his native soil, he found that something in it too had changed, or something in himself had changed toward it. The changes extended beyond the limits of the novel; what happens to Sor Matteo and his family is what has happened to Italy under Fascism and in the agony of the Resistance. As the novel proceeds the family falls apart spiritually and socially like the family in *The Cherry Orchard*. At the end of his life Pavese seems to have understood that the pagan instinct he had consciously sought for in his return to the *paese* ended in violence. "The people who practiced the worst and most frequent human sacrifices were the agriculturists," he entered in his diary in 1945. "Neither the shepherds, nor the hunters, nor the artisans were ever as cruel as the peasants." [26]

This violence is the opposite of the sterility which is the fatal vice of America. Santina ends in a bonfire, Rosanne ends coldly asking her former lover for money. Furthermore, the narrator's regret at not being present at the end of Santina is paralleled by Pavese's own regret at not taking a greater part in the events the novel recounts. Pavese was an anti-Fascist who paid for his ideas with jail and exile, but he was not active in the Resistance. The chief thing that his friend and biographer Lajolo finds to reproach him with is that in the worst months of the Occupation he "shut himself up in a trench made of books." [27] Pavese seems to have felt this himself. The one book other than *La luna e i falò* in which he treats the theme of the Resistance is called *Prima che il gallo canti* ("Before the Cock Crows"), and when he handed the volume to Lajolo he added the rest of the quotation: "Three times you will deny me." This sense of having failed to take part in the great experience of his generation probably played as large a part in his suicide as his sexual disappointments and his doubt in his own talent. It represented in his mind the triumph of betrayal over faith, of solitude over human solidarity. "He who does not know how to live in charity and embrace the suffering of others is punished in feeling his own suffering with an intolerable violence," [28] another diary entry notes in 1945. While his friends had fought in the hills he had sat in a warm room translating and writing literary essays. Now he knew the true meaning of the private America he had created for himself: it was solitude, isolation, shadow. The melancholy of the Pensive Barbarians, the quality he had admired in Melville and Masters, was perhaps only loneliness, the fear of empty space. The narrator of *La luna e i falò* had commented that even among themselves the Americans didn't know each other and suffered from their private loneliness. Out of this need to "touch something, make themselves known" they were brought even to the point of committing violence, against others and against themselves. It was possible to feel this in Turin as well as in Fresno.

10 *The Capri Letters*

Mario Soldati first came to the United States in 1929 in what he later described as "an attempt at emigration." He did not have a very pleasant time as a student at Columbia and he left after two years. In writing *American primo amore* in 1935 he got rid of most of his rancor, but it was obvious that the American experience had left a strong impression on him, and one he had not finished writing about. In many ways his situation was analogous to Pavese's. Both owed an important part of their formation to American culture, and both had an ambivalent attitude toward this influence, a nostalgia mixed with resentment. Like Pavese, Soldati seemed to be unwilling to come to grips with the problem for a long time, and then much later, over twenty years after the original experience, he wrote a novel which served to lay the ghost. *Le lettere da Capri* (*The Capri Letters*) was published in 1954, and it is one of the best international novels about Italians and Americans since James. It would be rather fruitless to try to find too many parallels between this novel and *La luna e i falò;* they are written by authors with different styles and different concepts of what a novel is. But insofar as they are documents of a personal experience of

America they are similar. In both cases the characters are not entirely autobiographical but the novels are; the America depicted is that of the author's own experience and resentments. Both are spiritual accounts of an emigration, one that ended in disenchantment and a return to the native soil.

There is an important difference between the two emigrations; Pavese's was only imagined and literary where Soldati had a firsthand experience of the United States and knew it thoroughly. He knew it, in fact, better than most Italians who visited America and even stayed there for some time; the reason was that his attraction to America was not that of a tourist or a journalist but that of an emigrant who hoped to become an American. For this reason, instead of merely studying Americans or "making friends" in the way a tourist does, he entered into intimate personal relations with them, or tried to, in the way a person does in his own country. This attitude toward America has persisted for the rest of his life. He does not, in the usual sense, regard them as foreigners. He is a kind of Henry James in reverse, and only a writer with this background and temperament could have written *Le lettere da Capri.*

The first remarkable thing about this novel is that it is written from the point of view of two Americans, a man and his wife. This in itself is a remarkable *tour de force* and one that James could never quite carry off; his Europeans are seldom as convincing as his Americans. The second is that the hero, Harry, is an odd autobiographical inversion. Where Soldati is an Americanized European, Harry is a Europeanized American. Each has at one point left his own culture and gone off in search of another, and each has acquired the surface manners and attitudes of the other culture so thoroughly that he seems half foreign to his own countrymen. As it happens, both are art historians, and both go to the other country originally to study the history of art. But Harry remains pro-Italian to the end, whereas Soldati by the time he wrote the novel had got over at least the overt phase of his love affair with America. In spite of his superficial Anglo-Saxon manners, his tweed jackets and his preference for whiskey, he remains at the bottom an Italian. It is therefore a kind of acrobatic stunt, and an impressive one, that he is able to portray Italy so convincingly as seen by an American.

The construction of the novel as well is Jamesian. The core of the story is told in a manuscript that Harry gives to his Italian friend Mario, a screen director. (Soldati's narrators are frequently named Mario and are frequently film directors or scenarists.) The manuscript is broken into two parts so that at one point Mario can intrude with a chapter of his own comments, and the climax of it is a long confession by Harry's wife Jane which takes up five chapters. At this point Jane is relating her story to Harry, who relates it in his manuscript to Mario, who passes it along to the reader. The point of view goes a step beyond *Daisy Miller* or *The Turn of the Screw* and approaches the Byzantine intricacy of *Lord Jim*. The plot is that of an old-fashioned novel which turns around some missing letters; as in *The Aspern Papers* the question is whether the possessor of the letters will give them up, and if so at what price.

The point of this novel is the contrast of national qualities, and all the characters are chosen with absolute economy to illustrate national traits. But since national traits are intricate and diverse even within a single culture, the characters are not two but several. Harry, the central character, is an art historian who comes to Italy first as a student in the Thirties and later as an officer during the war. Like his wife Jane, he is intelligent, energetic, and high-principled. Jane is the more puritanical of the two, or at least seems so at first. When Harry first meets her she is an army nurse in a hospital in Naples; he feels not that he loves her but that *it is his duty* to love her. "She seemed to me, small as she was, fragile, nervous, intelligent, sensitive, someone who needed protecting; I was drawn to her from the beginning by a bare melancholy emotion as simple as it was inexorable, something like my affection for my mother, an emotion which had, absurdly, the bitter taste of duty rather than the gentleness of love or the intoxication of desire." [1] This to Soldati is the mating instinct of Americans. The "melancholy emotion" leads to a marriage which, as might be expected, does not provide a complete physical satisfaction for either party. Meanwhile each has entered into a relation with an Italian lover, although the situation does not seem as obviously symmetrical in the novel as it does when it is summarized so flatly. Dorothea, Harry's mistress, is little more than a streetwalker, one of the ubiquitous adventuresses of the Liberation period in Rome, the kind the American GI's called *segnorine*. He knows this perfectly well and is attracted to her exactly by this vulgar sensuality, this degradation of the spirit which she appeals to in his own nature. The degradation, it should be pointed out, is in Harry and not in Dorothea, and Soldati makes this perfectly clear before the end of the novel. Dorothea is a native of Apulia, a provincial transferred to Rome, large, fleshy, and superb. There is no more evil in her than there is in the grand nudes of Rubens; if there is sin involved in their relation it is something in Harry's Anglo-Saxon mind. The relation between Jane and her lover Aldo is parallel. He claims to be a student but he is actually only the traditional Don Juan of lower-class Naples, the "handsome Italian" who preys on American girls in the Sixties as he did in the time of Daisy Miller. But "preys on" is a loaded term; Aldo is sincere and honest, more honest in his way than either Harry or Jane. If he has any fault it is simply that he is a thorough-going sensualist and vain about his skill as a lover. In short, Dorothea and Aldo are Italians *as seen by Americans*, the cinema stereotypes of Anna Magnani and Rossano Brazzi.

Harry came originally from Minnesota. In the middle of the novel he is seen as a professor of fine arts at Princeton, married to Jane who at this point seems a typical American wife. Soldati's own experience at Columbia was somewhat dismal, and university life in America as Harry describes it is the epitome of the petty, the philistine, and the boring. Twice a week he and Jane play bridge with their friends the Tutts, who unfortunately are types that anyone who knows American university life will recognize. "He was a tall thin young man, pink-faced and blond, who apparently dedicated his life to the care of his bushy moustaches, to his pipe collection, and to the cut of his tweed jackets. These three occupations were enough to satisfy his one ambition: to appear English while still remaining American, and proud of being an American. His wife on the other hand was not even vain. She was perfectly idiotic. Bridge was the whole aim of their existence. They had no children." [2] Harry's scholarly activity does not seem to provide him with any very great satisfaction, and if there are any students at Princeton they are never mentioned. To Harry it is simply the place where he plays bridge with the Tutts. At one point he remarks to Mario that he might have been happy in America if he could have lived by a Minnesota lake or in a hunting lodge in Wyoming. The America of Fenimore Cooper still has its attractions for the European, or for the Europeanized American like Harry. But Princeton with its pretension to culture and its bourgeois respectability is impossible. As for his physical relation with Jane, it is "reduced to a mechanical function in which sentimentality and intelligence predominated without going any deeper or without merging in a single experience with the act itself." [3]

The exact antithesis of this bridge foursome is the four-way relationship of Harry and Jane with their Italian lovers. It is one of the peculiarities of the novel that it succeeds in making matrimony seem typically American and concubinage typically Italian. Although Soldati contrives matters in this way to emphasize the contrast between the two cultures, the circumstances are actually rather special. Jane is a Catholic and therefore not a "typical" American but a member of a minority. If she had been Protestant she could have divorced Harry and married Aldo and there would have been no problem. In fact she considers marrying Aldo at one point before she is engaged to Harry. But the plot turns around the fact that divorce is impossible for her, and so she is forced to take Aldo as a lover. As for Harry, he is not "normal" either. His aesthetic training and his special interests set him apart from most Americans even more than Jane is set apart by her Catholicism. He is a university professor in America and a bohemian in Italy. If it had been the other way around he might have encountered quite different people and the plot would have been different. But it is difficult for Harry and Jane in the American army in 1944–1945 to meet respectable Italians, and so in the natural course of things they meet Dorothea and Aldo. If Jane had fallen in love with, say, a professor of Assyriology at the University of Rome and Harry with a Florentine contessa, love in Italy might not have seemed so simple and so frankly sensual. But probably it is the function of novels to simplify things, even to oversimplify them to the point of falsification. Daisy Miller did not fall in love with a professor either, but with the "beautiful Giovanelli" who is the prototype of Aldo.

Jane and Harry keep their secret from each other for a long time. As in Conrad and James the thread of the story is picked up near the end and then traced back to the beginning. When Harry is first seen he is living in an artist's studio in Via Margutta with Dorothea. Mario, who has known him several years before as an art historian and an apparently happy husband, is curious about what has happened to his wife and his career. For the moment he is left in the dark. All Harry will tell him, with an ironic smile, is that he has "chosen freedom." In Harry's old jeep the three of them go to the beach at Tor San Lorenzo on the coast south of Rome. While the two Italians swim lazily and bask in the sun Harry goes to work "with the methodical air of Robinson Crusoe" to construct a hut out of boughs and pine branches. The pioneer instinct is always under the surface in the American blood, Mario thinks. Harry is remembering his childhood camping trips in Minnesota, but in a deeper sense he is expressing a racial archetype, the instinct shared by the Deerslayer of Cooper and the boy scout of the twentieth century. This is the other side of Harry. On the one hand he is attracted to the most traditional and esoteric side of Europe—he is an expert on Jacopo Torriti and Piero Cavallini, two rather obscure frescoists of the Duecento—and on the other hand he is the Pensive Barbarian hacking down pine branches to make a hut in the forest. To the Italian mentality Robinson Crusoe seems very Anglo-Saxon; finding himself on a desert island he can think of nothing better to do than work. This, in the Italian view, accounts for the material prosperity of America but also makes it impossible for the American to enjoy it. Having made a hut out of pine branches he will then want, perhaps, to construct a bathtub out of driftwood. While Harry is building his hut, Mario is trying, unsuccessfully, to seduce Dorothea.

The reasons for Dorothea's inexplicable fidelity to Harry come out later in the plot. They are involved with her attitude toward America and thus are connected to the basic theme of the novel; Italy as Americans see it and vice versa. In contrast to Jane, Dorothea is the model of the unemancipated woman. Whether or not she is Soldati's ideal, at least he offers her as an Italian type. His heroines are frequently lower-class women and often of dubious virtue, and their lovers are usually intellectuals. Dorothea's specialty is knowing how to please men. She is cheerful, healthy, uncomplaining, good in bed, and an excellent cook. The only thing that anyone could possibly object to in her character is that she is a prostitute. Jane is certainly not this; she is a product of a careful and highly moral education and her virtue is a part of her physical nature. Her virtue, in fact, is her personality; it defines her as a human being and it defines her position in relation to others. When she is drawn helplessly into the intimacy with Aldo the sense of sin makes her physically feverish and almost kills her. James could not have drawn her because James could never have portrayed so successfully the power of physical flesh; if she has a prototype in American literature it is Hester Prynne. Like Harry she is not totally American; she went to school in Switzerland and speaks several foreign languages, and this along with her long stay in Italy as an army nurse has given her an international viewpoint, at least on the surface. This accounts for the conflict in her characer and her whole irrational attraction toward Aldo. In this she is contrasted to her friend Edith, another nurse who is totally, primly, and puritanically American. It is Edith who calls Aldo, with a simper, "that handsome Italian," but when she learns of Jane's relations with him the simper turns to a cold disapproval.

This is one of the important peculiarities of the four-way relationship, and one of the insights the novel offers about Italian-American relations. Harry and Jane are not totally American in their attraction to Italians, whereas Aldo and Dorothea are typically Italian in their attraction to Americans. In other words it is natural for an Italian to be fascinated with America, but it is not quite as natural for an American to be fascinated with Italy; or at least insofar as he is fascinated with Italy he is less American. It is possible to be fascinated with America and Americans and still remain completely Italian. There is nothing "international" about Aldo and Dorothea at all; they are indigenous and unsophisticated creatures seen in their natural habitat. As for Harry and Jane, their un-Americanness is seen particularly when they come back from Europe to be married and go to visit Jane's family in Philadelphia. Jane's mother is an admirer of European culture and her father is not. But to both of them Harry seems half a foreigner—he explains that his wife's parents considered him "European in my open-mindedness, in my habit of not considering the States the center of the world, European in the high respect I consistently showed for art and everything connected with art; European for my total inability to talk about anything but painting, music, and literature." [4] Probably the proportion of people who are interested in these things is no greater in Europe than it is in America. But it seems so to Harry and undoubtedly it seems so to Soldati, who came to America as a student of art history and spent two lonely years in what seemed to him an intellectual wasteland. If there is any objection to make to this neat oversimplification it is that Dorothea, who is typically European, is not characterized by her "total inability to talk about anything but painting, music, and literature." On the contrary she has no notion who Piero Cavallini is but she is very good at making *scarcella*, a regional pastry from her native Apulia. It is not as easy to sum up national characteristics as Harry thinks. Later she serves as an excellent stepmother for Harry's children. By the end of the novel she might pass for a typical American Mom except that she makes love too well.

The secret affairs of Harry and Jane go on for a number of years. The bulk of the story is told through Harry's manuscript, and therefore we see his side of it in detail whereas Jane's story is concealed until the end of the novel. Several years after their marriage they come back to Italy; while Harry travels on a research project Jane stays on Capri with her infant child. It is here that she writes the letters to Aldo around which the plot turns. The letters are abased, frankly sensual, "shameful." Rather than send them through the island post office, which has the reputation for opening mail, Jane uses the intermediary of Don Raffaele, a kind of minor politician and local eminence who has also found them their villa and their servants. Don Raffaele is another Italian type well known to Americans, the Neapolitan cicerone: vociferous, oily, aggressive, and insincere. He has a finger in everything on the island and it is impossible for anything to happen, in public or in private, without his being aware of it. Therefore when Jane several years later receives an anonymous telephone call in her hotel in Rome it is natural for her to imagine she is being blackmailed by Don Raffaele. Harry is aware of the telephone call too, and this leads to the confession in which Jane reveals the whole secret of her past to her husband. There is some danger that if the letters are made public they will damage Harry's career; by this time he is a highly paid consultant for UNESCO. Harry, who has been on the point of confessing his own secret to his wife, is so dazed by this that it is some time before he can pull himself together and decide what to do about it. Finally Harry and Jane decide to go together to Capri and confront Don Raffaele, pay him whatever he asks for the letters, and end the impossible situation in one way or another. By this time Don Raffaele has become mayor of Capri and receives them in his impressive office in the city hall. To their surprise he refuses to accept any money for the letters and insists that he mailed them as he promised Jane. They—the Americans—are in the wrong; they have unjustly accused this proud, clever, and egotistical man of blackmail. And yet instead of taking offense he is unexpectedly humble; he swears on the Crucifix that he is innocent and speaks with tears in his eyes of his own family. "There are so many misfortunes, so much pain in life. But compared to an illness, to an incurable illness of someone who is dear to you, a member of your family, what are these troubles, even the scandal? Nothing, believe me, nothing. I am a widower; my wife died of cancer. Seven years of torture. Those are the misfortunes of life, Signor Maggiore. Thank Heaven and the Madonna that your wife is well, that you are well, that your children in America are well. And for the rest . . . for the rest try to remedy it with calm, with deliberation, without exciting yourself so much." [5] The oily Neapolitan is transformed and under the surface is a human being. In this scene Don Raffaele speaks truer than anyone else in the novel and shows more insight than even Mario the narrator. The scandal the Americans fear is a purely verbal danger; it is all words. In fact Harry and Jane end by wondering literally whether the threat on the phone was only a verbal misunderstanding. Jane had the impression that the mysterious caller told her the letters had never been sent, and this led her to believe that they were still in the possession of Don Raffaele. But it is possible that what the caller said was "*Lettere? mai sentito.*" "The letters? Never heard of them." Jane with her imperfect knowledge of Italian, and in a high state of nervous tension, perhaps mistook *sentito* for sent. Harry and Jane never learn who it was who called on the telephone, but in any case it was not Don Raffaele.

In short, Don Raffaele as seen by the Americans is like Dorothea. At first these plebeian Italians seem mysterious and sinful, then they are revealed as normal, simple, with quite human weaknesses, and it is clear that the evil has been in the eye of the beholder. The cunning and avaricious Don Raffaele, undoubtedly guilty of much baseness in his life, is accused wrongly and responds only with tears. Harry concludes that this is the Italian character: "always human, never heroes, sometimes saints." [6] Neither Dorothea nor Aldo is a saint but neither is quite as dark and sensual as their American lovers imagine them. It is Soldati's remarkable accomplishment that he is able to portray Italians convincingly this way as seen through the eyes of Americans. If it had not been for their typical American limitations—Harry's streak of bourgeois respectability and Jane's puritanism—they might have accepted their Italian lovers freely and simply from the beginning and there would have been nothing to write a novel about. What Harry and Jane get from Italy is something very valuable, the experience of the flesh that frees them from the asceticism of their heritage. Unfortunately they cannot share this knowledge with each other; if they could it would be a novel by Colette instead of one in the manner of Hawthorne and James.

Harry learns his lesson and achieves a limited kind of happiness with it in the end. Jane, more religious and more deeply puritanical, dies before she can make use of the experience; symbolically she is destroyed by it. In a rather contrived *deus ex machina*, the weakest point in the novel, she is killed in an airline accident on her way back to America. This makes the ending of the novel possible; she would never have consented to a divorce, but once she is dead it is natural for Harry to go back to Dorothea. In this he is carrying out the wise Italian advice of Don Raffaele: "What are these troubles, this scandal? Nothing. Thank Heaven you are well." In the end the important thing is simply to be alive and to feel. And life can be felt only by those who are aware of the constant presence of death: Don Raffaele remembering his wife, Harry haunted by Jane's death in the plane. A basic part of Soldati's portrait of the Americans is the idea that they are unwilling to face the reality of death because they have never learned how to savor life. After Jane's death Harry, now in Via Margutta with Dorothea, tells Mario that before he has lived among people "who lived as though they were going to live forever" but that now in Italy he lives among people who are always aware of the presence of death. Although Harry does not make the point, the first is the attitude of savages and the second that of philosophers.

After Jane's death Don Raffaele is heard from no more and Aldo drops out of sight. At this point Dorothea comes to the forefront of the action and is seen clearly for the first time. So far the one inexplicable fact about her has been her rejection of Mario's overtures and her loyalty to Harry. To Mario's experienced eye she is obviously a streetwalker, or something very close to it, and he expects her to be as cynical as she appears. But there is something the urbane Mario does not understand about the provincial Italian character. Harry does understand this, and finally he explains it to his friend. Dorothea has a "grand project," one that is so important to her that for years she has sacrificed everything else to it and hung all her hopes on the frail thread of her relationship with Harry. "From the time of the Liberation, and perhaps even earlier, when she was a child in her village and saw the emigrants leave for America and come back millionaires, she had dreamed of America as an earthly paradise. It was a firmly rooted and fixed idea and nothing could dislodge it. Anyone who knows southern Italy will understand." [7]

But America is almost as hard to get into as that other Paradise, the heavenly one. For a girl of Dorothea's social class the American soldiers were angels who had the power to open the gate of this paradise, and Harry as an officer and professor was the archangel of them all. From the beginning Dorothea has had this plan in the back of her mind. But she knows that if Harry ever guesses her real motives she will lose him, and that even any jealousy or possessiveness on her part will endanger her "project." It is not really an insincerity, because she genuinely likes Harry. It is simply that America for her is a mystical and powerful emotion, and Harry is mixed up in her mind with this emotion and serves as its immediate and concrete symbol. Later Harry understands this attitude and half-humorously accepts it. "Superimposed on my face she always saw the Statue of Liberty," [8] he tells Mario. In a person with a logically trained mind this would be hypocrisy; in Dorothea it is simply the animus that gives direction to her life. Without the dream of America her relation with Harry would be mercenary; with the dream of America it becomes almost idealistic. She is simply a person without means or social advantage who is trying to better herself with the only expedients available to her.

Harry himself does not understand this for a long time. Dorothea conceals her aims shrewdly; she knows of Harry's engagement to Jane but says nothing, and she makes no objection when he marries. At this point her hopes are reduced to a frail thread, but she is content to play on even this slight chance of achieving her ambition. After Jane's death her hopes again have some chance of being realized. Harry comes back to live with her in Via Margutta. She knows that he thinks of her as promiscuous and expects her to be unfaithful whenever she has the chance. Perhaps he even wants her to act like this; there will be scenes, he will beat her, and they will end by making love. This is what a certain kind of American expects, and seeks, in his relations with a certain kind of Italian mistress. But Dorothea knows how this will end: After a time the scenes and quarrels will become boring, Harry will throw her out, and then "addio America." This is the secret of her absolute, almost bourgeois, virtue, and the reason why Mario is unable to seduce her. To Dorothea sex is not an end in itself but a means to an end, and the end is a higher one than money. Another risk to her project comes when Harry, who is on the UNESCO staff in Paris, gets the notion of bringing her there and installing her in an apartment. He is baffled when she refuses to come, but she knows she would be out of her element and at a disadvantage among the chic Parisians, in a place where everyone speaks a foreign language and all the values and customs are strange. Better to stay in Rome where she can deal with Harry on her own terms. Dorothea has the persistence of a fanatic and the patience of a philosopher, and she never loses sight of the target. "Paris, what was Paris? It wasn't worth the last village in Arkansas." [9]

Harry gives up his UNESCO job to live with her in Rome, but this situation has no future to it. When he finally runs out of money there is nothing to do but go back to America; a position as a professor is waiting for him in New York. By this time Dorothea has become a physical necessity to him. The logical if somewhat unconventional solution is to marry her, and he does. To his surprise she makes a good impression on Jane's family—the Philadelphia father-in-law is won over by her cooking—and they willingly hand over Jane's children to her. These Chestnut Hill society leaders find the Roman prostitute a fine girl—"from the people, of course," but honest and likeable. Dorothea settles down blissfully in a Long Island house among her pots and pans and her American appliances. Everyone is happy now but Harry, who finds that he is the victim of a curious irony. Dorothea as an American housewife has lost all of her fascination, which for him had been simply the attraction of evil. Once his father-in-law has called her "a fine girl" she seems as banal and sexless as Jane had been. And Jane's parents are absolutely right; it was Harry who had been wrong about Dorothea. She is a fine girl, a happy housewife out of *The Ladies' Home Journal.*

The final scene of the novel is a kind of caricature of Long Island life as it seems to the half-Europeanized Harry. One evening when he finishes teaching an irrational impulse comes over him to walk home to the Long Island house, a symbolic protest against the culture in which nobody walks and everybody travels in buses and cars. It is more than ten miles, and it is after midnight when he gets home. The landscape he walks through is that of a nightmare or a surrealist vision. Movie theatres, garages, apartment houses, drugstores, and more movie theatres succeed each other with an obsessive monotony. Bluish street lights, the endless asphalt pavement, billboards. It is the city Soldati described twenty-five years before in *America primo amore,* the New York "where sandwiches are the only nourishment and subways the only means of locomotion." At a deserted intersection he stops and sits on the curb to smoke a cigarette. Then he remembers that he still carries in his pocket the letters Jane wrote to Aldo; he had found them after her death at the mail desk of the Hotel Excelsior in Rome where Aldo had never claimed them. He takes them out now and burns them, feeling that he is finally ending not only the story of Jane's encounter with Aldo but also the story of his own relations with Dorothea. The woman who waits for him in his Long Island house is someone else, an American wife. As the letters burn Harry's only thought, a need that grows to an obsession, is to return to Rome. But now he wonders whether he will ever escape. Dorothea has fulfilled herself in becoming an American housewife; Harry has betrayed himself in accepting the rôle of an American husband. Now he wonders whether the powerful spell that Dorothea cast over him was only a "radioactive charge" that bewitched him and made him serve her own purposes. At the end of the novel the reader sees that from the beginning it has been simply the story of Dorothea's emigration.

11 *Moravia's America*

The childhood of Alberto Moravia was one of introspection, suffering, and boredom. He came from a middle-class family that provided him with every possible material comfort, but he was isolated from the normal world by illness and forced to rely for amusement on reading and on his own imagination. This illness is the single most important event in Moravia's life. He was stricken with bone tuberculosis at the age of nine and was an invalid during his whole adolescence; he spent three years in bed at home and another two years in a sanatorium at Cortina d'Ampezzo. A period of false cures and relapses lasted until he was sixteen, and he still suffered from the effects of the disease until he was twenty-five. It was under these conditions that his character as a writer was formed; the remarkable psychological insight of his early work is simply the hypersensitivity of the sickroom. He began to write his first novel, *Gli indifferenti,* at Bressanone in 1925 when he was not yet fully recovered. At this time he was only eighteen, and when it was published in 1929 he was still only twenty-two. The hero of this novel, Michele, has the mentality of the sickroom without being actually sick himself. He is only a passive machine for reflection, a camera, and he finally recognizes himself as such: "I didn't love Lisa . . . I didn't kill Leo . . . I've done nothing but think . . . and that was my mistake." [1] Michele is the first of a long series of Prufrocks in Moravia's work. His protagonists are often weak or passive characters who envy the strong and healthy people around them; for some reason they are unable to do what is natural and easy for others. Since Moravia is particularly adept at portraying and analyzing sexual behavior, this pathology often takes sexual forms. Impotence, either real or symbolic, is a dominant theme of his work from *Gli indifferenti* through *La noia* in 1960.

Especially in his later work, that published after 1947, the theme often takes the form of a stylized conflict. The hero is passive, ineffectual, and unconfident, and he tends to overanalyze his problem—often very shrewdly—instead of doing something about it. What he wants is near at hand—sometimes it is something he already owns, his own wife, as in *L'amore coniugale*—but for some reason he cannot reach out and take it. Meanwhile another character, one who is vigorous, simple, and often vulgar, does reach out and take it, but instead of drawing courage from this example the hero only becomes more self-conscious and aware of his own ineffectiveness. Moravia's favorite adjective for this virile antagonist is *prepotente*; the dictionary translation is "overbearing" or "arrogant," but in Moravia's private psychology it takes on a special meaning of masterful, virile, instinctive. The *prepotenza* of the antagonist is contrasted to the *impotenza* of the hero. Like Prufrock, he longs to be "a pair of ragged claws scuttling across the floors of silent seas," but he ends by measuring out his life with coffee spoons. Finally somebody else's ragged claws seize the very thing he has desired, often in front of his eyes. This personal way of regarding the world that Moravia acquired in his childhood has persisted throughout his lifetime. The sick are condemned to have things done to them and to watch other people doing things; they do not do things themselves.

Moravia himself has remarked that this illness was one of the two great experiences that formed his character. The other experience was also a passive one; in fact he believes it is precisely the things in our lives over which we have no control that make us what we are. "I attribute much importance to this sickness and to Fascism because through sickness and Fascism I had to submit to and do things I would never otherwise have submitted to or done. The things that form our character are those we are obliged to do, not those we do out of our own will." [2] Moravia was regarded with suspicion by the Fascists from the time of his first novel. When he published his second novel *Le ambizioni sbagliate* in 1935 the critics were forbidden by the government to review it and it passed almost unnoticed. After this misadventure Mondadori, his publisher, rejected his next book, a collection of stories under the title *L'imbroglio,* on the grounds that he was too busy publishing the memoirs of Marshal Badoglio, who had just come back from exterminating the Abyssinians. In 1941 the second printing of his satirical novel *La mascherata* was seized by the censor, and he turned to writing under a pseudonym. Shortly after this he was forbidden to write at all. By autumn of 1943 he realized that Rome was no longer safe for him; he heard rumors that his name was on a list of anti-Fascists marked for arrest. This was a curious situation considering that his own origins were thoroughly bourgeois and his writing had not been particularly political, at least in the beginning. In later years he wrote, "I think this development is inevitable in any totalitarian state, at any rate for the intellectuals. The choice is between becoming a paid adulator or being driven day by day into a complete silence and finally to prison. All the rest is idle chatter and sophism." [3] Shortly after the German occupation of Rome in September, he tried to make his way to Naples but found it was impossible to cross the Allied lines; instead he spent nine months hiding with the peasants in the mountains near Fondi. Moravia was a person of fixed habits and had always been in frail health, and he was not used to discomfort. The suffering, cold, and danger of this winter left on him one of the strongest impressions of his lifetime. This was what he meant by "submitting to and doing things I would never otherwise have submitted to or done." In the mountains he ate peasant food and slept in a stable, and was in constant danger of his life from the German patrols who searched the hills looking for partisans. After the breakout at Cassino in the spring he was liberated by the American Second Army and came back to Rome. This critical experience of his lifetime was therefore climaxed by a firsthand contact with American soldiers. These impressions of the Liberation he later used for *La ciociara* in 1957.

This experience with the American army in 1943 was by no means his first encounter with American culture. He knew English thoroughly and began reading American literature early in the Thirties; his translation of "The Killers" in *L'Italiano* in 1934 was one of the first Hemingway stories to appear in Italy. Moreover he had traveled in the United States, which few other Italian writers had. Under Fascism he spent as much time out of Italy as he could, traveling on a press passport as a foreign correspondent or simply as a tourist. In this way he managed to visit England, France, Greece, China, Mexico, and several other countries between 1930 and 1938. He spent the period of the Abyssinian War in the United States; a photograph dating probably from 1935 shows him standing on a snowy Park Avenue with his hat in his hand, looking awkward and rather lonely. It is doubtful whether American literature had any direct effect on his own writing; certainly it is not immediately apparent in his style. In 1941, in one of the *Prospettive* articles he signed with a pseudonym, he noted the influence of journalism and the cinema on the American novel and yet called it "the most vigorous because it has remained the most faithful to the fixed and ancient premises of the novels of all time." [4] But the paradox was only apparent; Moravia was speaking of the classic narrative from Homer to Stendhal and tacitly opposing it to the D'Annunzian fakery of the "official" Fascist style. At least in this sense his own style belonged with Homer and Hemingway. In theme, however, he had no need to borrow from the Americans or anyone else, because the thematic development of his own work follows a direct line from *Gli indifferenti* to the fiction of the Sixties. On another visit to the United States in 1955 he told an interviewer, "Good writers are monotonous, like good composers. Their truth is self-repeating. They keep trying to rewrite the same book. That is to say, they keep trying to perfect their understanding of the one problem they were born to understand." [5]

For Moravia this "one problem" was basically that of activity and passivity, or to put it in his own terms, *prepotenza* and *impotenza.* His work over a period of twenty-five years expresses this polarity in many forms; sometimes it is political, sometimes sexual, sometimes simply the direct physical domination of one character over another. Before 1957 he had not treated America or Americans in any major way in his fiction. But his encounter with America and American culture, especially during the war and immediately afterward, was evidently important to him precisely because it fitted into this scheme of energy and impotence which had dominated his work ever since *Gli indifferenti.* Although this title is translated in the American edition as *The Time of Indifference,* its literal meaning is "those who are indifferent," that is, unable to feel passions. To Moravia, as to many other Italians in the Thirties, Italy seemed corrupt, weak, "sick," trying to cover up its impotence through a false bombast. Like many of Moravia's heroes, Italy had tried to imitate the strong and virile actions of others, but the North African campaign and the invasion of Greece were fiascos. Moravia himself might have written the farcical dénouement of the Greek adventure. In an effort to imitate Hitler and demonstrate his own *prepotenza* Mussolini set out to invade Albania and Greece, but the Greeks counterattacked and almost drove him back into the sea. Finally the true *prepotente* Hitler had to come to the rescue. The events of 1943 and the Liberation strengthened this impression of the impotence of Italy. During the winter Moravia spent in the mountains it was obvious that the real powers in the peninsula were the Germans and the Allies, and that the Italians could only watch passively while these two forces decided their destiny for them. In the spring, when the Second Army broke out at Cassino and liberated Rome, there was no doubt which of these forces was the stronger. Moravia's encounter with the American motorized column on the road near Fondi left a strong impression on him, an impression he was later to describe in thinly fictionalized form in *La ciociara*.

In this novel, as in many of the stories and tales written after 1945, American culture plays an important part, and it is the part of the *prepotente*. It stands for strength, vigor, and success, and in this sense it is contrasted to Italian culture which represents the opposite: weakness, decadence, and failure. But this neat contrast is valid only in a limited sense. By 1943, and even more by the time he wrote the novel, there were signs of a new vigor in Italian culture. Two examples were the anti-Fascist Resistance and the remarkable resurgence of Italian fiction, in which Moravia himself had taken part along with Vittorini, Pavese, Silone, and others. Another was the "economic miracle" of the Fifties, the new industrial prosperity that had transformed Italy, or at least the northern half of it, in ten years. In his fiction Moravia often associates these phenomena with America; to him they are part of the "Americanization" of Italy that includes everything from Coca-Cola to the new fiction style of the postwar writers. All this new progress and energy are concentrated in northern Italy and particularly in Milan, and Moravia is a Roman. Traditionally Rome is conservative, picturesque, and easygoing, and this is the Italy out of which Moravia himself came. Considering his background and tastes he ought to be hostile to "Americanization," and he is in a certain sense. Other aspects of it he admires, but this is at a deeper and less rational level. Politically he is leftist and opposes NATO and American foreign policy; in the back of his mind he admires American *prepotenza*. In an ordinary man this would be confused thinking, but the task of the writer is precisely to convert this confused thinking into art. Moravia is very well aware of the contradictions in his attitudes and frequently uses them as a framework for conflict in his fiction. In this sense his work like that of all true artists is autobiographical; he exteriorizes his inner struggles.

This conflict is seen most clearly and obviously in his stories, especially the *Racconti romani* (*Roman Tales,* 1954) and *Nuovi racconti romani* (*New Roman Tales,* 1959) and those included in the Italian version of *L'amore coniugale* in 1949. The two volumes of Roman tales, most of them written for the literary page of *Il Corriere della Sera,* are simply miniature studies in the theme of *prepotente* and *impotente,* and almost invariably the central character is somebody who wants to do something but cannot. There is not a single protagonist in these two volumes of stories who consummates anything. In a comic story called "Il pupo" ("The Baby") an impoverished couple fail even in their efforts to abandon an infant in a church ("Lady, you left your package on the seat"). They then try to leave it in a parked car, change their minds and come back for it, and end in a furious argument with the owner of the car, the baby still in their possession. Moravia's characters are powerless even to *give* something away.

These people are examples of one kind of "Roman" character. There are two Romes superimposed in these stories. The first is the old Rome of Trastevere, Piazza del Popolo, the antiquaries in Via Margutta, the aristocratic families and small shopkeepers, the Rome of which Moravia himself is a product. The other is the slick modern Americanized Rome of Parioli and Via Veneto, along with its parodies in the lower classes—the rock-and-roll devotees of the slums, the boys who wear levis and have their hair cut "alla Marlon Brando." To Moravia this second Rome is vigorous and successful but vulgar. One of its symbols is the portable radio—rock-and-roll which can be hung from the shoulder and carried around the city, pseudo-American culture in its most moronic form. Another is the automobile. Moravia's early fiction is full of cars and motor trips; his heroes frequently have chauffeurs or are chauffeurs themselves. Probably this is connected to the fact that in the Thirties his frail health made the automobile his only means of mobility. Symbolically the automobile stands for power, prestige, and mastery over the physical elements, in short for *prepotenza.* In the Roman stories the cars, especially if they are powerful, are often American or driven by Americans. In "Scherzi di Ferragosto" ("August

Holiday Fun") the would-be-*prepotente* hero Torello wants to pass all the cars on the Via Aurelia but is beaten by a huge black American car. The driver is a powerful and vulgar man who smokes black cigars and is evidently an Italo-American. From the car his blonde companion smiles at Torello, and the American slaps her. Later at the beach Torello goes on trying to court the blonde woman in the style of the traditional Italian Don Juan (his name means "little bull") but gets nowhere. At the end the American beats him in a casual but savage manner, striking him several times in the stomach, and then drives off with the woman. When an American car appears in these stories, it invariably means that its owner is *prepotente* and will get what he wants before the story ends, usually by forceful or brutal means.

By way of contrast, in a story called "Le risate di Gioia" the car is Italian and as *impotente* as its occupants. The title means "The Laughter of Gioia" but also implies, ironically, "Joyous Laughter." Two working-class youths, Mario and Ruggero, set out on New Year's Eve to find some excitement, although they have no money. They finally end up at a rather wild artist's party with a girl called Gioia, followed by a melancholy taxi driver who wants to be paid. Gioia, who knows most of these international bohemians, goes about among them blithely trying to raise a thousand lire. None of the Italians has it. Finally she approaches a blond and bespectacled youth in a windbreaker and tells him, in Italian for Americans, "Percy, you lend me thousand lire pay driver." [6] Percy, who is rather drunk, offers to give her even three thousand for a kiss, then he flings himself on her "like a savage." When Ruggero tries to interfere, the American calmly takes off his glasses and knocks him flat. There is a brawl and all three Italians are thrown out of the party, but when they are out in the street somehow Gioia has the money. "Who knows where it came from," Ruggero wonders. This story is a model of Moravia's *prepotente-impotente* theme as it involves Americans. Not only has Percy physically dominated Ruggero, who fancies himself as rather tough and dangerous, but Gioia has sold herself to him for money before the eyes of her Italian escort. It is clear that Gioia is on her way to the international café society of Via Veneto. The evening ends with two flat tires on the (Italian) taxi.

The Roman tales were written for newspapers and most of them are rather slight; they remind the American reader of O. Henry. Often they are sketches for themes developed more fully later in the novels. One even has the same title as a later novel: "La ciociara" (the Italian title of *Two Women*). The stories collected in the 1952 *Racconti* (*Tales*) and in the Italian version of *L'amore coniugale* are more substantial. Most of the *L'amore coniugale* stories are set in the immediate postwar period and several of them involve foreigners in Rome; one is called "La messicana" and another "L'ufficiale inglese." One of the finest of these stories, "Il negro e il vecchio dalla roncola" ("The Negro and the Old Man with the Scythe"), is simply a more subtle variation on the theme of "Le risate di Gioia." Cosimo, another one of the endless young Italians in Moravia who fancy themselves as lovers, goes to the beach with Cora at a place where the coast is lined with pine woods, probably Ostia or Fregene. The beach is being used as a rest camp for soldiers, and the pineta is full of American trucks. Hoping to make love to Cora, Cosimo takes her down the beach to a deserted spot where the only signs of life are a few fishermen's huts. After a while an old fisherman comes down the beach selling mussels, but Cora only comments that it is a good way to catch typhus. She tells Cosimo about an American officer in Rome who tried to seduce her; she says she doesn't mind soldiers but "wants to be respected." Cosimo tries to kiss her but she rejects him ("Uff, all these kisses") and he decides she is frigid. They lie face down on the sand to sunbathe; Cora loosens the halter of her bikini. The next time Cosimo looks at her he sees a black hand in the middle of her back. A huge Negro soldier is repeating in a singsong voice, "Signorina . . . signorina."

To Cosimo's surprise Cora obeys the touch of this hand immediately and without hesitation. She gets up quite calmly and goes away with the Negro, who threatens Cosimo with a knife.

Cosimo, lying flat on the sand behind a dune, watches him leading Cora away by the arm. He has the odd impression that he is watching not a woman being abducted by force but a pair of lovers going for a walk on the beach. "Terrified and indignant, he began to curse her in a low voice: 'Bitch . . . with me no, with the Negro yes.' "[7] But as the two go off down the beach they pass the old fisherman, who is standing in the sea raking for mussels. Suddenly Cora runs to him and takes refuge behind his back. The old man comes out of the water with a *roncola*, a kind of scythe that peasants cut brush with. (The word is translated in one American version as "bill-hook.") Holding this tool which is also a weapon in his hand, he talks calmly to the Negro. "The gestures of the *roncola* were more oratorical than menacing and it seemed the Negro was listening with attention." Persuaded by this discourse, the Negro goes off down the beach. The old man stands watching him for a while with his *roncola* and then goes back into the sea, and Cora comes back to Cosimo. When Cosimo apologizes for his conduct she says simply, "What could you do? He was a giant. I was afraid."

The three males in this story stand at the points of a triangle with Cora in the center. Cosimo is the conventional Italian Don Juan, a type Moravia usually views with irony. His virility is not convincing; the notion that the professional seducer is subconsciously afraid of his own impotence is very old and goes back as far as the Don Juan legend itself. The Negro stands for *prepotenza*, here frankly sexual. The fact that he is an American is essential to the story, but it is also significant that he is made a Negro. In his effort to exaggerate the contrast between the two men Moravia deliberately selects the kind of American considered the most virile, the most highly sexed, and the least intellectual—a stereotype often shared, paradoxically, by American racists and European intellectuals. When Cora goes off with the soldier, Cosimo "remembered having heard of the attraction Negroes aroused in certain white women and thought that Cora was perhaps like this." Cosimo is perfectly right in suspecting that Cora's abduction is not entirely involuntary. Cora, in fact, with her complex and rather cryptic motivations, is the only psychologically complicated character in the story. Moravia's heroes never understand women very well, and Cosimo is typical.

The third male in the story, the old fisherman, is thoroughly Italian, even more Italian than Cosimo because he is less modern. When Cosimo first sees him he points out to Cora how beautiful he is, although she merely grimaces and says, "An old man." Moravia is careful to point out his resemblance to a classic sculpture. He is old, wiry, mild on the surface but with a quiet power underneath; he comes out of the sea like Proteus, and at the end of the story he goes back into it. It is significant that he uses his *roncola* not for brute violence but to persuade "oratorically" in the Latin tradition. In short he represents the ancient and traditional virility of Italy that lies under its superficial, and modern, impotence. Whatever Cora's attitude toward these two figures may be on the surface, she passively allows herself to be overpowered by the Negro and then turns instinctively for protection to the fisherman. Between them, Cosimo does not cut a very impressive figure. As he and Cora leave the beach in the car she allows herself to be kissed, but in the ardor he has waited for so long "he sensed something that had nothing to do with him and had been awakened by the insistent singsong voice of the Negro and the *roncola* of the fisherman. And he felt at the same time remorse and jealousy."

Although Moravia's encounter with the American army in 1944 had obviously made a strong impression on him, "Il negro e il vecchio dalla roncola" is one of the very few of his stories involving American soldiers. In the three volumes of tales published between 1952 and 1959 there is nothing that deals directly with the war or the Liberation. It was thirteen years after his winter in the mountains before he wrote directly about this experience and the effect it had on him. When he did he made a curious change in the autobiographical material. *La ciociara,* published in 1957 and translated into English the following year as *Two Women,* is the story of a winter spent in the mountains near Fondi by refugees from Rome. It takes place in 1943–1944 and the outward details are those of Moravia's own experience, including the encounter with the American army in the spring. The change that Moravia made was to reverse the sex of his narrator and write about his war experiences from the point of view of a woman. The story is narrated by Cesira, a widow who owns a small shop in Trastevere, and Moravia's experiences are portrayed as happening to her and her daughter Rosetta. Technically the novel represents a return to the lower-class monologue Moravia had not used in a major work since *La romana* in 1947. *La romana* has been compared by critics to *Moll Flanders,* and *La ciociara* is told in the same style. There are limitations to this technique, especially in the problem of conveying complicated mental states through a narrator with a limited vocabulary, but there are also advantages. Besides the obvious one of concealing the autobiographical material the change to a lower-class female narrator offers the advantage that the writer can show fear, confusion, and joy in his characters in a way that might seem effeminate in a male narrator. Cesira's emotions are close to the surface and her thoughts flow from her naturally and ingenuously, like the thoughts of a child. This is especially useful when Moravia portrays her elation over the Liberation and her awe of the American army, emotions he undoubtedly felt himself but would not be likely to describe so candidly in his own voice.

Many of Moravia's characters are small shopkeepers; they are a race that interests him. He admires their shrewdness and tenacity but he despises their pettiness. Cesira is shopkeeper-shrewd but almost illiterate; she is totally ignorant of politics and the causes that lie behind the war. At the beginning of the novel she has two simple impulses: petty-bourgeois avarice and protectiveness toward her daughter. She doesn't care who wins the war, Germans or Allies, as long as they leave her shop alone, and she is obsessed with the idea of protecting Rosetta from the evil reality of the world. It is because Rosetta is afraid of the air raids, in fact, that Cesira decides to leave Rome. In the mountains she finds other people like herself: refugees from the city, mostly small shopkeepers, and peasants who see in the war only a chance to rent their stables to the refugees at exorbitant prices. The one unselfish person she meets is the young Michele, a shopkeeper's son who has gone to the university and become an anti-Fascist intellectual. Michele is something incomprehensible both to the shopkeeper mentality and to the peasant: an altruist. He is also the only one who sees the true causes of the war—that evil produces evil in return, that foreigners are killing and destroying in Italy because the Italians killed and destroyed in Abyssinia. Why should you complain when your houses are bombed? he asks the others. Did you protest when the houses of others were bombed? "What is done to me today will be done to you tomorrow." At first his paradoxes only confuse Cesira, and it is not until after his death that she realizes the full meaning of what he had said.

During the long winter the refugees, Cesira and Rosetta among them, look forward with a kind of messianic hope to the arrival of the Allies. In their reveries they imagine the liberating army as a long line of trucks full of food and clothing, with soldiers on top throwing everything down to the Italians. The problem of political liberty doesn't interest them, and their idea of the Liberation is like the typical Italian peasant's idea of America: an endless abundance earned without working. Michele's intellectual ideas have little effect on them. Instead it is the actual events of the winter that force a political education on the refugees, especially Cesira and Rosetta. In the beginning they are only worried about whether their salami will last the winter and whether the peasants are charging them too much to sleep in their hovel. But when the Nazis begin arresting hostages and shooting civilians they perceive that human life has a value in the abstract, and that this and other ideal values are more important than material possession. Along with Michele they listen while a German officer describes the aesthetic sensation he received from "cleaning out" a cave full of enemy soldiers with a flame-thrower. When Michele is shot by the retreating Germans, their political naïveté comes to an end. By then they know they are against the Germans, but they are not quite sure what they are for. They still imagine the Allies as "like saints," unreal and indistinct. It is at this point that they encounter the American army.

The first Americans they see are two "small dark young men" who are moving toward a German machine-gun position on the mountain. One of them calls a casual "Hello" to them. Cesira had imagined that all Americans were tall and blond, but she is soon to find out they are all races and all colors, white and black, dark and light. These first two, she learns later, were Italian-Americans. The offhandedness of their "Hello" in the middle of a dangerous military operation is typical of the Americans in the novel, the opposite of the disciplined fanaticism of the Germans. A little later they meet a whole column advancing up the road into the mountains. "They walked in Indian-file and this time I saw they were really Americans, different from both the Germans and the Italians. They had a tired slouching way of walking that was almost resentful and each one wore his helmet in a different way, some on one side, some down over the eyes, some on the back of the head; many of them were in shirtsleeves, and they all chewed gum. They looked as though they were making war against their will but without fear, not like people who are born to make war, the Germans for example, but as though they had been dragged in by the neck." [8] Anybody who has seen American soldiers in combat will recognize the accuracy of this description. Here Moravia is writing from firsthand memory.

These first Americans are only a detached patrol on a country road. When the two women reach the Via Appia near Fondi, they see the full force of the Second Army, and for the first time they understand why the Germans will lose the war. More than an army of men it is an army of machines. The whole highway, the main road from Naples to Rome, is packed solid with trucks and machines of every kind. The machines are painted green and they all have the same five-pointed star, the American star different from the star of Italy which was supposed to bring good luck but brought only defeat, whereas this one "seemed *prepotente* and gave strength to those who followed it." [9] The soldiers sitting on the machines are chewing gum and reading comic books; they seem indifferent and almost bored. Before this, Cesira has imagined war as something like the colored pictures in the Italian Sunday supplements: the heroic Bersaglieri of 1915 charging with fixed bayonets. Now she understands it is fought not with men but with machines. First came the airplanes and the cannon and knocked everything down, then the soldiers came seated comfortably in automobiles with their rifles between their knees, chewing their gum and reading their comic books. Sometimes they were killed, but it was not the enemy that killed them but other machines. The soldiers that had the more powerful machines would win the war, and these were the Americans.

As Moravia describes it the war seems less a struggle than a pageant or a ritual. The outcome is determined in advance, and each party acts according to its predetermined rôle. There is a puppet-like mechanicalness in the behavior of the Americans as well as the Italians. In the town of Fondi the two women find a great crowd of peasants and American troops, almost like a fair. But there is nothing to buy and nothing to be sold except "the hope of better days," and the peasants and the refugees walk about aimlessly as though they are uncertain how this is bought. The Americans speak English and the Italians speak Italian, and neither understands the other. Other Americans, standing on a balcony, throw candy and cigarettes to the Italians who scramble for them in the dust, not because they want them but because they sense this is what the Americans expect from them. For their part the Americans are throwing the candy and cigarettes not because they want to give but because this is the rôle expected of them. Most of the houses in Fondi have been wrecked by the bombardments. Cesira shouts at an American, "Is this your Liberation? Die of hunger and go without a house as we did before, or worse than before?" [10]

Finally the refugees are taken to an army supply center and given some canned food. But Cesira finds something obscurely annoying in the way these Americans act. It is true they are polite and better than the Germans, but their politeness is indifferent and distant; they treat the Italians like bothersome children who have to be given candy so they will be good. It is an ironic inversion of the usual European stereotype in which the Americans are children and the European the adults. But for all their boyish slouching and their comic books these Americans are the *prepotenti,* because of their machines and because they are the victors. The few who are arrogant are the ones who are the least *prepotenti* and therefore the least sure of themselves: the Italian-Americans. Moravia is almost alone among Italian writers in finding Italian-Americans less likeable than Americans. Cesira calls the others "the real Americans, the *americani-inglesi,*" [11] and comments that they are always well-bred. These English-Americans have no need to bluster because they are sure of their power. They have exactly the assurance of the Percy in "Le risate di Gioia" who first took off his glasses and then knocked the Italian flat.

For shelter Cesira and Rosetta find an abandoned house on the outskirts of Fondi which for some reason nobody has occupied. When they try to go to sleep in it they find out why: there is an American artillery battery in the woods a hundred yards away. Every five minutes a shattering explosion shakes the walls of the house, and even exhausted as they are sleep is impossible. But Cesira finds an odd pleasure in these rhythmic and deafening explosions. The cannon are described as "thick as tree-trunks at the base and tapering to a narrow mouth, painted bottle-green and so long they disappeared in the foliage of the big plane-trees under which they were hidden." [12] These cannon are the climax of Moravia's long effort to find a symbolism for American culture, an effort which had begun with the stories of the early Fifties. Even to the unsophisticated reader their phallic significance is obvious: the rhythm of the explosions is "regular, monotonous, and obstinate," driving away the winter, the suffering and danger, the Fascists and Germans and all the ugly things they had brought with them. As the barrage goes on Cesira feels "a joy that increased with every explosion," and gradually this joy becomes mixed with an odd and hallucinatory hatred of the dictatorship she has lived under for twenty years. It is the first real political passion she has ever felt. Half asleep, she dreams or imagines a casual unhurried American pushing a huge projectile into the cannon and pulling a handle, the shell whistling through the air and falling in a salon where all the

Fascists and Nazis are standing, Hitler and Mussolini among them. With each explosion the scene is repeated in her mind like a childish movie, and each time she takes a greater pleasure in it. All the Nazis and Fascists are standing at attention: Mussolini with a fat broad face and a chest covered with medals, and next to him "his friend Hitler with his cuckold's face and his black mustache like a toothbrush and his eye like a spoiled fish and his pointed nose and his arrogant bully's lock hanging over his forehead." [13] ("Arrogant" is *prepotente* in the original.) And all this is smashed into powder by a gum-chewing American pulling a handle. Lying in the deserted house, Cesira feels the Liberation as a physical experience that happens to her body and leaves a physical sense of well-being, like the feeling of being untied after being tied up for a long time with a rope.

But if the novel ended at this point it would be excessively optimistic and would give an untrue picture of the war as it seemed to the average Italian. There is another and bitter side to the "Liberation" that Cesira has yet to learn. A few days later the two women are attacked by Moroccan soldiers in a church and Rosetta is subjected to a multiple rape. This scene caused a violent polemic in Italy when the book was published; some critics accused Moravia of sensationalism and others of a leftist bias against the Allies. The fact is that such incidents did happen during the so-called Liberation, and plenty of them, so many that they added a new word to the Italian language, *marocchinata*, a Moroccanade. But this is not the point. This scene is necessary in Moravia's scheme to complete the pattern of *prepotente-impotente* as it applies to Italy's part in the war, and to balance the positive side of the Liberation as it is seen in the cannon episode. After their encounter with the American troops Cesira and Rosetta are in an unnatural state of euphoria, the mental state of Italy itself in the first few days after the Liberation. The *marocchinata* is necessary to produce in them a symbolic parallel to the cynicism and disenchantment that followed after the immediate enthusiasm of the Liberation was over. To intensify this sexual symbolism Moravia attributes the overt violence to the dark-skinned Moroccans, as he used the device of the Negro in "Il negro e il vecchio dalla roncola" for the same purpose. The Moroccans represent the irrational, savage, "dark" side to the Allied occupation of Italy, a side that is always present when any army conquers a country by force. It is the end of the fairy tale of the Liberation as a long line of trucks carrying food.

The reactions of Cesira and Rosetta to this incident are quite different. In Cesira it produces a brief spasm of hatred for the Allies and a compassion not only for her daughter but for all those who have suffered in the war. She knows now the meaning of Michele's prophecy: what is done to me today will be done to you tomorrow. She has lost everything she sought to protect and seen her daughter's innocence violated before her eyes, and now she knows there is no security in material possessions and no final defense against evil. It is impossible for anyone, an individual or a nation, to come into contact with forces like those of the giant cannon and not be harmed by them; it is impossible to go through a war and come out a virgin. This is the wisdom that Cesira learns, and for this the rape scene is necessary.

At first it seems that Rosetta has been even more deeply damaged by the experience. She falls into an apathetic silence which her mother at one point mistakes for the beginning of insanity. But Rosetta is young and her nature is resilient. After the first shock is over the experience produces in her a cynical and precocious kind of maturity. Cesira has always been indifferent to physical love, but to Rosetta it now becomes a daily necessity. She goes with any man who happens to be near at hand and brazenly shows off her new clothes, fine underwear, and nylon stockings to her mother. This is the most terrible of Cesira's discoveries—that her daughter's reaction to the force that has violated her is to accept and even seek out this force instead of defending herself against it. It is as though the evil forced on her by the Moroccans is a drug to which she too has now become addicted. Rosetta represents a younger generation which was psychologically unprepared for the shock of war and reacts to it with an unnatural and precocious cynicism. She is the prototype of the Dolce Vita youth of postwar Italy, a type Moravia himself often portrays in his stories. Like the girl in "Le risate di Gioia" she is attacked by a *prepotente* aggressor but instead of being destroyed by the experience finds a way to turn it to money. And like Cora in "Il negro e il vecchio dalla roncola" she is ambivalent toward the dark sexuality of her attacker, fearing it on the surface but attracted to it underneath. In both stories the Italian lovers are humiliated by Americans, just as the sham-*prepotenti* Hitler and Mussolini are destroyed by the American soldier in Cesira's dream. America is maleness, force, *prepotenza,* success. There is no moral judgment implied in this and Moravia is neither for nor against America; it is simply a fact.

The Italians react to this collision of cultures in various ways. Some, like Michele, die in order to bring about its consummation. Some are destroyed by it, "knocked flat" like Ruggero in "Le risate di Gioia," and some like Cesira are dazed and unable to adjust. The others, the younger generation like Rosetta, suffer the immediate shock most keenly but quickly "Americanize," if Americanization means nylon stockings, fast cars, and easy sex. In any case they accept; with an odd passiveness they seem to recognize the historical inevitability of what is happening. There is only one character in these three works of fiction who stands up to the *prepotenza* of American culture. The old fisherman who gestures with his scythe in a way "more oratorical than menacing" while the Negro listens with attention represents something very traditional and very deep in Italian culture, deeper than the fake Romanità of the Fascists. Who this Old Man of the Sea is Moravia does not explain. The only thing that is clear is that he resembles Proteus, who changed shape under any attempt to overwhelm him by force.

12 *Two Plays*

It is the nature of drama to simplify conflicts and convert them to some sort of concrete antithesis that can be represented by actors on a stage. What is internal in the novel must be externalized in the theatre; the invisible, the general, the analytical, the philosophical, must be seen and made concrete. A play made from a novel often seems stereotyped and obvious by comparison. But this is only when it is badly dramatized. The stage has means and possibilities denied to mere words on a printed page: an aliveness, a power to clothe ideas in tangible flesh. Where the novel tends toward subtlety and complication the drama tends toward immediacy and vividness. There are only two postwar plays in Italy that deal with America and Americans to any extent, but these are in a way more valuable than any novel because they show the Italian image of America with a great clarity, free from the technical and stylistic complications of fiction.[1] These two plays are Ezio d'Errico's *Tempo di cavallete* ("Time of Locusts"; 1956) and Luigi Squarzina's *La sua parte di storia* ("Her Part of History"; 1955). They are quite different as dramas, one fantastic and one realistic, and their picture of American culture is also diametrically opposite: myth in d'Errico, reality in Squarzina. Which is truer, myth or history, is a question still being debated by wise men. Each expresses its own kind of truth, and taken together they show a picture of America as seen from Italy which otherwise would be lacking a dimension.

Ezio d'Errico was a painter and popular novelist before he turned to the drama. Between 1948 and 1960 he wrote over twenty plays, beginning in a more or less realistic style (he had also been a commercial screenwriter) and gradually working into a vein of surrealistic-expressionistic fantasy. His later drama has been called apocalyptic theatre, theatre of solitude, absurd theatre, theatre of *Angst*. The last term is probably the most accurate. But his Existentialism is like Kafka's—symbolic and implied—rather than the overt and intellectual version of Sartre. His three best-known plays, *Tempo di cavallette, La foresta,* and *Il formicaio,* show the same grotesque and dehumanized modern civilization in which men live in the shadow of fear: dread of the unknown, of nothingness, of infinity. *Tempo di cavallette* is set in an Italian village immediately after the war, a time of dislocation and broken values, and its mood is apocalyptic. Another disaster, no one is quite sure what, seems to hang over the action. In the ruins of the village live a handful of survivors: the Hunter, the Employee, the Director, the cynical postwar teen-agers Mattia and Giunchiglia, and several others. In a corner of a wall the old woman Serafina mumbles about her three sons who were shot "for a better world"—but where is this better world? Who has seen it? In the middle of the ruins nothing has changed; it is still the same old prewar Europe with the same pettiness, the same boredom, the same class hatreds. Each of the characters plays his rôle in the allegory. The Employee is the pompous and petty bureaucracy, the Mechanic is the working class, the Hunter is the philosopher or intellectual, often a spokesman for d'Errico's own ideas. The bombed village is to be rebuilt, or so says the Employee. There will be schools and new houses for all, and they will even put up an ersatz classical statue, since every Italian town must have its piece of Romanità. The Director, who represents the capitalistic-manager class and is also mayor of the town, endeavors to disseminate a kind of forced cheerfulness. "In America," he tells the others, "smiling is a subject taught in the schools." [2] Meanwhile they await the coming of the locusts. Some say they will come and some not, but no one doubts the locusts exist. In this biblical image d'Errico sums up the fear and uncertainty of the postwar world. In plain terms the locusts are simply the Bomb. "They may come from the East or the West," the Mechanic says. "They may even come from both sides and happen to meet right here." [3] The Hunter remarks that they are very likely living in a time of the changing of seasons of the world, a kind of Spenglerian sunset. But what new time will come nobody knows. Then, shortly after a regiment in parade order has passed by, Joe appears on the scene.

Like the other characters, Joe is allegorical rather than real. He represents the myth of America as seen by the uneducated Italian, the Dream of Emigration in the flesh. He emigrated to America as a penniless boy, a stowaway. Now he has come back a middle-aged man to visit his native town again and marry the daughter of the local baron. He stops at the village only because his Cadillac breaks down. Or rather, since American cars never break down, it merely has a noise in the transmission. Joe is genial, offhand, and uninhibited. He is impatient with any kind of formality; he calls all the men Joe and all the girls Baby. He speaks a crude immigrant Italian full of American idioms; he says *moneta* for money, *non fa materia for* "it doesn't matter" instead of the correct Italian *non importa*, and *giobba* for job. He makes friends with everyone immediately and gives the keys of his Cadillac to Mattia so he can go for a ride, and he has no false modesty about his wealth. "Yes, I have a lot of money," he tells the Hunter, "and so I come back to my people. Here all friends. Even the stones, even the telegraph poles. And you, *simpatico*, say beautiful things I don't understand, but it's like you had music in your voice. All this I've always carried inside me, without telling anybody, because nobody understands in America. Understand business, money, building, subway, elevated . . . understand all the big things, but can't understand the little things that a man carries inside." But then he laughs; even his stereotyped criticism of America is easy-going, generous, benevolent. In America, he tells them still laughing, the Italians are "not specialized" and do everything: making music, singing, dancing, digging, driving nails, washing windows, directing banks, inventing new machines. "Good for any *giobba*, goodbye gentlemen and ladies . . . good bye." [4] He then goes off in his Cadillac and comes back with a picnic for his friends: roast chicken, canned lobster, sweets, cigarettes, champagne. Then, getting out his guitar, he sings an American song for them, a Whitmanesque ballad that tells about his wandering in "the waste places of the Far West." The song and the action that accompanies it are a kind of stylized ballet of the homecoming of the emigrant; if Joe is not as eloquent as Odysseus he is just as fabulous.

Joe's real message is friendship, but none of the Italians is capable of understanding this. To each his own America. The Director wants to import compulsory smiling because it is "taught in the schools in America." For the juvenile delinquent Mattia, America is the land of gangsters; in fact it is because he suspects Joe of gaining his fortune illegally that he admires him. But in Italy there is nothing for a gangster to do. If you pulled out a pistol they would only begin shrieking, Mattia complains, whereas in America they all put up their hands. "They're organized," he says admiringly. His own ambition has always been to be an American-style gangster. As a start he waits until Joe is asleep and then callously breaks his skull with a bottle. Then he steals the American's money out of his Cadillac and runs off with Giunchiglia. For a while they wander over Italy dancing to rock-and-roll music, then when the money is gone they go their separate ways, indifferently, "as people do after a dance." The murder of Joe is simply the latest version of The Goose That Laid the Golden Egg.

In the second act Mattia, Giunchiglia, and Joe reappear in a tableau. Joe is in the center, "pale, ecstatic, his hands raised in the gesture of surrender," a gesture which is also the pose of the Cross. This is an extraordinary scene; d'Errico is the first and last

Italian to portray America as a Christ-figure. A kind of a trial takes place; Joe tells the others, "What I had in me was hope." But in spite of the urging of their better selves the Italians have betrayed this hope; they have slain Joe for his money, for immediate easy wealth. The money is quickly spent and they have nothing left. Now they begin to think that perhaps Joe did not exist at all; the only ones who still believe in him are the Hunter and the young Baroness, Joe's fiancée. The Mechanic offers to kill Mattia for his crime, but the Hunter answers in the logic of Camus' philosophical rebel: "No, we must not kill even to prevent killing. And anyhow the rebel does not demand a life but the reason for life itself." [5] Then he hands down a judgment on the murderers: they stand before him to defend themselves, but they have carried their sentence inside them from the time of their birth. It was fated that they should reject the message of Joe, and it was fated that they should be lost, both in the Existentialist sense and the political. In their bickering they have forgotten the locusts, and at the end of the play they finally come. At first they look like pieces of paper; the Director says reassuringly that they are only propaganda. Instead they fall like the ashes on Pompeii, burying everything and everyone. Only a boy is left, shooting "absurdly" at the sky with a toy gun: the hope of tomorrow.

Naturally it is not certain that Joe could have prevented this holocaust even if they had accepted his canned lobster and his friendship. America is not usually viewed by Italians as a great force for world peace. More often it is a vague menace, one of the two directions from which the locusts may come. But Joe in this play is not America in any literal or political sense. If he were the Christ-symbolism would be presumptuous or sacrilegious. Instead he is simply the hope of human brotherhood, as Christ said, "I am the life and the hope." The idea of America as hope is so deeply rooted in the Italian mentality that it is natural, and valid, for d'Errico to personify this force as an American. Although Joe is only a symbol, the fact that d'Errico conceives his symbol in these terms is the positive side of his attitude toward America, an attitude which is also found in the typical Italian. The other side, the negative side, is that America is shown as a mechanical culture (the Cadillac never breaks down, and Joe calls America "a world where mechanics have great importance") and the falling ashes at the end are accompanied by the rumbling of motors. The catastrophe that ends the play is a mélange of a biblical plague, *The Last Days of Pompeii,* and the Strategic Air Command. The fear of the Bomb is the fear of nothing, *nihil,* emptiness. To this fear the men of good will oppose hope, even though they are not sure what it is they are hoping for. But in this play at least the hope is represented by Joe. "I believe in everything," the Hunter tells the Baroness. "In spirits, in ghosts, in horoscopes, in good and bad luck, in angels." And she answers, "I believe in everything too, and that's why I believe in Joe." [6]

Squarzina's *La sua parte di storia* treats a new aspect of America that so far no other Italian writer had dealt with: the foreign aid mission in a depressed region, the theme of Lederer and Burdick's *The Ugly American.* His style as a dramatist is essentially realistic, but he handles this subject with a great sublety and political sophistication. Where d'Errico is a highly imaginative experimentalist Squarzina is a practical man of the theatre, director of the Teatro Stabile di Genova and producer of, among other things, Shaw, Pirandello, and Sartre. Where d'Errico is deliberately naïve he is sophisticated; where d'Errico creates myth he destroys myth. In the end his image of America is not basically different; it is simply seen with more complexity.

Squarzina had two sources for the writing of *La sua parte di storia:* a visit to America as a scholarship student in 1951–1952 and a newspaper clipping about the murder of a postman in a depressed region of Italy. In the play American culture and the culture of the primitive region collide, and out of the contrast comes the dramatic conflict. It takes place on an island which is not named but is easily identifiable as Sardinia. To the most primitive part of this island comes an American medical aid mission which wins the struggle over a polio epidemic and saves the lives of hundreds of children. The mission is headed by

Dave Fletcher, an efficient and unemotional administrator. But his assistant, the younger doctor Gail Tibbett, is another type of American. Out of a sense of consecration she gives not only her technical skill but her emotions, her whole being, to the people of the Island. She is soon regarded almost as a saint; if the Islanders do not light candles to her it is only because there happens to be no shrine with her picture in it. She disregards Fletcher's warning that she is losing "the necessary detachment from the environment" and goes on working to rehabilitate the crippled children until she is at the point of exhaustion.

At this point her sympathy for the Islanders leads her a step too far. She learns that the local postman has been stealing money from the mail, mostly remittances from emigrants and conscripted soldiers. Many families depend on these remittances for their food, for their very existence. At first she makes up the money to the families out of her own pocket, hoping the postman will have a change of heart. When the thefts continue she finally confronts him one evening in the piazza, at the head of a group of villagers. Gail's emotions betray her; her voice rises and she begins to shout. When the frightened postman tries to escape he is beaten by the villagers and later dies of his injuries.

This incident occurs on the eve of a celebration which is to congratulate the mission on its success, a ceremony in which Gail is to be given a medal for her work. The inspector of the Foundation that finances the mission, Patricia Taylor, is to come from America, and reporters and television cameramen will be present. Gail could easily deny her part in the crime, since she would never be suspected and the Islanders with their tradition of *omertà* (absolute silence toward the police, especially in cases of vendetta) will never reveal her name. But her dogged idealism leads her to an almost masochistic sense of guilt; she insists on accepting her responsibility for the crime even though this will wreck the ceremony and damage the work of the Foundation. The rest of the play consists of a struggle between Gail and those who try to bring her to reason and persuade her to repudiate her confession so the ceremony can take place as planned.

Most of those who surround her in these critical hours are Americans. But each is a different type, just as Gail herself is different from them all. The first is Patricia Taylor, who arrives the morning of the ceremony. She is a type of highly efficient American woman who has rejected the usual tea-party philanthropy to go out and compete successfully in a world of men; to do this she has had to train herself to a rigid self-discipline and objectivity. To do good you must remain outside, she tells Gail. This is the essence of her personal code, which she repeats several times: "Near them, but outside—with us." Only in this way can you conserve your strength and go on working for the good of others; as soon as your emotions become involved you are useless. She herself has suffered a great personal tragedy—her daughter was killed in an automobile accident before her eyes—and it is only her work for the Foundation that keeps her alive. In her secret thoughts she associates this daughter with Gail, who is about the same age, and for this reason she has looked forward to the ceremony in Gail's honor. But in spite of this personal commitment her attitude is ruthlessly objective. Soon after she arrives she discovers that the mortality rate of the mission is slightly higher than she had expected, specifically .29 percent higher than the Mellon Foundation in Puerto Rico whose record she had hoped to beat. "Where did this twenty-nine thousandths of a dead child come from?" [7] she demands. The reason is explained to her; one evening a dying child was brought to the mission by peasants. Although Fletcher told them nothing could be done for the child, Gail insisted on accepting it. Because of this the mission failed to break the record; it is only "publicity" but as a result the Foundation may lose thousands of dollars in gifts. "I know how you feel, I have consecrated my whole life to the good of others," she tells Gail. "But everything must have a limit." [8] To Gail's idealism she opposes American pragmatism, the spirit of practical compromise that gets things done.

When Mrs. Taylor fails to convince Gail she hands her over to an expert: Ezra Shaber, psychoanalyst and consultant to the Foundation. Here for the first time Gail's conviction begins to weaken. In a simple ten-minute conversation with her he demolishes her high principles one by one and shows them for what they really are. He forces her to admit that collective violence is unjustified in any form, even to prevent a greater evil. The real reason she took part in the attack on the postman was that she felt a guilt over her own comfort and security and subconsciously wanted to share the condition of the Islanders. Her true wish was therefore not to end injustice but to have injustice inflicted upon her. Her imagined dedication and self-sacrifice were really only a girlish desire for martyrdom. "It's not so easy to be burned at the stake, little Saint Joan," [9] he tells her. Gail is shaken by his arguments but still refuses to recant. She is defended almost to the end by Amsìcora, the local archivist and amateur scholar who is a spokesman for the Italian cultural tradition. Like Gail he is an idealist, and he has faith in Gail and what she stands for because her America seems to him the last hope of human ideals. He tells Gail his theory of why she had shared in the violence against the postman: "Because it was love you felt for him . . . love which is the enemy of pity." [10] He and Gail exchange their love and agree to marry, but only after she has expiated her guilt in prison.

When her will is finally broken it is not through the arguments of others but through an incident that follows inevitably out of her act. In the Island tradition of vendetta the relatives of the postman carry out their own justice, and another man is murdered. The chain of revenge will move from family to family and many more will suffer before it is broken. This is the result of Gail's attempt to end an "injustice" which is deeply rooted in a culture. In the end even Amsìcora is convinced by the Americans and abandons her, and she weakly signs a repudiation of her confession. Now the ceremony can go on. But something is shattered inside Gail; she falls into a hypnotic trance, asking in a childish voice for ice cream and mistaking Mrs. Taylor for her mother. Like an obedient puppet she is led out on the stage to receive the medal. Gail represents an America which is in constant danger of spiritual collapse because its unreal principles are constantly menaced by reality. It is possible to tear away the illusions of an idealist and make him see the world as it really is, but only at the price of destroying a personality.

In the middle of this pathos another American, the psychoanalyst Shaber, remains detached and ironic. As a technician he is cynical about America's divine call to do a good to others which they have not asked for and will not appreciate. He says to Mrs. Taylor, "You ask me what I think of the tasks we have assumed. I think they're unworthy of us. These pathetic stories weighed down with all the imprecision of the human element—let's leave them to the Old World." [11] The third American, Mrs. Taylor herself, is less pessimistic; at the bottom there is something in her of Gail's idealism. In Shaber's "pathetic stories," even in the superstition and suffering of the Islanders, she sees something that is useful and necessary to an America from which tragedy has been banished. She tells Amsìcora, "We have need of you. It is your past that gives sense to our present. Our rightness is a mold growing on your ruins." [12] Mrs. Taylor is the most complicated character in the play and the most admirable. She has found out how to do something that few Americans have learned: how to do good to others without destroying yourself. She has managed to be both saint and technician, idealist and pragmatist. Her admiration for European tradition and its values does not prevent her from working to destroy it when it causes human suffering. In the end it is she who stands as the most valid symbol of her culture, an America which wanted to do good and is only hated for it, and in this sense she is a tragic figure where Gail is only melodramatic. In the last line of the play she replies to Shaber's sarcasm in words that express America's whole coming of age in a world in which tragedy seems inevitable. "You're bitter, Shaber. And I wanted others to be happy. . . ." [13]

Mrs. Taylor is not all of America. No one figure, in a book or anywhere else, can stand for all of America, and this is one thing Italian writers had learned by the time of d'Errico and Squarzina. It is a long way from Guareschi's funny-paper caricature in *Il destino si chiama Clotilde* to the complexity and psychological depth of *La sua parte di storia*. The picture did not really change; the Italians had been "right" about America from the beginning, insofar as an oversimplification can ever be right. But the truth about anything is never simple; truth lies in complexity. In this sense the Italian writers of the mid-century, who are aware of the complexity of America and the impossibility of summing it up in a neat formula, are closer to the truth than the writers of the Thirties who were excited and driven to creation by the "American myth." A myth is something invented by primitive people and is always a simple explanation of a phenomenon, too simple. Myths are also full of fear, hope, awe, and other emotions which interfere with an accurate judgment of the facts. By the middle of the century the Italians had got over their awe of America, and instead of hoping they were working hard themselves to get some of the things they had envied in the America of the Thirties. Many of them now saw that their fear of America, of the "locusts," was insecurity that was inherent in the twentieth century itself, and that America could not be blamed for this fear, that in fact many Americans felt it themselves. And that perhaps America's "immaturity," its naïve effort to save the world for democracy and provide a bottle of milk for every Hottentot, came from a genuine generosity and was more sincere than it seemed. Squarzina was not exactly pro-American, perhaps not any more than Cecchi in the Thirties, but at least he understood that America wanted others to be happy.

APPENDIX

Three Documents

These three pieces of writing deserve to be published here in full if only because they are three personal testimonies of the Italian discovery of America. They are also interesting reading for any American with enough curiosity to want to see himself and his culture through foreign eyes. One of them, Soavi's preface, has never before been published in English. The other two have appeared in the same translations in *The Western Humanities Review*: the Pavese article in the Summer, 1957, issue (11:3) and the Pintor essay in Summer, 1963 (18:3). A fuller discussion of all three articles will be found in the text preceding.

Pintor's "Americana" originally appeared in *Aretusa,* 2:5–14 (1945) and was reprinted with slight revisions in his *Il sangue d'Europa,* published by Einaudi in 1950. Pavese's "Yesterday and Today" first appeared on the literary page of the Turin *L'Unità* (August 3, 1947) and was reprinted in his *La letteratura americana e altri saggi,* also published by Einaudi in 1953. Soavi's short piece appeared as a preface to his *L'America tutta d'un fiato,* published by Mondadori in the Arcobaleno Collection in 1959. The three pieces are published here by permission of Giulio Einaudi Editore, Arnoldo Mondadori Editore, and *The Western Humanities Review*. For the Pintor translation special gratitude is due to Italo Calvino, who provided one of the last copies of *Il sangue d'Europa* in the publisher's stock, and Elio Vittorini, who lent his copy of the rare *Aretusa* version. I am indebted to Jack Garlington for *The Western Humanities Review* permissions.

"Americana"

GIAIME PINTOR (1943)

A book counts always for what it does not propose—for that margin of the unforeseen it contains in itself like a reserve of energy and vigor. Vittorini's *Americana* appears in a collection of classics which are easy to lump together in a single critical judgment. The terms German fiction or religious drama refer to scholarly units, to pretensions to culture. The book we are discussing is important for another reason: it represents the spontaneous message of a people to other peoples who are far from its shores, the justly proud response of America to the problems of a new world. It is in this that Vittorini has succeeded, and this polemic success opens the way to a more important set of meanings than would be expected from a mere textbook. *Americana*: the brevity of the name suggests the richness of the intentions. There is more of the fantasy of the traveler here than the research of the scholar.

For us America has always stood for a single set of values. Perhaps its geographical unity and its isolation across the sea have contributed to this myth of a country which grew like a single body and produced patterns and attitudes unique to itself. Immigrants came there from all the countries of Europe, but the strong American voice quickly replaced the many tongues and molded the diverse peoples into a single race. By the two oceans a new architecture sprang up, different from that of our cities. And when this burst of life had surmounted its initial phase, when it passed beyond the prairies and mines to industry and power, the indulgent curiosity of the Europeans took on a querulous note. It seemed to some that a genuine conflict was about to take place between the two civilizations, something like the violent and inevitable struggle between two historical periods.

This mixture of diffidence and curiosity coincided with a phase of copious sociology, especially after the war when America entered intimately into European life and began to impose its own tastes and tendencies. At that stage the abstraction was studied in its most obvious phenomena, total democracy and the cinema, Negro music and advertising art. The other aspects remained vaguely in the shadows, too embryonic or too remote to strike the untrained eye. Sociology has never flourished among Italians anyhow, and the relations between the two peoples remained at the crude mass level of the poverty of the emigrants and the more flashy aspects of advertising. Still the shape of America was too obvious on the horizon not to attract the attention of intellectuals. Along with the lyrical books like Soldati's and the inept documents of political journalism there appeared a few years back *America amara,* the first important statement of our intellectual reaction to the already mature forms of American culture.

America amara exemplifies the tendency of its time. Pure in style as few European writers are and sensitized to the value of words through a refined literary education, Cecchi is limited by his own cultural regionalism: for him space is an insurmountable obstacle. The overcivilized flavor of Tuscany is present in all of his judgments, the familiar patterns of the Tuscan landscape are his measure for all other lands. This indefatigable traveler is one of the least equipped men in the world to adapt himself to the surprises of travel, one of the most obstinately shut up in the prejudices of his own country.

In addition to this geographical difficulty Cecchi is hampered in his political judgment by another weakness: the characteristic inability of his generation to comprehend any value that eludes aesthetic appreciation, the tendency to regard social customs as curiosities and cultural differences as motives for fantasy. In a writer this tendency can be a quality of superiority; in fact it has liberated our literature from ponderous ideological complexes and breathed a new life into it. But at the same time it is the first symptom of an obscure danger. In our literature it coincided—after the collapse of a handful of courageous experiments like those of *La Voce* and Gobetti—with a school whose talent was soon expended and whose greatest historical mistake will be to have lived in peaceful contemporaneity with Fascism. In France, the mother-country of all modern literary colonies, the same phenomenon was even more conspicuous and obvious. We only have to recall the total superficiality of the political pretensions of Gide, the weakness of Valéry as soon as he ventured into discussing practical matters, the charming and fruitless arabesques traced by Giraudoux in *Pleins pouvoirs*. Like these others, Cecchi is a rigorous and often faultless critic in the realm of the printed page but is utterly unsound when he tries to expand in other directions, when he leaves the familiar ground of nuances to venture into the more difficult terrain of judgment. At which point we observe the vain efforts of a scene-designer trying to make his stage-sets into houses, of a mathematician trying to set up his formulas on the shifting sands of political economy.

Only reasons this powerful, and another which lies outside the discussion but is no less important—the age which separates us—can explain the contrast between his mentality and ours toward this name of America. Where Cecchi painstakingly assembled a museum of horrors and decadence and drew a world it is impossible to believe in, we heard a voice profoundly similar to our own, the voice of true friends and immediate contemporaries.

This image of America was all we had to fill the darkness and void of our minds. The childhood myths, faded and worn in their folklorish simplicity, came forth again with a new freshness from the American highways; the childhood of the Armenian-American Saroyan was our own, with the same discoveries and the same desires, a childhood in which bicycles and newspapers had a power of enchantment denied to the time-worn trappings of fable. The new legend sprang to life among pianos and songs in the tremendous cinemas of our youth. The abstract women of those times, the first to appear on the horizon of our adolescence, were the heroines of the adventures we saw in our provincial movie theatres; the unpronounceable names of American stars marked the glorious steps of our sentimental education. And after the war of 1914 had confused our minds with a dubious legendry, before another war had revealed the true significance of that episode out of which our maturity had come, Hemingway in *A Farewell to Arms* had given us our first example of how individual man can liberate himself from an obsolete code of values and escape through his own efforts from the ambushes of society.

Cecchi was unable to grasp the enormous importance of all this, the value of the precious cargo of spices and gold the new vessels had brought back from America. In his criticism of American writers he was condemned to the dubious scholarly task of trying to reconcile a basic existential incompatibility: that between a mind formed in an artificial atmosphere and the free expanse of America. Cecchi had too frankly confessed his respect for the "Carabinieri on horseback" to be able to understand the impulses and reactions of a popular mass in ferment.

Now his name appears again in this anthology, signed to a preface which is genuinely bitter in its refusal of any understanding with the adversary. But the following pages which Vittorini dedicates to the various periods of American culture stand as a clean antithesis to Cecchi's formula, demolishing both his ideological content and his critical method. Vittorini knows that a mere "musical" reading of the texts is no longer valid, that to persist in this path after recent developments in European criticism is to lose the real sense of the written word and to surrender to pure sensibility. (And in France, where the same cultural evolution has gone a step farther, non-journalistic criticism is going around in a whirlpool it may never work its way out of.) Vittorini performs the exact reversal of values necessary to keep alive any history of literature which is to continue to be a universal history. Perhaps he proposes a more radical thesis than he knows, a path to salvation in which the object itself, the concrete origin of the inspiration, determines the scale of values and guides the interest of the critic.

Such a formula would be excessively vulnerable and call forth arguments long since dead and buried if it were *only* a formula, if it represented only some kind of doctrine or neorealistic aesthetic. But more than this it is a breakthrough to a new kind of creativity: a turn to the living creatures and things of our environment in that mood of objective curiosity which is the basis of all valid judgment. For after all what is a poetic revelation if not basically the discovery of a new world, the glance which unexpectedly fixes on figures which had before been indistinct, the emerging from the dark of unknown words? We remember all true poets, the true masters of the past, as the governors of provinces, the discoverers of treasures they pass on to us as a heritage. Certain hours of the day belong to them as certain landscapes belong to the painters who have brought them to life through their art: every book, every finished work stands like a sign of man set up against the surrounding jungle.

In this progressive task of conquering and civilization, in this expansion of man beyond the borders of his primitive experience, America stands today as the most fertile and promising soil. A century and a half ago Germany emerged finally from its cultural prehistory and assumed its well-known shape in the geography of the European people. Fifty years ago a group of intellectuals and writers of genius brought to its climax a labor of historical reconciliation which gave to the western world Russia, its landscape and its religious experience, its mass ecstasies and its maladies. America has now reached that critical point in which its literature is no longer merely things seen and has not yet become academic tradition. The writers who live in this period have the right to call themselves classics, because they express for the first time an image of America which is self-explanatory and sufficient unto itself.

Hawthorne and Melville, the major figures of the past century, had offered the basic material for such an American history, had occasionally spoken out with an authority it was impossible to mistake, but there is always in them the heritage of an earlier history. Conscious of the fetters of their religious tradition, they sensed in some way the coming of a new morality but were unable to take the crucial step toward new manners and customs. Only the present generation has made out of its means of expression, its films and its books, a weapon of total war, has matched with the force of its words the progress of a century which has called forth all its energies. This generation alone has succeeded in celebrating the new works of man in the same instant they were created. As in every true literary renaissance, the key figures among the present-day American writers—Hemingway, Faulkner, Saroyan—are above all the inventors of a style. But it is a style in which the earthy materials are still fresh, which owes its richness to the presence of new objects: new machines, new houses, new human relations. To be aware of these special circumstances is perhaps not the only task of the critic, but it is the first condition for understanding this effort that a people and a generation are making to express themselves. Vittorini meets this challenge in the notes which he provides for each group of writers. Free from all academism, infused with a keen and vigorous imagination, the notes are a remarkable example of a literary history as *lived* by a writer. In this they are closer to classic examples, like Mme. de Staël's *L'Allemagne* or Heine's *Die romantische Schule,* than they are to the usual work of professional critics. The fact that Vittorini wrote these pages only a few months after *Conversazione in Sicilia* shows the force he exerts in our culture, demonstrates that his name has already passed beyond a vigorous friendship to make its deeper and more lasting mark in our history.

Perhaps because I read this book while the Bavarian plain passed before my eyes beyond the train window, I gradually began to see Germany as the natural antithesis of this world and in a broader sense of the new world as it is reflected in Europe. No people is closer to the American in the youthfulness of its blood and the candor of its desires, and no people celebrates its own legend in words more different. As always, the ways of corruption and purity are dangerously close, and a chronic madness seems to distract the Germans from their path and involve them in difficult and inhuman adventures. Thus these two peoples, who only a few years ago met amicably on athletic fields and competed in industrial production, face each other today as the protagonists of a cruel struggle. Each has taken on itself responsibility for the future of the world, and each is ready to batter down the last obstacle to the fulfillment of its destiny. For this is the real significance of the war which is now being fought. In the formalities of diplomacy and the fantasies of generals the same old clichés are dragged out: the balance of power, *France éternelle,* the Hapsburg monarchy, the buffer states. But these figures of speech belong to the Peace of Westphalia and the Treaty of Versailles; behind their intangible presences those who search for the real value of words will see other names: America and Germany, Russia, China.

The forces involved on both sides are powerful enough to deflect the whole course of our experience, to cast us aside as useless rubbish or lead us together into some haven of safety. But America will win this war because its basic impulse comes out of a more genuine strength, because it believes in the possibility and the justice of what it is setting out to do. *Keep smiling*: this peacetime slogan came to us from America wrapped in edifying music at a time when Europe was an empty shop-window, when the forced austerity of totalitarian countries showed us only the face of a desperate and bitter Fascist reaction. The extreme simplicity of such American optimism was viewed indignantly by some who felt the duty of going around in mourning as a sign of their humanity, those who preferred a pride in their own dead to the welfare of the living. But the pride of America today for its sons lies in the knowledge that they have climbed the steepest road in history and have avoided the traps and dangers lying in the path of this unceasing progress. The quick riches and bureaucratic corruption, the gangsters and the depressions, were absorbed naturally in the growing body. And this is the real history of America: a growing people, burying under its enthusiasm the mistakes that lie behind it and arming with good will against the dangers of the future. The greatest evils men know are found on the American soil, disease and poverty, but the risks and fears end in something positive, and with each struggle man is exalted.

Naturally such adventures are not proclaimed at the top of one's voice; they appear behind a mask or hidden in a cipher. There is too much of the old English blood in the American race to reveal so shamelessly a weakness for abstract morality. And so physical comfort, wealth, and money are made to serve as masks for these abstract furies; they are simply the concrete expression of the humanism of this young American culture. And all the leisurely aesthetes who feel themselves the contemporaries of Pericles, the pseudo-philosophers wound up in their metaphysical distinctions, the journalists who have taken on themselves the defense of the western world turn their backs on a people so obviously degenerate.

There weighs over American society the stupidity of a phrase: materialistic civilization. A civilization of producers: this is the pride of a race which has not sacrificed its own strength to ideological subtleties and has not fallen into the easy trap of "spiritual values," a race that has made technology a part of its life, that has found a new world of sentiment in the commonplace fact of daily labor and built new legends out of the horizons it has conquered. Whatever the romantic critics may think, such a profoundly revolutionary experience has not remained without a voice to express it. While postwar Europe was taking up again the clichés of a decadent culture or inventing formulas like that of surrealism which by their very nature led into blind alleys, America was creating a new narrative language and inventing the new medium of the cinema.

Everybody knows what American movies are; we regard them with that mixture of sympathy and condescension which has been described as one of our most basic European traits. But the real point has perhaps not yet been made, or not vigorously enough. Today, when a forced abstinence has cured us of the abuses of advertising and the boredom of habit, we can perhaps understand for the first time the significance of the cinema in our education and recognize in the American motion picture the most important message our generation has received. It is true that the cinema was born and developed first in Europe, but as soon as it emerged from the infantile stage it turned into a mediocre appendage of our literature. The limitations of a rigid aesthetics, and one based on dubious premises, kept us for years arguing about non-existent problems: who was to write the film, what the relations were to be between the actor and the director. Only in Russia did the cinema seem to get on the right track and follow it, with the naturalness of one who instead of resting on his heraldic laurels entrusts himself to the strength of his own powers. And when a few years later the same easy spontaneity was reborn in America with an even greater technical sophistication, it was the signal for all the guardians of pristine literary taste to start weeping over mechanization, the decline of the silent film, and similar industrial accidents.

Here as in other fields American capitalism and Russian proletariat met in their determination to explore an undiscovered world, to take up with confidence and energy these new instruments of man. The American cinema came into being as a luxury industry subject to the most rigid laws of the capitalistic economy, but it soon became not only a product for mass consumption but the expression of the needs and preferences of the masses themselves, the first influence of a unified culture on the whole population of the world.

At that point the cinema became an indispensable presence in our lives; it grew up with our own youth, taught us to see and create by new standards, modified the history and geography of our brains, educated us while it set us to arguing, served us as amusement and provided us with a mythology. As it spread and expanded its function was above all social; it was a quiet revolutionary weapon that abolished political frontiers and guided us in the most important inner struggle of our time, that of the unity of humanity. But its aesthetic aspect was hardly less significant. Without these movies our eyes would have seen the world in another light; today it is clear that the anonymous makers of the American films were the first to respond to Baudelaire's call for the modern artist, the first to show us how young and fine we were with our patent-leather shoes and our bourgeois neckties.

We needed to know this if we were going to find our way out of a mediocre aestheticism. To a greater or less degree according to the affinity of tastes, the lesson was absorbed by the whole civilized world. Today only Germany, obstinately shut up inside its medieval complex, refuses to accept it. The posthorn of Eichendorff sounds again in the verses of the bad poets of the Third Reich: not one of them recognizes any aesthetic value outside the traditional framework, not one of them can hear any music unhallowed by academism. Every German girl discovers over again the same autumn sunsets her great-grandmother discovered, goes into ecstasy over the same landscapes, finds *fabalhaft* and *wunderbar* the same archeological relics. A fascination with wilderness, exoticism, the blue sky of Italy are still today the limits of an aesthetics which has served these incorrigible philistines for more than a century. Not one of them has grasped that a factory on the outskirts of Berlin is just as much "nature" as the cliffs of Capri and that a window glimpsed from an Unterbahn train has even more right to be admired, even on the same standards by which we admire a baroque garden.

The romantic universe, that dangerous toy of men insulated in their lofty irony, has passed on intact into the hands of their descendants, reduced to a common formula and venerated as though it were a museum piece. All the counterreactions of more than a century of European intelligence, from Heine to Thomas Mann, have failed to alter this fundamental vice of the German soil. The romantic aesthetic stands in the way of the development of any new sensibility; a romantic politics conceals the basic uncertainty of a people who have passed through the severest historical trials without ever gaining a true political experience.

Out of this confusion was born the National Socialist regime, the absurd hallucination of a proletarian country trying to live by petit-bourgeois ideals. Through this confusion the most productive country in Europe has set up an artificial distinction between production and culture, turned its industry to the needs of war, and given the miracle of organization over into the hands of the military. Germany today perpetuates the cult of an unreal anthropology; on the shabbiest Nietzschean grounds it hails the revolt of myth against man and indulges in other unhealthy comparisons. Blood and soil have become the symbols of a people who owe their very civilization to their mixture of blood and their indifference to territorial problems; the country which was the first to discover the power of a modern centralized industry has nothing more to offer future generations than a village communalism. It is this irreconcilable difference of faith and doctrine that lies at the bottom of the conflict between America and Germany. To the mystics of the domestic hearth a pioneer people replies: the important thing is to travel. The old idol of Fatherland collapses and passes into the realm of memory; the earth is something to be used and believed in, not to make men slaves. Along with this idol perish other deeply rooted patterns, all the meanness and laziness we conceal behind noble words. America has no cemeteries to defend. In this battle against the idols it finds its true mission: the struggle against the Gentiles who continually repeat their error of subjecting man to an orthodoxy or a rite, a political machine or a doctrine.

Through the example of this generous mission the dreams of a utopian world take heart again. Here America demonstrates the Marxist ideology: the concrete proof is seen wherever man does not surrender to the dark perils of mysticism and regret—wherever he does not take refuge in neutrality and indifference but comes to grips, freely and through his own means, with the problems of a precarious existence. This can happen in America or it can happen in Russia. In our words dedicated to America much may be ingenuous and inexact, much may refer to arguments extraneous to the historical phenomenon of the United States as it stands today. But this does not matter because even if the continent did not exist our words would not lose their significance. This America has no need of Columbus, it is discovered within ourselves; it is the land to which we turn with the same hope and faith of the first immigrants, of whoever has decided to defend at the price of pains and error the dignity of the human condition.

"Yesterday and Today"

CESARE PAVESE (1947)

Toward 1930, when Fascism commenced to be "the hope of the world," a lot of young Italians looked in their books and discovered America: an America pensive and barbaric, blissful yet quarrelsome, dissolute, fecund; burdened with all the past of the world, yet youthful, innocent. For several years these young people read, translated, and wrote in a mood of joyful discovery and revolt that scandalized the official culture. But the thing was so overwhelmingly successful that the regime was obliged to tolerate it, if only to save face. What was this, a joke? We were the heirs of the Roman tradition, the land where even mathematicians studied Latin; the land of warriors and saints, the land of Genius by the Grace of God, and these brash ragamuffins, these colonial merchants, these hordes of yokels dared to give us a lesson in taste? dared to put themselves forward to be read and admired? The regime swallowed its rage and tolerated. Meanwhile it lurked in the breach, waiting for a false step, for a slightly cruder page, for a more direct curse, so it could catch us red-handed and slap our wrists. They did slap us a few times, but that didn't stop the thing. The odor of scandal, of facile heresy, which permeated the new books and their ideas—the fury of revolt, of sincerity which even the most superficial readers felt pulsating in those translated pages—irresistibly appealed to a public not yet fully cowed by conformity and academism. There is no denying that, at least in the area of style and taste, the new fad helped more than a little to keep alive and nourish the political opposition, as diffuse and feeble as it was, among the Italian reading public. For many, the encounter with Caldwell, Steinbeck, Saroyan, and Lewis broke open the first breathing-hole to liberty, offered the first hint that not everything in the culture of the world finished with Fascism.

It goes without saying that for the more sophisticated reader the lesson was more basic. Anyone who goes beyond merely leafing through the dozen or so most striking books which arrived from overseas in those years—anyone who shakes the tree to make the hidden fruit fall, anyone who digs down to uncover the roots—will soon be aware that the rich expressiveness of this people was born, not so much out of its splendid quest for new social forms, which was after all banal, but out of a dogged determination, already a century old, to convert the experience of daily life completely into verbal form. This is the source of their continual effort to adjust their language to the new reality of the world—to create in substance a new language, material and symbolic, whose only justification is in itself rather than in some passive traditionalism. And it is not hard to identify as the inventors and pathfinders of this style—a style often cheapened, but one which still strikes us even in the latest books through its unusual clarity—the poet Walt Whitman and the storyteller Mark Twain in the mid-nineteenth century.

At that point American culture became for us something very serious and precious, a sort of great laboratory where others were working, under different conditions of liberty and with different means, in the same task of creating a taste, a style, a modern world as the best of our writers were, perhaps with less immediacy but with the same stubborn will. And so this culture seemed to us an ideal place for work and experiment, of strenuous and embattled experiment, rather than a mere Babel of clamorous efficiency, of crude neon-lit optimism that stunned and blinded the naïve—an image that even our provincial-minded rulers found of some use when they came across it in certain hypocritical writers. After several years of study we comprehended that America was not *another* land, *another* historical beginning, but merely the gigantic theatre where, with more frankness than was possible anywhere else, the drama of everybody was being enacted. And if at that point it seemed worthwhile to repudiate ourselves and our past to surrender ourselves body and soul to this free world, it was only because of the absurd, the tragic and comic situation of civil death in which history had for the moment confined us.

In those days American culture enabled us to see our own drama unfolding as though on a gigantic stage. It showed us a furious, a conscious and incessant, struggle to impart a sense and a name and an order to the new reality and the new impulses of individual and social life—to reconcile a dizzily transformed world with the traditional feelings and the ancient words of men. As was natural in a time of political constraint, we all limited ourselves to studying merely how those intellectuals across the sea had *expressed* this drama, how they had succeeded in *speaking* this language, in *telling,* in *singing,* this story. We could not take part openly in the drama, the story, the problem; and so we studied American culture the way the past centuries are studied, the Elizabethan drama or the poets of the *dolce stil nuovo.*

Now the times are changed and everything can be said, and in a certain sense everything has been said. So it happens that the years go by and more books come to us from America than ever before, but today we open them and read them without excitement. There was a time when even a minor book from over there, even a mediocre film, stirred up and posed living questions, stripped away our complacency. Is it we who grow old? or is this little liberty we have enough to distract us? The creative and narrative triumphs of the American twentieth century remain—Edgar Lee Masters, Anderson, Hemingway, and Faulkner have taken their place among the classics—but for us not even the long fast of the war years is enough to make us genuinely love what comes to us nowadays from over there. Sometimes it happens that we read a vivid book which provokes our imagination and speaks out to our conscience, and then we notice the date: prewar. In short, to be frank it seems that American culture has lost its mastery, that wise and innocent fury that thrust it to the forefront of our intellectual world. And one cannot help noting that this coincides with the end, or the suspension, of its struggle against Fascism.

Now that the more brutal restrictions are at an end we have come to understand that many lands today, in Europe and throughout the world, are laboratories where new forms and styles are created—that there is nothing to prevent anybody who wants to, no matter if he lives in an old convent, from saying a new word. But without a Fascism to oppose, without a progressive historical ideal to personify, even America—for all its skyscrapers and automobiles and soldiers—will no longer be in the vanguard of anybody's culture. Without an ideal and without a progressive struggle, it even runs the risk of surrendering itself to its own form of Fascism, though it be in the name of its best traditions.

Preface to "*America All at One Breath*"

GIORGIO SOAVI (1959)

In 1954 I was in America for three months. Ever since I came back the memory of the America I saw has fascinated me—the myth of this Country is something I can't forget. What is it about America? and why do I think about it so often? "Would you like to live there?" my friends keep asking me. We Italians are excitable and dramatic and probably, the way things stand right now, we're not made for America. But we have this affection for it, we keep watching it, and even if we don't like it we know so many things about this Country by heart that every so often we have a feeling that we're living there. This is because Italians, the young ones, the exhibitionists, in their fantasy often live the lives of Americans. I don't remember that Italians ever mimicked any other people this way. The French? Absolutely not. And not the Russians, the Japanese, or the English. The Germans. . . . The Americans yes. We look at them with sentiments of astonishment and irony, and we more or less want to imitate them.

I didn't know what to do when I came back, but I did know one thing: I didn't want to write journalism about them. Fine, I know that America keeps changing like lightning and nobody but a journalist can keep up with the daily revolution. I wrote poetry because poetry, even when it's more or less narrative like mine, hits you in the same way as lightning.

Of all the people in the world the Americans are the ones who, more than any others, have not lost sight of the world of fantasy, of the future. The Americans started making their future right away and they made it with all the means they had at their disposition. Going with Lindbergh to the airport that rainy morning, creating economic machines capable of rebuilding entire regions like the Tennessee Valley Authority, filling up the sky with skyscrapers: the things America has done are well known. Even the tragedies and brutality; they have the worst underworlds in the world too. Would it be better or worse than Siberia? Either one would be terrific. We're in the middle. Anyhow America is generous, it offers more than other people do. In the middle of all the confusion everybody is eating while America goes on giving or selling all of itself, as flashy as its neckties and as durable as its Constitution.

I've loved and hated it the way you love and hate a person, and now that my book is finished I'm sorry to have written certain cruel and petty things. A little cruelty does no harm to a healthy person as long as it's inflicted with good will. I have good will and perhaps some day I will write a little more joyfully about America.

NOTES

1. CHATEAUBRIAND, THE MOVIES, AND OTHER MYTHS

1 *La letteratura americana e altri saggi,* Turin, Einaudi, 1953, p. 193.

2 *Saggi critici di letteratura inglese,* Florence, 1897, p. 99.

3 *Il Corriere d'Informazione,* May 5, 1953, p. 3.

4 See Francis J. Brown and Joseph Slabey Roucek, eds., *One America,* New York, Prentice-Hall, 1945; Federal Writers Project, *The Italians of New York,* New York, Random House, 1938.

5 Carlo Levi, "Italy's Myth of America," *Life,* 23:1 (July, 1947), p. 84.

6 *Ibid.,* p. 85

7 *Ibid.,* p. 90.

8 *Immigrant's Return,* New York, Macmillan, 1951, p. 181.

9 *Ibid.,* p. 159. This somewhat dubious Italian is thus in the original, including "Americana" with capital A.

10 *Ibid.,* p. 161.

11 *Ibid.,* p. 203.

12 A detailed account is found in Ed Reid, *Mafia,* New York, Random House, 1952.

13 *Christ in Concrete,* Indianapolis, Bobbs-Merrill, 1939, p. 279.

14 "Americana," in *Il sangue d'Europa,* Turin, Einaudi, 1950, pp. 216f.

15 *Ibid.,* p. 211.

16 "Il mito di Hollywood e la cultura cinematografica in Italia," *Galleria,* 4:5–6 (December, 1954), p. 288.

2. THE TRAVELERS

1 *America primo amore*, Milan, Garzanti, 1956, p. 6.
2 *Ibid.*, p. 103.
3 *Ibid.*, p. 66.
4 *Ibid.*, p. 65.
5 *Ibid.*, p. 233.
6 *Ibid.*, p. 52.
7 *Ibid.*, p. 78.
8 *Ibid.*, p. 162.
9 *Ibid.*, p. 207.
10 *Ibid.*, p. 260.
11 Letter to writer, November 26, 1962.
12 Giaime Pintor, "Scrittori a Weimar," *Il sangue d'Europa*, Turin, Einaudi, 1950, p. 198.
13 *America amara*, Florence, Sansoni, 1946, pp. 81f.
14 *Ibid.*, p. 128.
15 *Ibid.*, p. 48.
16 *Ibid.*, p. 298.
17 *Loc. cit.*
18 *Ibid.*, p. 43.
19 *Scrittori inglesi e americani*, Milan, Mondadori, 1953, vol. II, p. 158.
20 *America amara*, p. 255.
21 *Ibid.*, p. 253.
22 *Ibid.*, p. 255.
23 *Ibid.*, p. 140.
24 *Ibid.*, p. 300.
25 "America and Italy: Myths and Realities," *Italian Quarterly*, 3:9 (Spring, 1959), p. 5.
26 *Questa è l'America*, Milan, Edizioni Alpe, 1945, p. 103.
27 *Ibid.*, p. 226.
28 *Ibid.*, p. 87.
29 *Ibid.*, p. 126.
30 *De America*, Milan, Garzanti, 1959, p. 156.
31 *Ibid.*, p. 359.
32 *Ibid.*, p. 366.
33 *Ibid.*, p. 94.
34 *America allo specchio*, Bari, Laterza, 1960, p. 11.

35 *America 1962: Nuove tendenze della sinistra americana,* Florence, "La Nuova Italia" Editrice, 1962, p. 2.

36 *Ibid.,* p. 91.

37 *Ibid.,* p. x.

38 *America a passo d'uomo,* Milan, Rizzoli, 1962, p. 143.

39 *Ibid.,* p. 93.

40 *L'America tutta d'un fiato,* Milan, Mondadori, 1959, pp. 78ff.

41 *Fantabulous: Racconti americani,* Milan, Mondadori, 1962, p. 122.

3. THE AMERICANISTI

1 Quoted in Julien Benda, *The Betrayal of the Intellectuals,* Boston, Beacon, 1955, p. 28.

2 Quoted in Oreste del Buono, ed., *Moravia,* Milan, Feltrinelli, 1962, p. 35.

3 *Scrittori anglo-americani d'oggi,* Milan, 1932, p. 63.

4 "Walt Whitman, poeta," *Nuova Antologia,* June 16, 1908; reprinted in *Scrittori e artisti,* Mondadori, Milan, 1959, pp. 1100f.

5 From a radio broadcast June 12, 1950; reprinted in *La letteratura americana e altri saggi,* Turin, Einaudi, 1953, p. 293.

6 *Pesci rossi* 3, Bompiani, Milan, 1949. The best source of Vittorini's biography is still this sketch he wrote for a Bompiani advertising brochure. It was reprinted in *Diario in pubblico,* Bompiani, 1957, pp. 170ff., and a translation appeared in *Italian Quarterly,* 1:3 (Autumn, 1957), pp. 46ff.

7 Pavese, *Il mestiere di vivere,* Turin, Einaudi, 1955, p. 245.

8 Preface to *Il garofano rosso,* Milan, Mondadori, 1947. This excerpt is from my translation in *The Western Humanities Review,* 9:3 (Summer, 1955), p. 203.

9 Giovanni Cecchetti, "Elio Vittorini," *Italica,* 29:1 (March, 1952), p. 8.

10 John Steinbeck, "Flight," from Warren and Erskine, eds., *Short Story Masterpieces,* New York, Dell Books, 1954, p. 455.

11 In "Cesare Pavese and the American Novel," *Studi Americani,* 3 (1957), pp. 347ff., the British novelist Richard H. Chase maintained that Pavese's interest in the Americans was substantially technical and that his themes were drawn from the Proust-Joyce psychological school, while Nemi D'Agostino in a later number of *Studi Americani* (4:399ff.) found this conclusion "profoundly erroneous."

12 *Diario in pubblico,* p. 94 (September, 1938).

13 From the seized *Americana* prefaces; reprinted in *Diario in pubblico,* p. 146.

14 *Il mestiere di vivere,* p. 368.

15 *The Short Stories of Ernest Hemingway,* New York, Modern Library, 1942, p. 174.

16 *Paesi tuoi,* Turin, Einaudi, 1954, p. 69.

17 *Diario in pubblico,* p. 178.

18 "Un'antologia tedesca," *Primato,* April 15, 1940; reprinted in Pintor's *Il sangue d'Europa,* Turin, Einaudi, 1950, p. 123.

19 "Sulle scogliere di marmo," *Primato,* September 15, 1942; reprinted in *Il sangue d'Europa,* p. 192.

20 "Americana," *Il sangue d'Europa,* p. 217.

21 *Aretusa,* II, March, 1945. The entire essay is reprinted in this volume in the appendix.

22 See particularly "Giaime Pintor," *Rinascita,* Naples, 1:2 (July, 1944); Aldo Garosci, "Un mese e mezzo con Giaime Pintor," *Mercurio,* 16 (December, 1945); Luigi Pintor, "Ricordo di Giaime Pintor," *Rinascita,* Rome, 4:3 (March, 1947); Giorgio Amendola, "Significato di un ritorno," *L'Unità,* Rome, November 18, 1948.

23 *Il sangue d'Europa,* p. 246.

24 *Ibid.,* p. 248.

25 *Ibid.,* p. 217.

26 *Ibid.,* p. 214.

27 *Ibid.,* pp. 209f.

28 *Ibid.,* pp. 210f.

29 *Ibid.,* p. 215.

30 *Ibid.,* p. 219.

4. "THE TIME IS PAST IN WHICH WE DISCOVERED AMERICA"

1 Letter to writer, January 30, 1957.

2 "Un'inchiesta tra i narratori," *Galleria,* 4:5–6 (December, 1954), pp. 314ff.

3 Introduction to *Il sentiero dei nidi di ragno,* Turin, Einaudi, 1954, p.8.

4 "Hemingway e noi," *Il Contemporaneo,* November 13, 1954, p. 3.

5 *La letteratura americana e altri saggi,* Turin, Einaudi, 1953, p. 189.

6 *Ibid.,* p. 193.

7 Letter to Mario Camerino, May 30, 1950, quoted in *Il "vizio assurdo": Storia di Cesare Pavese,* Milan, Il Saggiatore, 1960, p. 360.

8 *Il "vizio assurdo,"* p. 340.

9 "Last Blues," *Poesie,* Turin, Einaudi, 1962, p. 174.

10 *Il "vizio assurdo,"* p. 340.

11 *Il mestiere di vivere,* Turin, Einaudi, 1955, pp. 400f.

12 *Diario in pubblico*, Milan, Bompiani, 1957, p. 209.
13 *Ibid.*, p. 263.
14 *Ibid.*, p. 151.
15 *Ibid.*, p. 360.
16 Fernanda Pivano, *La balena bianca e altri miti*, Milan, Mondadori, 1961, p. 10.
17 *Ibid.*, p. 72.
18 Letter to writer. December 31, 1962.
19 "Poesia americana e cultura americana," *Aut-Aut*, 21 (May, 1954), p. 223.
20 Alberto Arbasino, *L'anonimo lombardo*, Milan, Feltrinelli, 1959, p. 127.

5. GUARESCHI: AMERICA OR CASTOR OIL?

1 Guareschi, *Il destino si chiama Clotilde*, Milan, Rizzori, 1941, p. 129.
2 *Ibid.*, p. 132.
3 *Ibid.*, p. 140.
4 *Ibid.*, p. 143.
5 *America amara*, Florence, Sansoni, 1946, pp. 145f.
6 *Il destino si chima Clotilde*, p. 270.

6. SILONE: EMIGRATION AS THE OPIATE OF THE PEOPLE

1 *Fontamara*, Milan, Mondadori, 1962, p. 42.
2 *Ibid.*, pp. 12f.
3 Interview in *La Fiera Letteraria*, 18:2 (January 13, 1963), p. 1.
4 *Bread and Wine*, tr. by Gwenda David and Eric Mosbacher, New York, Penguin, 1946, p. 56.
5 *Ibid.* pp. 217ff.
6 *Vino e pane*, Milan, Mondadori, 1955, p. 221.
7 *Bread and Wine*, pp. 220ff.
8 Quoted in Kenneth Alsop, "Ignazio Silone," *Encounter*, 18:3 (March, 1962), p. 51.
9 *Bread and Wine*, p. 62.
10 *Ibid.*, p. 203.
11 *Vino e pane*, p. 211.

7. EMIGRATION: LEVI, ALVARO, AND OTHERS

1 *Cristo si è fermato a Eboli*, Turin, Einaudi, 1962, p. 9.
2 *Ibid.*, p. 109.

3 *Loc. cit.*
4 *Ibid.*, p. 110.
5 *Ibid.*, p. 115.
6 *Le parole sono pietre*, Turin, Einaudi, 1961, p. 35.
7 *Cristo si è fermato a Eboli*, p. 86.
8 *Passione di Rosa*, Milan, Mondadori, 1958, p. 97.
9 *Ibid.*, p. 104.
10 *Ibid.*, p. 138.
11 *Ibid.*, p. 143.
12 "Il rubino," *Gente di Aspromonte*, Milan, Garzanti, 1960, p. 105.
13 *Ibid.*, p. 107.
14 *Ibid.*, p. 102.
15 "L'ospite americano," *Il Messaggero*, October 8, 1963, p. 3.
16 "Posta dal New Jersey," *Il Messaggero*, October 4, 1962, p. 3.

8. "LIBERATION"

1 Quoted in Charles F. Delzell, *Mussolini's Enemies: The Italian Anti-Fascist Resistance*, Princeton University Press, 1961, p. 566.
2 *Uomini e no*, Milan, Bompiani, 1949, p. 5.
3 *Diario in pubblico*, Milan, Bompiani, 1957, p. 179.
4 *Guerra in camicia nera*, Milan, Garzanti, 1955, pp. 91f.
5 "Un nuovo romanziere italiano: Giuseppe Berto," *Il Libraio*, December 15, 1946. This is one of several accounts written by Berto of his prison experience; see also "Animali in prigionia," *Il Tempo*, January 26, 1948; "Avvenimento a Hereford," *Il Giornale d'Italia*, December 9, 1956; "La conversione," *Il Giornale d'Italia*, December 5, 1959. There is also a short story about the Hereford camp, "Il seme tra le spine," in his *Un po' di successo* (Milan, Longanesi, 1963).
6 From "La conversione," the *Giornale d'Italia* sketch cited above.
7 *Il cielo è rosso*, Milan, Longanesi, 1957, p. 79.
8 *Ibid.*, pp. 79f.
9 *Ibid.*, p. 339.
10 *Ibid.*, pp. 400f.
11 A *Farewell to Arms*, New York, Modern Library, 1952, pp. 351f.
12 *Il cielo è rosso*, p. 132.
13 *Un po' di successo*, Milan, Longanesi, 1963, p. 55.
14 *Il cielo è rosso*, pp. 240f.
15 *Ibid.*, p. 241.
16 *Ibid.*, pp. 242f.

17 See Armando Boscolo, *Fame in America,* Milan, Edizioni Europee, 1954, p. 94. This is an account of the Hereford camp written by one of Berto's fellow officers, badly biased but valuable as a source of information.

18 *Il cielo è rosso,* p. 452.

19 "L'umorismo come salvezza," *La Fiera Letteraria,* October 20, 1963, p. 1.

20 *Un po' di successo,* p. 243.

21 *Ibid.,* p. 266.

22 *Ibid.,* p. 270.

23 *Il clandestino,* Milano, Mondadori, 1962, p. 187.

24 *Ibid.,* p. 251.

25 *Ibid.,* pp. 418ff.

9. THE MOON AND THE BONFIRES

1 Massimo Mila, preface to Cesare Pavese, *Poesie,* Turin, Einaudi, 1962, p. vii.

2 "I mari del sud," *Poesie,* p. 5.

3 *Ibid.,* p. 8.

4 Quoted in Davide Lajolo, *Il "vizio assurdo,"* Milan, Il Saggiatore, 1960, p. 226.

5 "I mari del sud," *Poesie,* p. 5.

6 "Sherwood Anderson," *La Cultura,* April, 1931; reprinted in *La letteratura americana e altri saggi,* Turin, Einaudi, 1953, p. 36.

7 *La luna e i falò,* Turin, Einaudi, 1955, p. 14.

8 Letter to writer, October 2, 1962.

9 *Il mestiere di vivere,* Turin, Einaudi, 1955, p. 362.

10 *La luna e i falò,* p. 13.

11 *Ibid.,* p. 16.

12 *Ibid.,* p. 23.

13 *Ibid.,* p. 113.

14 *Ibid.,* p. 114.

15 *Ibid.,* p. 115.

16 *Loc. cit.*

17 *Ibid.,* p. 62.

18 *Ibid.,* p. 64.

19 *Ibid.,* p. 52.

20 *Ibid.,* p. 21.

21 *Ibid.,* p. 25.

22 *Ibid.*, p. 53.
23 *Ibid.*, p. 95.
24 *Ibid.*, p. 158.
25 *Ibid.*, p. 175.
26 *Il mestiere di vivere,* p. 302.
27 *Il "vizio assurdo,"* p. 281.
28 *Il mestiere di vivere,* p. 303.

10. THE CAPRI LETTERS

1 *Le lettere da Capri,* Milan, Garzanti, 1954, p. 36.
2 *Ibid.*, p. 80.
3 *Ibid.*, p. 81.
4 *Ibid.*, p. 73.
5 *Ibid.*, p. 272.
6 *Ibid.*, p. 274.
7 *Ibid.*, p. 336.
8 *Loc. cit.*
9 *Ibid.*, p. 337.

11. MORAVIA'S AMERICA

1 *Gli indifferenti,* Milan, Bompiani, 1962, p. 342.
2 "Autobiografia in breve," in Oreste del Buono, ed., *Moravia,* Milan Feltrinelli, 1962, p. 10.
3 *Ibid.*, p. 14.
4 "L'uomo e il personaggio," *Prospettive,* 22, 1941. (Signed "Pseudo.") Quoted in Oreste del Buono, *Moravia,* p. 164.
5 Unsigned, "One Good Tune," *The New Yorker,* May 7, 1955, p. 39.
6 *Nuovi racconti romani,* Milan, Bompiani, 1961, p. 131.
7 *L'amore coniugale e altri racconti,* Milan, Bompiani, 1958, p. 278.
8 *La ciociara,* Milan, Bompiani, 1961, p. 306.
9 *Ibid.*, p. 307.
10 *Ibid.*, p. 312.
11 *Ibid.*, p. 315.
12 *Ibid.*, p. 316.
13 *Ibid.*, p. 320.

12. TWO PLAYS

1 In 1963 a third play was presented by the Teatro Stabile di Torino: Luigi Candoni's *Oedipus at Hiroshima,* a study of the moral and psychological conflicts of an American bomber pilot.

2 *Tempo di cavallette,* with *La foresta* and *Il formicaio,* Bologna, Cappelli, 1962, p. 67.

3 *Ibid.*, p. 18.

4 *Ibid.*, p. 36.

5 *Ibid.*, p. 91.

6 *Ibid.*, p. 77.

7 "La sua parte di storia," in Luigi Squarzina, *Teatro,* Bari, Laterza, 1959, p. 263. Squarzina is a little confused about percentages; .29 percent is twenty-nine hundredths of 1 percent of a child, or twenty-nine ten-thousandths of a child.

8 *Ibid.*, p. 268.

9 *Ibid.*, p. 292.

10 *Ibid.*, p. 284.

11 *Ibid.*, p. 296.

12 *Ibid.*, p. 329.

13 *Ibid.*, p. 279.

BIBLIOGRAPHY

This bibliography is not complete, nor does it represent all the research materials that went into the writing of the book. Its purpose is to provide the American reader with some of the background material that will facilitate a better understanding of the text, and to suggest further reading in those aspects of the subject which particularly interest him. A number of other bibliographies have been consulted, and in some cases borrowed from; particularly the excellent one in Sergio Pacifici's *Guide to Contemporary Italian Literature* (Cleveland, Meridian Books, 1962). The dates of novels and other works are usually those of the most easily obtainable editions; for dates of first publication see the preceding text. Since the bibliography is intended chiefly for the convenience of the nonspecialized American reader, novels and other works are usually listed in English-language version when available. For bibliographical description of Italian editions see the preceding text with its corresponding notes. In general the most easily obtainable editions were used in the preparation of this book. Certain critical materials unavailable in English are here listed in Italian, along with important novels and other works not yet translated.

Chapter 1: Chateaubriand, the Movies, and Other Myths

THE ITALIAN MYTH OF AMERICA: For a general study see Carl Wittke, "The American Theme in Continental European Literature," *Mississippi Valley Historical Review*, 28 (June, 1941), pp. 3ff. Also valuable are Andrew J. Torielli, *Italian Opinion of America as Revealed by Italian Travelers, 1850–1900*, Harvard University Press, 1941; Carlo L. Golino, "On the Italian 'Myth' of America," *Italian Quarterly*, 3:9 (Spring, 1959), pp. 19ff.; Joseph Rossi, "The American Myth in the Italian Risorgimento: The *Lettere* from America of Carlo Vidua," *Italica*, 38:3 (September, 1961), pp. 227ff. For an Italian view from the Fascist era see A. La Piana, *La cultura americana e l'Italia*, Turin, 1938.

ITALIAN EMIGRATION TO AMERICA: A good general study of Italian-American immigrants is found in Francis J. Brown and Joseph Slabey Roucek, eds., *One America*, New York, Prentice-Hall, 1945. For a more detailed account see Federal Writers Project (WPA), *The Italians of New York*, New York, Random House, 1938. Angelo M. Pellegrini's *Immigrant's Return*, New York, Macmillan, 1951, is a good personal account. For a novelized treatment see Jerre Mangione, *Mount Allegro*, Boston, Houghton Mifflin, 1942. Other useful works are Constantine Maria Panuzio, *The Soul of an Immigrant*, New York, Macmillan, 1921; Giuseppe Prezzolini, *I trapiantati*, Milan, Longanesi, 1963.

CHATEAUBRIAND: The classic authority on Chateaubriand and America is Gilbert Chinard, who published mainly in French; see *L'exotisme américain dans l'oeuvre de Chateaubriand*, Paris, Hachette, 1918; and "Chateaubriand, Les Natchez, livres I et II: Contribution à l'étude des sources de Chateaubriand," *University of California Publications in Modern Philology*, 7 (Berkeley, 1919), pp. 201ff. In English see Emma K. Armstrong, "Chateaubriand's America," *PMLA*, 22 (1907), pp. 345ff. A sound modern study is included in Durand Echeverria, *Mirage in the West: A History of the French Image of American Society to 1815*, Princeton University Press, 1957.

PIETRO DI DONATO: *Christ in Concrete* was first issued by Bobbs-Merrill (Indianapolis) in 1939, and was translated into Italian as *Cristo fra i muratori*, Milan, Bompiani, 1941. For criticism and biography see Louis Adamic, "Muscular Novel of Immigrant Life," *Saturday Review of Literature*, 20:18 (August 26, 1939), pp. 5f.; *Time*, 33:77 (April 10, 1939), pp. 77f.; Olga Peragallo, *Italian-American Authors*, S. F. Vanni, 1949, pp. 89ff.

FELLINI AND "LA DOLCE VITA": For documentary material see Tullio Kesich, ed., *La dolce vita Federico Fellini*, Bologna, Cappelli, 1959.

Chapter 2: The Travelers

MARIO SOLDATI: *America primo amore*, Milan, Garzanti, 1956, is untranslated except for an excerpt which appears as "Sixth Avenue" in *Italian Quarterly*, 3:9 (Spring, 1959), pp. 13ff. For other materials see notes to Chapter 10.

EMILIO CECCHI: *America amara*, originally published in 1938, was reissued after the war by Sansoni, Florence, 1946. For a sample of Cecchi's American criticism see "Two Notes on Melville," *Sewanee Review*, 68:3 (Summer, 1960), pp. 398ff. Two more short sketches by Cecchi are found in Marc Slonim, ed., *Modern Italian Short Stories*, New York, Simon and Schuster, 1954, pp. 106ff. His untranslated *Scrittori inglesi e americani* has been recently reissued in a two-volume edition (Milan, Il Saggiatore, 1962).

GIUSEPPE PREZZOLINI: See his "America and Italy: Myths and Realities," *Italian Quarterly*, 3:9 (Spring, 1959), pp. 3ff.

GUIDO PIOVENE: *De America*, Milan, Garzanti, 1953, has not been translated. For a sample of his fiction see "The Dressmaker's Daughter," in P. M. Pasinetti, ed., *Great Italian Short Stories* (New York, Dell Laurel, 1959), pp. 368ff. The concluding chapter of his Italian travel book *Viaggio in Italia*, Milan, Mondadori, 1957, is translated as "Conclusions of the Journey" in *Italian Quarterly*, 1:4 (Winter, 1958), pp. 5ff.

Chapter 3 The Americanisti

AMERICAN STUDIES AND AMERICAN LITERATURE IN ITALY: See Sigmund Skard, "Italy," in *American Studies in Europe*, University of Pennsylvania Press, 1958; Mario Praz "Hemingway in Italy," *Partisan Review*, 15:10 (October, 1948), pp. 1086ff.; Elio Vittorini, "American Influences on Contemporary Italian Literature," *American Quarterly*, 1:1 (1949), pp. 3ff.; Leslie Fiedler, "Italian Pilgrimage: The Discovery of America," *Kenyon Review*, 14:3 (Summer, 1952), pp. 359ff.; Donald Heiney, "American Naturalism and the New Italian Writers," *Twentieth Century Literature*, 3:3 (October, 1957), pp 135ff.; Lowry Nelson, "Americanisti italiani," *Italian Quarterly*, 2:2 (Summer, 1958), pp. 77ff.; Sergio Pacifici, "America and Italy: An Encounter," *A Guide to Contemporary Italian Literature* (Cleveland, Meridian Books, 1962), pp. 293ff. See also the special issue of *Sewanee Review* (68:3, Summer, 1960) devoted to Italian criticism of American literature, and including contributions by Cambon, Cecchi, Chiaromonte,

D'Agostino, Montale, Moravia, Orsini, Pavese, Praz, and Vittorini; the introduction by Agostino Lombardo is particularly valuable. Two other special periodical issues of interest are the Spring, 1959, *Italian Quarterly* (3:9), including pieces by Prezzolini, Fiedler, Soldati, Golino, Della Terza, and Liciani; and the Summer, 1961, *Texas Quarterly* (4:2), dedicated to the theme "Image of Italy" and including contributions by Alvaro, Levi, Soldati, Silone, and Pavese.

The material in Italian is copious. See particularly Vito Amoruso, "Cecchi, Vittorini, e letteratura americana," *Studi Americani,* 6 (1960), pp. 9ff.; Glauco Cambon, "La critica americana in Italia," *Galleria,* 4:5–6 (1954), pp. 257ff.; Raffaele Crovi, "Vittorini, l'America e la giovane letteratura italiana," pp. 307ff. in the same special issue of *Galleria* devoted to American literature; Nemi D'Agostino, "Pavese e L'America," *Studi Americani,* 4 (1958), pp. 399ff.; Claudio Gorlier, "Poesia americana e cultura americana," *Aut-Aut,* 21 (May, 1954), pp. 117ff.; Agostino Lombardo, "La critica italiana sulla letteratura americana," *Studi Americani,* 5 (1959), pp. 9ff.; Salvatore Rosati, "Gli scrittori italiani e gli Stati Uniti," *Il Veltro,* 4:1–2 (1960), pp. 29ff.; H. Marraro, "Relazioni culturali tra l'Italia e gli Stati Uniti," pp. 103ff. in the same special issue of *Il Veltro;* Sergio Pacifici, "La riscoperta italiana dell'America," *Quadrivio,* 2 (March, 1962), pp. 23ff.

CESARE PAVESE: His criticism of American literature is collected in *La letteratura americana e altri saggi,* Turin, Einaudi, 1953. His fiction available in English includes *The Moon and the Bonfires,* 1953; *Among Women Only,* 1959; *The Devil in the Hills,* 1959; all published by Farrar, Straus, and Young (New York); and *The House on the Hill,* Walker, 1961. A Pavese story, "Suicides," is included in Ben Johnson, ed., *Stories of Modern Italy* (New York, Modern Library, 1960), pp. 159ff.; and another, "The Leather Jacket," is found in Marc Slonim, ed., *Modern Italian Short Stories* (New York, Simon and Schuster, 1954), pp. 280ff. For samples of his criticism see "Yesterday and Today," *The Western Humanities Review,* 11:3 (Summer, 1957), pp. 225ff.; and "Literary Whaler," *Sewanee Review,* 68:3 (Summer, 1960), pp. 407ff. Parts of his *Dialoghi con Leucò* (Turin, Einaudi, 1953) are translated in *Texas Quarterly,* 4:2 (Summer, 1961), pp. 58ff.

The only adequate biography of Pavese to date is Davide Lajolo, *Il "vizio assurdo,"* Milan, Il Saggiatore, 1960. The first critical study in English was Leslie Fiedler, "Introducing Cesare Pavese," *Kenyon Review,* 16:4 (Autumn, 1954), pp. 536ff.

See also Richard H. Chase, "Cesare Pavese and the American Novel," *Studi Americani*, 3 (1957), pp. 347ff.; Sergio Pacifici, "America and Italy: An Encounter," *A Guide to Contemporary Italian Literature* (Cleveland, Meridian Books, 1962), pp. 293ff.

ELIO VITTORINI: His fiction available in English includes *In Sicily*, Norfolk, Conn., New Directions, 1949 (also translated as *Conversations in Sicily*, Penguin, 1962); *The Twilight of the Elephant*, New Directions, 1951; *The Red Carnation*, New Directions, 1952; *The Dark and the Light* (includes *Erica* and *La Garibaldina*), New Directions, 1960. An excerpt from an untranslated novel *Le donne di Messina* appears as "Uncle Agrippa Takes a Train" in Marc Slonim, ed., *Modern Italian Short Stories* (New York, Simon and Schuster, 1954), pp. 402ff. "Autobiography in Time of War," extracted from *Diario in pubblico* (Milan, Bompiani, 1957), appeared in *Italian Quarterly*, 1:3 (Fall, 1957), pp. 40ff. The preface to *The Red Carnation*, an important statement of Vittorini's literary principles, was revised for English translation by Vittorini himself and appeared as "Truth and Censorship: The Story of *The Red Carnation*," *The Western Humanities Review*, 9:3 (Summer, 1955), pp. 197ff. See also his "Outline of American Literature," *Sewanee Review*, 68:3 (Summer, 1960), pp. 423ff. (material based on the suppressed *Americana* prefaces of 1941).

For American comments on Vittorini see R. W. B. Lewis, "Elio Vittorini," *Italian Quarterly*, 4:15 (Fall, 1960), pp. 55ff.; Donald Heiney, "Vittorini, the Opera, and the Fifth Dimension," *College English*, 17:8 (May, 1956), pp. 135ff.; Sergio Pacifici, "Elio Vittorini," *A Guide to Contemporary Italian Literature* (Cleveland, Meridian Books, 1962), pp. 87ff.; Glauco Cambon, "Elio Vittorini: Between Poverty and Wealth," *Wisconsin Studies in Contemporary Literature*, 3 (1962), pp. 20ff. For an excellent review of *Diario in pubblico* see Sergio Pacifici, "Understanding Vittorini 'Whole,'" *Italian Quarterly*, 1:4 (Winter, 1958), pp. 95ff.

GIAIME PINTOR: Pintor's criticism of American literature is collected in *Il sangue d'Europa*, Turin, Einaudi, 1950, which also includes a biographical and critical essay by Valentino Gerratana. The only biographical information of any value in English is found in Charles F. Delzell, *Mussolini's Enemies: The Italian Anti-Fascist Resistance*, Princeton University Press, 1961. Pintor's essay "Americana" appears in a translation with introduction by Donald Heiney in *The Western Humanities Review*, 17:3 (Summer, 1963), pp. 203ff.

Chapter 4: "The Time Is Past in Which We Discovered America"

NEOREALISM AND THE NEW ITALIAN WRITING: For two good anthologies see Marc Slonim, ed., *Modern Italian Short Stories,* New York, Simon and Schuster, 1954; and Ben Johnson, ed., *Stories of Modern Italy,* New York, Modern Library, 1960. For criticism see Dante Della Terza, "Italian Fiction from Pavese to Pasolini: 1950–1960," *Italian Quarterly,* 3:11 (Fall, 1959), pp. 29ff.; Sergio Pacifici, *A Guide to Contemporary Italian Literature,* Cleveland, Meridian Books, 1962; P. M. Pasinetti, "The Incredible Italians," *New World Writing,* 1 (1952), pp. 183ff.; Donald Heiney, "American Naturalism and the New Italian Writers," *Twentieth Century Literature,* 3:3 (October, 1957), pp. 135ff.; Sergio Pacifici, "From Engagement to Alienation: A View of Contemporary Italian Literature," *Italica,* 60:3 (September, 1963), pp. 236ff.

ITALO CALVINO: His fiction available in English includes *The Path to the Nest of Spiders,* Boston, Beacon, 1957; *The Baron in the Trees,* New York, Random House, 1959; *The Non-Existent Knight, Random House,* 1962. Calvino also edited *Italian Fables,* New York, Orion, 1959. For samples of his short fiction see "Night of Numbers," *The Reporter,* 24:1 (January 5, 1961), pp. 34ff.; "The Adventure of a Near-Sighted Person," *Cesare Barbieri Courier,* 4 (Fall, 1961), pp. 12ff.; "Going to War," *Odyssey,* 1 (March, 1962), pp. 9ff. Three more Calvino stories are found in anthologies: "UNPA Nights" and "Last Comes the Raven" in Ben Johnson, ed., *Stories of Modern Italy* (New York, Modern Library, 1960), pp. 204ff.; and "One Afternoon, Adam . . ." in Marc Slonim, ed., *Modern Italian Short Stories* (New York, Simon and Schuster, 1954), pp. 391ff. A lecture by Calvino, "Main Currents in Italian Fiction Today," is reprinted in *Italian Quarterly,* 4:13–14 (Spring/Summer, 1960), pp. 3ff. For a good study of Calvino's fiction see Sergio Pacifici, "From Engagement to Alienation: A View of Contemporary Italian Literature," *Italica,* 60:3 (September, 1963), pp. 236ff.; also Edward Williamson, "The Sobriety of the Italian Novel," *Cesare Barbieri Courier,* 5 (Spring, 1963), pp. 18ff.

FERNANDA PIVANO: *La balena bianca e altri miti,* Milan, Mondadori, 1961, is untranslated.

Chapter 5: Guareschi: America or Castor Oil?

There are a number of English editions of the *Don Camillo* sketches. See especially *The Little World of Don Camillo*, New York, Farrar, Straus, 1951; *Don Camillo's Dilemma*, New York, Grosset, 1957; *Don Camillo and His Flock*, New York, Pellegrini and Cudahy, 1952. For Guareschi's account of his German prison camp experiences see *My Secret Diary*, Farrar, Straus, 1958. *Il destino si chiama Clotilde*, Milan, Rizzoli, 1941, is untranslated.

There is not very much serious criticism of Guareschi in English. For a review of *My Secret Diary* see Ned Calmer, "Open Letter to the Gray People," *Saturday Review*, 41:28 (July 12, 1958), p. 18.

Chapter 6: Silone: Emigration as the Opiate of the People

Silone's fiction available in English includes *Fontamara*, New York, Harrison Smith, 1934; *Bread and Wine*, New York, Harper, 1937; *The Seed Beneath the Snow*, Harper, 1942; *A Handful of Blackberries*, Harper, 1953; *The Secret of Luca*, Harper, 1958; *The Fox and the Camellias*, Harper, 1961. See also the political dialogue *The School for Dictators*, Harper, 1938. Revised versions of the earlier novels have appeared as *Fontamara*, New York, Atheneum, 1960; *Bread and Wine*, Atheneum, 1962. For samples of Silone's shorter fiction see "The Parting of the Ways," Ben Johnson, ed., *Stories of Modern Italy* (New York, Modern Library, 1960), pp. 146ff.; "Return to Fontamara," Marc Slonim, ed., *Modern Italian Short Stories* (New York, Simon and Schuster, 1954), pp. 187ff. A short sketch, "a Courageous Priest: A Note on Don Lorenzo Milani," is included in *Texas Quarterly*, 4:2 (Summer, 1961), pp. 197ff.; and an article, "Fiction and the Southern Subsoil," in *Italian Quarterly*, 1:2 (Summer, 1957), pp. 32ff. For Silone and Communism see his contribution to Richard Crossman, ed., *The God That Failed* (New York, Harper Colophon, 1963), pp. 76ff.

Criticism of Silone in English is copious. See particularly R. W. B. Lewis, "Ignazio Silone: The Politics of Charity," *The Picaresque Saint* (Philadelphia, Keystone Books, 1961), pp. 109ff.; Paolo Milano, "Silone the Faithful," *New Republic*, 129:12 (October 19, 1953), pp. 16ff.; Irving Howe, "Silone: The Power of Example," *New Republic*, 139:12 (September 22, 1958), pp. 18ff.; A. Kingsley Weatherhead, "Ignazio Silone: Community and the Failure of Language," *Modern Fiction Studies*, 7 (1961), pp. 157ff.; Kenneth Alsop, "Ignazio Silone," *Encounter*, 18:3 (March, 1962), pp. 49ff.; Nathan A. Scott, "Ignazio Silone: Novelist of the Revolutionary Sensibility," *Rehearsals of Discomposure* (New York, King's Crown Press, 1952), pp. 66ff.

Chapter 7: Emigration: Levi, Alvaro, and Others

CARLO LEVI: *Cristo si è fermato a Eboli*, Turin, Einaudi, 1962, is translated as *Christ Stopped at Eboli*, Grosset, 1947. Other works by Levi available in English include *Of Fear and Freedom*, New York, Farrar, Straus, 1950; *The Watch*, Farrar, Straus, 1951; *Words Are Stones*, Farrar, Straus, 1958; *The Linden Tree*, New York, Knopf, 1962. A Levi story, "The Massacre of Vallucciole," is included in Marc Slonim, ed., *Modern Italian Short Stories* (New York, Simon and Schuster, 1954), pp. 237ff.; and a short sketch, "Bread," is translated in *Texas Quarterly*, 4:2 (Summer, 1961), pp. 117ff. For two articles by Levi, the second one extremely important in regard to the Myth of America, see "Peasants Stir in Groping Italy," *New York Times Magazine*, September 14, 1947, p. 18; "Italy's Myth of America," *Life*, 23:1 (July 7, 1947), pp. 84ff. For criticism of Levi see Lawrence Grant White, "Time and the Man," *Saturday Review of Literature*, 34:26 (June 30, 1951), pp. 8ff.; Harold Rosenberg, "Politics as Dancing," *Tradition of the New* (New York, Horizon Press, 1959), pp. 199ff.

LIVIA DE STEFANI: Her fiction available in English includes: *Black Grapes*, New York, Criterion, 1958; *Passion of Rosa*, London, Eyre and Spottiswood, 1963. There is no important criticism in English. For a good article in Italian see Gino Raya, "Viaggio di una sconosciuta," *La Fiera Letterari*, July 21, 1963, pp. 2–5.

CORRADO ALVARO: *Gente in Aspromonte*, Milan, Garzanti, 1960, is translated as *Revolt in Aspromonte*, Norfolk, Conn., New Directions, 1962. An Alvaro story involving emigration "The Black Mare," is found in Ben Johnson, ed., *Stories of Modern Italy* (New York, Modern Library, 1960), pp. 68ff.; and another story, "The Wedding Journey," appears in Marc Slonim, ed., *Modern Italian Short Stories* (New York, Simon and Schuster, 1954), pp. 182ff. For Alvaro's comments on regionalism and southern Italian literature see "Fitting into the Present," *Italian Quarterly*, 1:2 (Summer, 1957), pp. 29ff. Three fragments by Alvaro, "Last Journal," "Roman Spring," and "Venice in Winter," are translated in *Texas Quarterly*, 4:2 (Summer, 1961), pp. 49ff., 107ff., and 127ff.

GIUSEPPE CASSIERI: His satirical novel *La cocuzza*, Milan, Bompiani, 1960, has been translated as *So It Goes*, New York, Pantheon, 1963.

Chapter 8: "Liberation"

THE RESISTANCE AND THE LIBERATION, GENERAL: The best account in English is found in Charles F. Delzell, *Mussolini's Enemies: The Italian Anti-Fascist Resistance,* Princeton University Press, 1961. In Italian see Renato Carli-Ballola, *Storia della Resistenza,* Milan-Rome, 1957.

GIUSEPPE BERTO: *Il cielo è rosso,* Milan, Longanesi, 1957, is translated as *The Sky Is Red,* Norfolk, Conn., New Directions, 1948, and Signet, 1952. Other fiction by Berto in English includes *The Works of God and Other Stories,* New Directions, 1950; *The Brigand,* New Directions, 1951. "Aunt Bess, In Memoriam," probably Berto's best short-fiction treatment of the American Myth, is found in Marc Slonim, ed., *Modern Italian Short Stories* (New York, Simon and Schuster, 1954), pp. 326ff. For other stories see "The Seed Among Thorns," a fictionalized treatment of his Texas prison-camp experiences, in *New World Writing,* 1 (1952), pp. 163ff.; "Midnight Trysts," in Ben Johnson, ed., *Stories of Modern Italy* (New York, Modern Library, 1960), pp. 272ff. Good criticism of Berto in America is rare. For a review of *The Sky Is Red* see Unsigned, "Bitter Ashes," *Time,* 52:17 (October 25, 1948, pp. 114ff. The present writer's "Berto: Texas and Treviso" in *Cesare Barbieri Courier,* 6:2 (Spring, 1964) is merely a version of the material in Chapter 8 of this book.

MARIO TOBINO: *Il clandestino,* Milan, Mondadori, 1962, is untranslated. A sketch by Tobino, "Oscar Pilli," appears in *Texas Quarterly,* 4:2 (Summer, 1961), pp. 69ff. For a critical comment see Sergio Pacifici, "Italy 1962: Literary Trends and Books," *Cesare Barbieri Courier,* 5:1 (Fall, 1962), pp. 3ff.

Chapter 9: The Moon and the Bonfires

For Pavese in general see bibliography to Chapter 3. *La luna e i falò,* Turin, Einaudi, 1950–1955, is translated as *The Moon and the Bonfires,* New York, Farrar, Straus, and Young, 1953. There are a number of good studies of this novel in English. See particularly John Freccero, "Mythos and Logos: The Moon and the Bonfires," *Italian Quarterly,* 4:16 (Winter, 1961), pp. 3ff.; Paolo Milano, "Pavese's Experiments in the Novel," *New Republic,* 128:18 (May 4, 1953), pp. 18ff.; Peter M. Norton, "Cesare Pavese and the American Nightmare," *Modern Language Notes,* 77:1 (January, 1962), pp. 24ff.

Chapter 10: The Capri Letters

Soldati's *Le lettere da Capri*, Milan, Garzanti, 1954, is translated as *The Capri Letters*, New York, Knopf, 1956. Other fiction of Soldati available in English includes *Dinner with the Commendatore*, Knopf, 1953; *The Confession*, Knopf, 1958; *The Real Silvestri*, Knopf, 1960. A Soldati story, "The Father of the Orphans," is included in Ben Johnson, ed., *Stories of Modern Italy* (New York, Modern Library, 1960), pp. 304ff.; and another, "Nora," appears in Marc Slonim, ed., *Modern Italian Short Stories* (New York, Simon and Schuster, 1954), pp. 369ff. A sketch by Soldati, "A Dinner in Rome," is translated in *Texas Quarterly*, 4:2 (Summer, 1961), pp. 129ff. For material relating to *America primo amore* see bibliography for Chapter 2. For a typical American review of *The Capri Letters* see Harrison Smith, "The Capri Letters," *Saturday Review*, 39:6 (February 11, 1956), p. 14.

Chapter 11: Moravia's America

Fiction of Moravia available in English includes *The Woman of Rome*, New York, Farrar, Straus, 1949; *Conjugal Love*, Farrar, Straus, and Young, 1951; *The Conformist*, Farrar, Straus, and Young, 1951; *The Fancy Dress Party*, Farrar, Straus, and Young, 1952; *The Time of Indifference*, Farrar, Straus, and Young, 1953; *A Ghost at Noon*, Farrar, Straus, and Young, 1955; *Roman Tales*, Farrar, Straus, and Young, 1957; *The Wayward Wife and Other Stories*, Farrar, Straus, and Young, 1960; *The Empty Canvas*, Farrar, Straus, and Young, 1961; *Two Women*, Farrar, Straus, and Young, 1962. An important Moravia story, "A Sick Boy's Winter," is found in Ben Johnson, ed., *Stories of Modern Italy* (New York, Modern Library, 1960), pp. 89ff. The story "The Negro and the Old Man with the Bill-Hook," discussed in the preceding text, is included in *The Wayward Wife and Other Stories*, cited above.

For two valuable interviews with Moravia see Malcolm Cowley, ed., *Writers at Work: The Paris Review Interviews* (New York, Viking, 1960), pp. 211ff.; and "One Good Tune," *The New Yorker*, 31:12 (May 7, 1955), p. 39. Also useful is Moravia's "About My Novels: A Fragment of Autobiography," *Twentieth Century*, 164 (December, 1958), pp. 529ff. In Italian an important source of biographical and documentary material is Oreste del Buono, ed., *Moravia*, Milan, Feltrinelli, 1962.

Good criticism of Moravia in English is plentiful. See especially Giovanni Cecchetti, "Alberto Moravia," *Italica*, 30:3 (September,

1953), pp. 153ff.; S. J. Pacifici, "The Fiction of Alberto Moravia: Portrait of a Wasteland," *Modern Language Quarterly*, 16 (March, 1955), pp. 68ff.; R. W. B. Lewis, "Alberto Moravia: Eros and Existence," *The Picaresque Saint* (Philadelphia, Keystone Books, 1961), pp. 36ff.; Sergio Pacifici, "Alberto Moravia," *A Guide to Contemporary Italian Literature* (Cleveland, Meridian Books, 1962), pp. 29ff.; Thomas Bergin, "The Moravian Muse," *Virginia Quarterly Review*, 29 (1953), pp. 215ff.; Frank Baldanza, "The Classicism of Alberto Moravia," *Modern Fiction Studies*, 3 (1958), pp. 309ff.

Chapter 12: Two Plays

EZIO D'ERRICO: His three plays *Tempo di cavallette, La foresta, Il formicaio*, Bologna, Cappelli, 1962, are untranslated. See Ossia Trilling, "Ezio d'Errico—A New Pirandello?" *Theatre World* (London), April, 1958.

LUIGI SQUARZINA: His plays are collected in *Teatro*, Bari, Laterza (Biblioteca di Cultura Moderna no. 534), 1959. There is no criticism of any importance in English. For an important statement by Squarzina on *La sua parte di storia* see "L'Isola povera e la nazione-balia," in *La Biennale di Venezia: XXI Festival Internazionale del Teatro di Prosa* (program, Venice, 1962), pp. 48ff. For Italian criticism see Tullio Kezich, "Il teatro politico di Squarzina," pp. 49ff. in the same biennial program; Nerio Minuzzo, "Il teatro è finito?" *L'Europeo*, 18:50 (December 16, 1962), p. 55.

Index

Where translations exist, the titles of more important literary works are listed in this index in both Italian and English. References to major discussions of authors, works, and themes are indicated by page numbers in italics.

U.C.W. LIBRARY ABERYSTWYTH